"Courageously harnessing the power of theatre to unmask our ignorance, fear, and immobility, this groundbreaking collection provides an artistic antidote to the social malaise that surrounds the HIV/AIDS epidemic, particularly as it affects women and people of color. The great reward of this anthology is a new perspective on a subject that perhaps we think we already know. With profound commitment, compassion and vision, these artists shake us loose from the grip of complacency and call us into the space of desire for change, for healing, for wholeness."

—*Sydné Mahone dramaturg and editor of*
Moon Marked and Touched by Sun

"*Positive/Negative* brings together the authentic voices of those we would all agree to be survivors. The premise put forth frightens us, but reveals the truth of the context in which this epidemic grows. It says the continuum of behaviors that separates HIV positive from HIV negative is a matter of consciousness. It is fluid and thus deadly. Lest we forget: we are one behavior away from being HIV positive. This epidemic has just begun. None of us is exempt."

—*Henri E. Norris, Esq.,*
Past Director of the Multicultural Alliance for the Prevention of AIDS

"This collection of plays explores the central problems faced by women of color with HIV/AIDS. A wonderful book…original and provocative."

—*Roya Sakhai, Ph.D.*

"*Positive/Negative: Women of Color and HIV/AIDS* is a brilliant and compelling anthology of plays that speak with powerful voices of truth and revelations rarely heard in contemporary theater. Voices of a marginalized, largely unheard segment of our society speak out with a power and a bravery that cannot be ignored. These plays bear witness to the beauty of truth. Their message is clear and it demands to be heard. Imani Harrington and Chyrell D. Bellamy are to be congratulated for bringing us an anthology destined to be a classic on the subject of the theater of AIDS."

—*Bill Jacobson, Theater Arts Editor of* A & U
(Arts and Understanding): America's AIDS Magazine

"Medical discourses are essentially ideological as well as material, determining where one looks to assign responsibility for sickness, often 'blam[ing] the victim' and obscuring the social and economic conditions which are at the root of the problem. Seizing the means of production of discourse on disease is necessary to challenge this hegemonic power. These narratives, collected by Harrington and Bellamy in *Positive/Negative*, enhanced by the dramatic and theatrical form of expression, produce a powerful and radical discourse that seeks not only to be individually healing, but also, through challenging the dominant ideology on these issues, creates necessary social change. Harrington, Bellamy and the authors anthologized in this volume are practitioners of 'Liberation Medicine.'"

—*Michael J. McAvoy, M.A.*
Critical Medical Anthropologist and Dean,
New College of California School of Humanities

Dearest Richard...
It's great to be back in
touch... Thanks for all your support
when my play Love + Danger was first being
workshopped - Enjoy this compilation of voices
Always - A friend
Imani

POSITIVE
a collection of plays
NEGATIVE
women of color and HIV/AIDS

edited by Imani Harrington & Chyrell D. Bellamy

First Edition

Aunt Lute Books
P.O. Box 410687
San Francisco, CA 94141
www.auntlute.com

Senior Editor: Joan Pinkvoss
Managing Editor: Shay Brawn
Production: Trisha Flanagan, Gina Gemello, Shahara Godfrey, Marielle Gomez, Tamara Martínez, Laura Reizman

Cover Photo: Copyright © 1995 by Debra St. John. Still from *Love & Danger* workshop production, directed by Abraham Celaya. Tina Marie Murray as Player D/Winter (front), Melanie Moore as Player A/Salome (middle), Seema Sodhi as Player C/Candice (back).

Cover Design: Amy Woloszyn
Text Design: Kajun Graphics
Typesetting: Amy Woloszyn

This book was funded in part by grants from the California Arts Council and the National Endowment for the Arts.

Library of Congress Cataloging-in-Publication Data

Positive/negative : women of color and HIV/AIDS : a collection of plays / edited by Imani Harrington and Chyrell D. Bellamy.–1st ed.
    p.cm.
    Includes bibliographic references.
    ISBN: 1-879960-65-6
    1. AIDS (Disease)–Patients–Drama. 2. American drama–Minority authors. 3. Women–United States–Drama. 4. American drama–Women authors. 5. American drama–20th century. 6. HIV-positive women–Drama. 7. Minority women–Drama. 8. Ethnic gourps–Drama. 9. Minorities–Drama. I. Harrington, Imani. II. Bellamy, Chyrell D.

PS 627.A53 P67 2002
812'.54080356–dc21
                                                                2002034517

Printed in the United States of America
10 9 8 7 6 5 4 3 2 1

december song

wind calls my hair the
willow tree and tosses
it through her
fingers
she wants me to be
happy
today. nonetheless the
Great Sadness tries to pinch,
pinch me for one last dance
it can feel its life force
dying
away. the rebirth of a century
is among us, my blooming
will not halt. suicide and
depression find themselves
forgotten. moonsister helps me
purge
the lovesickness with blood.
the
dawn awaits me, i will step
naked
on the horizon and see what
awaits me on the other side.
it is time to reclaim
the Beauty.
it is time.

—kehinde apara

Acknowledgments

Chyrell, thank you for your compassion, sisterhood, and the alchemy you brought to this relationship, as well as your undying loyalty and dedication to me, to your work in the AIDS pandemic, and for your years of immense commitment to the development of this project. I give special thanks to professors Ali Chavoshian, Louis Roussel and Kambiz Sakhai of New College of California Graduate School of Social/Clinical Psychology for stimulating my thinking about intersubjectivity, which helped me to come to the insight that there is such a phenonmon as a positive and negative consciousness. And a very special thanks to Theatre Bay Area-Mary Mason Memorial Lemonade Fund for helping me to improve the quality of my life, as it was during this process that I made lemonade.

—*Imani*

Imani—you are brilliant! It has been a true joy to work with you on your vision—thanks for keeping us on track. You are a blessing in my life! Thanks to the Rackham School of Graduate Studies, the Gender and Mental Health Training Fellowship (Susan Nolen-Hoeksema and Carol T. Mowbray), and The Institute for Research on Women and Gender at the University of Michigan for supporting this project.

—*Chyrell*

Also, Chyrell and Imani both would like to thank the New Jersey Women and AIDS Network (NJWAN) for their support and assistance. Thanks to all the contributors for their voice, vision, stories, bravery and honorable determination to shine the light they have cast on the lost, but now found, faces of the epidemic. A special thanks to Evelyn C. White for her unselfish acts given to this project and inspiration. Special thanks to our mothers, families, community members and friends for all their love and support while working on this task. We especially give our most sincere acknowledgment to all those writers whose work we regrettably had to leave out. Thank you for your commitment and for the honorable work submitted. We are grateful to and extend special thanks to all of our dedicated and loyal assistants on this project: Cherri Gregory, Katherine McCracken, Peggy Megivern. A special thanks to writer, editor, and playwright Laura Peoples who jumped in with a third eye to help with edits on the biographies and with editorial commentary on the plays, and to Theresa Thadani for her loyalty, hard work and graphic-computer quickness. A very special thanks to Abraham Celaya for his artistic loyalty, respect for theater, dramaturgy, and directing vision. A special thanks to dramaturgs Alice Elliot Smith and Patricia Schaefer and to Tony Taccone for his inspiration and dramaturgical insights on *Love & Danger* and Benny Sato Ambush for his artistic encouragement. Our most heartfelt appreciation goes to the women at Aunt Lute Books—Shay Brawn, Trisha Flanagan, Gina Gemello, Shahara Godfrey, Marielle Gomez, Tamara Martínez, and Joan Pinkvoss—for their exquisite knowledge in all of what they do and their compassion put forth in the development of this project as well as their vision and commitment to community and to helping emerging women writers to excel. Finally, we give thanks to the ancestors for their presence in guiding us through this project.

This anthology is dedicated to all the women who have died without a face or voice.

CONTENTS

SECTION 1: LOVE/RELATIONSHIPS

SECTION 2: SEX/SEXUALITY

SECTION 3: DANGER/DEATH

Trouble Don't Last Always

How can it be? Twenty years after the onset of the epidemic and massive prevention campaigns, black and brown people now comprise the majority of all AIDS cases. At a loss for words, personally, I am heartened by *Positive/Negative*, a collection of writings that not only answers the above question, but one that also provides a map to the distant milestone marked: How did the silence and death end?

For just as women and minorities have conquered other oppressors, we will one day vanquish AIDS, of this I am sure. As always, information is key. Truth is vital. Faith works. The ancestors anchor all who effort (however wearily) to anchor themselves.

Those who are guided to this book will find in it affirmation, provocation, enlightenment, laughter and much love. Embrace its offerings as if your life depended on it, because it does.

More than a century after the Emancipation Proclamation, people of color remain enslaved by prejudice, poverty, ignorance and fear. And yet and still, we know from our history that this too shall pass. Trouble don't last always.

Evelyn C. White
September 2002
Oakland, California

Unveiling Positive and Negative Consciousness

Imani Harrington and Chyrell D. Bellamy

In order for us to be fully realized as human beings, as ourselves, as sensual beings in the face of the epidemic, in order to deal with the prospect of death and have a dance with love, we must first be who we are. But how can we be who we are when so often it is on the basis of who we are that we are being judged? How can we be who we are without blame, stigma, and shame disturbing both our sense of ourselves and how others see us? Those who are HIV positive both live with a life-threatening disease and bear the added burden of protecting others from contracting the disease. And these tasks should not be confused with each other, because protecting others and managing oneself while knowingly living with HIV are not the same thing. They require working, to borrow W.E.B. DuBois' term, from a kind of "double consciousness," seeing the world from the standpoint of both positive and negative HIV status. And managing this binary position is complicated not only by intersecting factors of race, class, gender, and sexuality, but by individual consciousness as well. It is our belief that the behavior of both HIV-positive and HIV-negative people depends a great deal on the consciousness they bring to their actions: how HIV-positive and HIV-negative people think, act, and feel about their relationship to the world at large. If we are to understand the behaviors, we need to understand the consciousness that precedes them.

Since the beginning of the pandemic in the United States, our consciousness about HIV has evolved, particularly in terms of how we think about who gets the disease and how it is transmitted. Dispelling the myth that HIV is a "gay man's disease" and improving our understanding about how HIV is transmitted has transformed how HIV-positive and HIV-negative individuals think, act, and speak in daily social relations. Increased awareness that we are all at risk has integrated an awareness of HIV into more and more aspects of our daily lives. Furthermore, improvements in treatment have meant that people with HIV are living longer, healthier lives. And as the focus has centered less on dying from AIDS and more on living with HIV, this society as a whole has had to find more creative approaches to sexual intimacy, dating, and healthcare arrangements.

However, although significant changes have taken shape during the last decade of the pandemic, much of the ignorance about HIV and many of the negative attitudes toward people with HIV have unfortunately continued to be reflected both in our everyday lives and in developments in social policy and law. Because of this, many women and men who are HIV positive have chosen to remain silent both about their diagnosis and about the painful isolation they have experienced because of that diagnosis. The epidemic isn't over; in fact, for many of us, it has just begun. Thus, our consciousness about it must continue to evolve so that we may dispel the ignorance, denial, stigma, blame, and silence that still haunt our efforts to fight this disease. Until very recently, prevention messages have focused on changing behavior rather than addressing the factors that motivate behavior. Some behaviors were simply labeled as wrong or to be avoided, a strategy which not only did very little to help people think about why they might engage in risky behaviors, but also served to further stigmatize people who are HIV positive by implying that they must have done something "bad" or "wrong" in order to have become infected. In recent years, this simplistic approach to prevention has increasingly given way to more holistic approaches that look to motivations and context as significant determinants of how people behave.

It is our premise that all individuals living in relation to this pandemic, HIV positive and HIV negative alike, bring to bear on their experiences of the world both positive and negative consciousness. That is, rather than thinking of "positive" and "negative" as fixed and polarized identities determined solely by one's current health status, we consider "positive" and "negative" to be context-dependent modes of consciousness that shape the actions and perspectives of both HIV-positive and HIV-negative individuals. For instance, an HIV-positive person might shift along this continuum of positive and negative consciousness at any given moment depending on whether or not his or her status is known, whether the people she or he is with at any given time are themselves positive or negative, and the extent to which she or he is engaged in protecting others (physically or emotionally). Similarly, an HIV-negative person, whether or not he or she consciously understands that status as potentially temporary, might also engage the world from the perspective of positive and negative consciousness as he or she makes decisions about physical intimacy, and so on.

One of the reasons it is crucial to think about consciousness in this more fluid and contingent way is that it prevents us from operating out of an "us" and "them" mentality as we manage our relationships with each other in the midst of this epidemic. As long as we think of the world as simply divided between those who have HIV and those who don't, between the sick and the well, between the positive and the negative, we risk perpetuating both the epidemic and the oppressive, uncaring social attitudes that have come with it. And, importantly, we unfairly and dangerously place the burden of managing both the disease and its spread solely on the shoulders of those who are already infected. Coming to terms with HIV/AIDS is a task that must and should involve every human being.

The plays and poems gathered in this collection bear witness to the manifold and various ways the pandemic has impacted the lives of both HIV-positive and HIV-negative people. In creating this forum, we celebrate those who have learned to live with and cope with HIV/AIDS despite the continued challenges they face. We invite you to hear voices that have waited long to be heard, voices of people who have struggled long with AIDS, many of whom have found joy in the struggle, and others who have not.

Positive/Negative aims to raise awareness and give voice to those whose lives and work have remained hidden, silenced, and censored, while they fought for their lives and for the lives of others in the face of the pandemic. Who are they and how have they survived for so many years without *positive* acknowledgment from the larger society? How have they functioned under the oppressive forces of stigma and fear? What has been happening to women, especially women of color, with HIV or AIDS, who have been rendered particularly silent and invisible by the misinformation about and fear of this disease? Indeed, how is it that we are going into the third decade of AIDS and only recently have women begun to be considered forefront in the ravages of this disease? What truths have women not expressed because no one else has talked about them? What hopes and dreams sat before them as mere fantasies about someone that would come into their lives and love them, care for them, support them, and hear their cries? And when women—and people of color and gays of color—with HIV/AIDS have broken the silence, why has it been so difficult for them to be truly heard by the larger society? The authors in this collection of plays and poetry—both those who have personally battled with this disease and those who have watched others battle with it—bear witness to social and psychological realities that have long gone unexpressed or unheeded. In compiling this body of work, we honor and celebrate their achievements in creating meaning and seeking social change through their artistic quests.

Positive/Negative presents an understanding of the epidemic through a host of multicultural voices—writers, activists, and community caregivers. Witness a re-imaging of ourselves unveiled through the characters in this assorted body of plays and poetry. Hear the voices of younger and older generations of women and men—women who love women, men who love men, women who love men and men who love women—all demonstrating how theater can reflect and effect social and behavioral change.

Current Trends in the Epidemic

The works in this anthology represent the complex psychosexual, behavioral, and social relationships of the HIV-positive and HIV-negative consciousness. Here the broad themes of love, sex, and death are brought together, revealing some of the most hidden truths of the HIV-positive and HIV-negative experiences. This anthology comes at a crucial time, as many communities have either become complacent or are still in denial about the epidemic. For, even in the face of hope, there are still signs of danger, as shown both by the resurgence of HIV infections (up by 60%) and by new policy mandates and legislation.

Several of the works in this anthology reflect the impact that current laws and public policy have on the behavior of both HIV-positive and HIV-negative individuals. Because these laws generally regulate the behavior of HIV-positive people, they place a tremendous psychosocial weight on those individuals by laying the burden of responsibility for controlling the epidemic largely on them. Currently, over half of the states have implemented laws designed to prevent the transmission of HIV infection. This legislation falls under three broad areas: contact tracing, partner notification, and case reporting. Unfortunately, not only do these laws tend to further alienate already marginalized HIV-positive individuals, but also, in the name of protecting the broader public—a public which does not, apparently, include HIV-positive people—actually denies them equal protection under the law. While the laws concerning HIV vary from state to state, they are largely punitive and generally undermine or retard efforts to encourage good health and spiritual development for all. These laws do little to challenge the awareness and behavior of those who are assumed to be negative, as if they should be exempt and unaccountable for their own behaviors. Essentially, laws mandating contact tracing, partner notification, and case reporting dissuade people from getting tested and disclosing their status. They do little to encourage *positive* behavior and in fact influence one to be *negative*. Clearly, under a socio-political climate like this, to be *negative* is highly favorable. These laws have a great impact on the psychosexual attitudes between positive and negative individuals. A few cases in point show how unfair these statutes are: a woman from Tennessee received a 26-year sentence even though she disclosed her status to her sex partners, who consented to have sex with her; an Indiana woman was charged with attempted murder for biting and scratching a police officer; a mentally impaired woman who did not inform her sex partner that she was positive received four years for engaging in sexual penetration; sex workers have been charged for engaging in prostitution while being HIV positive (even if protection is used), while their partners have not been prosecuted (POZ, 2000). But even in these cases we see that disclosure may not prevent positive individuals from being prosecuted and charged with reckless endangerment, willful exposure, intentional transmission, sex crimes, or, in the extreme, attempted murder. Policies such as these encourage many positive people to live in denial, in effect preventing them from changing behavior that may warrant change. Ultimately, imprisoning, punishing, and imposing unfair penalties on a person, and treating her or him as an *it*, as the only thing to be feared, does not prevent her or him from transmitting the virus.

The World Health Organization's year-end 2000 global report estimates that there are 36 million children and adults living with HIV, with new infections up to 5.3 million. The cumulative number of deaths due to HIV/AIDS is projected at 21.8 million (WHO, 2000). Worldwide, people of color are disproportionately infected with HIV/AIDS, in many cases causing further destruction to families already ravaged by poverty and other social ills. We must continue to explore the psychosocial and political landscapes occupied by those becoming infected and ask why the epidemic has continued to intensify. It is clear that more must be accomplished to address the growing rates of HIV infection, a resurgence of HIV infection in the young, elderly, gay, straight, visible, invisible, and otherwise. The works in this anthology examine this phenomenon through their exploration of the relationship between individual dramatic characters and society. It is clear that even with the opposing trends in the epidemic, many people are now ready to talk about sex, death, and love in the era of HIV/AIDS.

The Use and Value of AIDS Theater

As Long and Ankra suggest in their book *Women's Experiences with HIV/AIDS: An International Perspective* (1996), in order to look at women's issues in the pandemic, different disciplines need to collaborate and, through a variety of approaches, allow the real experiences of women and their relationships to be contextualized. At its best, theater helps to facilitate such a process. Since HIV is a disease influenced by biological, social, and behavioral factors, then the living theater is a place for one to explore the broader socio-psychological forces influencing this same behavior. As Brazilian theater activist and director Augusto Boal has argued, theater allows a creative process to unfold in which individuals are empowered to question, test, explore, and intervene, to reject the old and rehearse the new by creating possibilities for social transformation. Theater provides both positive and negative individuals a safe place to engage in a conversation about social policies, attitudes, beliefs and behaviors concerning HIV, and, in the process, to construct meanings that underscore the quintessential value in human relationships. Given the complexity of the experiences of both positive and negative individuals, bringing the two into dialogue can have a profound effect on community cohesion and cultural expression.

It was Augusto Boal who coined the term "Theatre of the Oppressed," drawing on Paulo Freire's vision of collective/community empowerment through popular education (Schutzman and Cohen-Cruz, 1994). Boal's brilliant humanist vision has been about focusing on oppression through a series of techniques, such as imaginative games and exercises in theatrical forms. The most popular forms of Theatre of the Oppressed, many of which developed in the midst of repressive regimes in Brazil, are Newspaper Theatre, Image, Forum, Invisible Theatre, and Legislative Theatre. The main goal of Theatre of the Oppressed is to "break the oppression" through acts of personal and social transformation. All of the plays and poetry in *Positive/Negative*, by virtue of their themes and content, reflect the goals and strategies of Theatre of the Oppressed. They embody the essential ingredients needed to confront one's oppressor, to empower and liberate oneself from those forces that have sought to control or demean one's human existence.

Inherent in the techniques of the Theatre of the Oppressed are elements that engage, as Boal suggests, participants as active (listening) members rather than passive sitters watching a drama unfold. We propose, using Boal's terminology, that our contributors are both actors and "spect-actors." The actor is never without the consciousness of being who she or he is and at the same time another: "Humans are capable of seeing themselves in the act of seeing, of thinking their emotions, of being moved by their thoughts" (Boal, 1992). In Theatre of the Oppressed, participants are respected and supported for their attempts to write on their feet and to produce theater that speaks with and engages the audience as active participants in a dialectical exchange, not merely for show and entertainment, but for the purposes of social and community development. This dialectical relationship between audience, performer, and everyday social life dates back to the early traditions of Asian, African, and Latin cultures.

One of the main tenets of writing AIDS is that the writer carries the potential to educate her/himself as well as those who are not often afforded the means to access information. Like Paulo Freire, many advocates see awareness as a process brought about by education, by an increase in knowledge

(Knowledge=Power). The quest to ignite change within a given spectator is highly possible. And as more and more people develop critical consciousness, we propose that a positive and negative consciousness will ensue, engendering a process of personal insight and social change.

In the early 1980s, toward the beginning of the epidemic, many mainstream plays reflected the gay white and middle-class male experience. Since then, a number of plays and unique forms of writings, performance art, and ritual have begun to appear in the cultural landscape of art, AIDS, and theater. As those disenfranchised communities became more visible, the articulation and expression for addressing HIV/AIDS in the mainstream media increasingly flourished in the light of a grieving society. Thus, mourning art as ritual became the norm. Theater as an art form began to serve as a tool for self-expression and creative expression. Art that represented HIV/AIDS was reflected in paintings, photographs, collages, journals, letters, pendants, bracelets, quilts, narratives, and plays; created by those who felt the need to express their experience of the epidemic. A number of male artists of color whose work finally reached the depths of the community and subsequently made it to either film or the main stage were forefront in presenting the themes of life, love, sex, death, intimacy, and the joys and pain of suffering from HIV—to name a few: Sean San Jose Blackman, Wayne Corbitt, Essex Hemphill, Marlon Riggs, Assato Saint, Reggie Williams, and Chey Yew. For these writers, theater and AIDS narratives, which reflected HIV/AIDS concerns, helped to function as a method to fight the oppressive forces. Important to note are those writers of color who have been writing in the trenches and have yet to see their work surface from the underground and make it to any form of mainstream visibility. Women writers who have written about women with HIV include Sapphire, Cheryl West, Charlotte Watson Sherman, and Pearl Cleage, all of whom are established and published writers. Their works are about women and HIV; however, men also play significant roles, especially within the works by Cleage and West.

In *Positive/Negative* we emphasize the work of playwrights writing about AIDS, recognizing the difficulties playwrights have experienced in getting work about HIV/AIDS produced. AIDS theater has certainly challenged traditional Western theatrical norms as it has explored the nuances and the social and psychological articulation of the experience of the AIDS epidemic. As social action theater, AIDS plays are at least as serious in their efforts to not only entertain but educate, breaking boundaries of what has been considered "traditional" and "standard" theater. An AIDS play as narrative tells the authorial and imaginative story of the experience of being positive not necessarily in form and structure but in content. Unfortunately the works of ethnic and marginal communities which promote social change have not always been taken seriously by "American Theater." So how would they be taken seriously in the face of a raging epidemic? However, plays reflecting the voice of communities of color that previously had not been central to mainstream theatrical performance venues, have nevertheless managed to find their audiences.

Some established community-based programs have been building relation-ships between students, community activists and theaters, including West Coast theater programs such as BRAVA's Drama Divas, Community Education Program at TheatreWorks, Mark Taper Forum's Other Voices Project for writers with disabilities, and the New College Theater in San Francisco. Additionally, Berkeley Repertory Theatre, Medea Project, Geese Theatre, Soapstone Theatre, Black Repertory Group, and Oakland Ensemble Theatre have all taken some extraordinary leaps toward building community through education and cultural art, and building audience through produc-ing and developing the artistic minds of some promising writers and actors as they become writers of their own experiences in urban communities. While these programs do not specifically deal with AIDS as their main focus, they have taken up social issues and concerns of the community. On the rise are more theaters and organizations learning from these thought-provoking, stimulating, and progressive, social-based programs to expand their audi-ence base and/or educational programs. Thus today we might say that out of AIDS theater, a type of social theater providing knowledge-based interven-tion and prevention methods that aid in the education of the masses has been forged.

The San Francisco AIDS Theater Festival is one of the first major perform-ing arts events in San Francisco that sought writers from a diverse back-ground of sexuality, class, race/ethnicity, and gender to develop and showcase their works to both conference attendees and the general public. It was Hank Tavera, cultural activist, director and original founder of the San Francisco AIDS Theater Festival who was responsible for setting the theatri-cal agenda for nurturing artists over the past ten years. Tavera advocated that in order for the epidemic to be taken seriously and give voice and meaning to cultural artists fighting for their lives and the lives of those affected, a viable theater format should be implemented at the conference—to help educate and propel one's struggles into action. Works not initially embraced by local or professional theaters found a venue at the AIDS Theater Festival. The AIDS Theater Festival earned many of its successes by allowing artists the opportunity to work and grow in a community of other artists and activists. We accepted a few of the many promising plays from the festival. Tavera was instrumental during this process, answering questions about the history of the AIDS Theater Festival, and offering to bring some of these plays to the festival. While in the development and planning stages for the next festival, and awaiting an essay from Tavera on the history of the festival, a harrowing notice came and those final plans came to a sudden halt—Hank Tavera had passed away while in the development and planning stages for the next festival after a noble fight from a "non-AIDS related" condition. Many of the plays presented here would have found their way to the AIDS Theater Festival.

Unveiling Gender

At the time we solicited writers—known and emerging—for this anthology, few had written about the experience, perception, or image of women in the epidemic. Additionally, in a number of the oral interviews first conducted for this book project, we observed that few women writers (in our networks and other networks) had known women with HIV. We found this phenomenon particularly interesting given the invisibility of women in the epidemic. It is our hope that this anthology will inspire women to write about women in the HIV/AIDS epidemic.

Our natural and initial impulse was to include only work by and about women in this anthology, but writing the self is relative to what we live, know, and experience (Corrine Squire, 1999), and we came to believe that if we separated the women's voices from the full range of that experience then we would run the risk of denying what women think about themselves and others in the epidemic. Women writers write about men as friends, would-be lovers, admirers and even role models. We also recognized from a womanist's perspective that men writers (primarily men of color) should be included because HIV has had a devastating effect on communities of color as a whole. Therefore, we included the works of men who were willing to write about women's issues with a conscious awareness that women are forefront in this disease. We believe that collectively, the writers in this anthology contribute an unprecedented range of voices and perspectives to the landscape of HIV/AIDS dramatic literature.

Positive/Negative: The Process and Organization

We divided the anthology into three thematic sections: Love/Relationships, Sex/Sexuality, and Danger/Death. While these themes, of course, do not represent the full range of issues taken up by each of these works, and while all of the works, to some extent, treat each of these themes, we felt that organizing the works under these broad themes might help readers to see some of the important connections between the works.

Love/Relationships: Where Women Sleep. When we consider love and relationships in the era of AIDS, we find it impossible to separate them from issues of gender identity, sexuality, and sexual politics, because who we love, how we love, and why we love are all bound up within social psychology of gender. What happens to love when physical intimacy is understood to be dangerous? How and when and under what conditions is it safe for women to love? What happens to a woman when she thinks of her body as a source of contagion? How do women feel about skin-to-skin sex, pregnancy, and mortality? How do these feelings affect women's decisions about whether or not to disclose their HIV status? While some women find refuge in rejecting physical intimacy, others say they want to be touched. By looking into these issues as they are played out in the actions and thoughts of the characters depicted in this section, we get closer to the social experience and the psychology of HIV/AIDS.

Positive Women is a series of six short plays, each by a different writer, that specifically deals with how the AIDS crisis has been experienced by the Latina community. Commissioned by the Latino Experimental Fantastic Theater, these plays are based on a series of interviews of women with HIV conducted by Carmen Rivera and Cándido Tirado. Each playwright was given an interview to work with, and the whole series was designed, as Rivera puts it, to allow the audience to "experience the different emotional stages through the illness." Taken as a whole, the plays emphasize family issues, nurturance, love, life, and death—but mostly survival.

Sandra Rodríguez's *Prologue: Loves That Kill* focuses on the stage of *discovery* as four women who are grandmothers learn they have been infected with the virus and struggle to conceal their HIV status when they initially encounter each other in the waiting room of a doctor's office. Opening with a game-playing sequence that helps us to see these women in the context of their whole lives, the play explores how a community of women who have been marginalized by the larger society because of their ethnicity can find a space both to acknowledge their HIV status and to support each other in facing the emotional and practical challenges the disease brings to them.

Mariluz's Thanksgiving, written by Migdalia Cruz, closely examines love while in the face of *anger.* Through the main protagonist, Mariluz, Cruz lets the readers see how gender identity roles factor into how Latinas are impacted by HIV/AIDS. Through this character's vivid memory of her childhood we see her faced with feelings of loss, betrayal, isolation, and alienation. We come to see how Mariluz, who both as woman and as an HIV-positive immigrant lacking power and privilege, is nevertheless far from being a victim.

Delia's Race by Carmen Rivera is the story of a mother who, faced with *fear* after becoming infected with the HIV virus, became an AIDS activist. The story reveals how a mother's love for her daughter and her community are challenged by fears of death. For someone who has been very positive throughout her illness, the knowledge that her T-cell count is zero comes as a blow.

now and then, written by Michael John Garcés, explores the *hope* of a young pregnant woman, Monica, who is HIV positive. Here again the themes of love, sex, and danger are intricately connected as we witness Monica negotiating complicated relationships both with Eric, the partner who infected her, and with David, a later partner.

Ilka: The Dream, written by Cándido Tirado, is based on the life of actress, lawyer, and AIDS activist Ilka Tanya Payan. Exploring themes of *love* and connection, the play takes place in the surrealistic realm between life and death, where Ilka encounters her old friends Victor and Manolito, who also died from AIDS. Ilka is having a hard time letting go of the life she left behind, in part because she feels that she has left things undone. To help her find some resolution, she and her friends recreate her experiences both during the initial scare of the epidemic and later as she herself was diagnosed with HIV.

The closing play in the sequence is Louis Delgado's *Epilogue: Elba's Birthday*, which features the same four women introduced in the *Prologue*. In the *Epilogue*, we see how far these four grandmothers have traveled as they gather together to celebrate one of their birthdays.

Imani Harrington's *Love & Danger*, heralded as the first literary play to address women in the epidemic, explores the experience of five female protagonists who sojourn the underground after having fled a clinical trial that went awry. The women, at various times throughout the play, take on multiple roles, ranging from accuser to oppressor to target of blame. Together, they confront past loves and lies, revealing the various ways in which love has been associated with danger. As we experience the players' anxieties and finally the unveiling of each woman's desires, we come to understand the complexities of positive-negative consciousness. The simple duality as used to determine HIV status is much more complex when we witness the identity clashes between HIV-positive and HIV-negative characters.

The next piece in this section is Dorinda Welle's poem "Allah appears as an eyelash in brooklyn." Part of a larger series of interconnected poems, this poem uses the metaphor of an eyelash to stand in for an absent lover, whose whole being ("allah" in this context means "all of"), physical and spiritual, is somehow embodied in the eyelash left behind. The poem's treatment of themes of love and connection gives a sense of how important all the "sacred traces" of love, wherever we find them, are.

Like many other pieces in this section, the last selection, *I'se Married* by Ntombi Howell and Ernest Andrews (Sweet Potato Pie), represents the quest for love, intimacy, and relationships in the context of the epidemic. Even rapid medical and scientific advances do not change the reality that HIV-positive people live with the knowledge that they could die. *I'se Married* is a testament to a positive consciousness, one that is acutely aware of the prevailing possibility of death, but that invokes the marriage vow "Till death do us part" as a declaration of love and hope. It honors those who, despite the challenges the epidemic has brought on over the years, have nevertheless had the courage to choose, as Howell and Andrews put it, "to enter into the space of love."

Sex/Sexuality: Unveiling Touch. The experience of abuse, the act of sex, and the consequences of sex are just a few of the themes in this section concerned with the body politic. These themes are centered in the various characters' need to touch, have intimacy, express desire, and confront their own sexuality. Here we find connection and pleasure wrapped in seduction, and even moments of eroticism. Politically speaking, women of all sexualities have had to pay a price for such expression. It should come to us as no surprise that women who feel censored often fail to assert their power about their sensual selves. These plays, monologues, and poetry as narrative voices directly challenge the current conflicts and concerns about the expression and meaning of one's sexuality, one's identity as a sexual person, and the consequences of that expression.

Migdalia Cruz's short play *So…* explores the body through four voices: a fatalist, pragmatist, romantic, and realist. We see the pathos and humor found in a positive and negative consciousness of both female and male experiences of love, longing, belonging, and the obsessive need for intimacy and desire even if it's in the face of death. In this meditation of voices speaking to God in a confessional manner, we find how love brings more than closeness; the body is something sacred and is objectified by the phenomenon of love.

Mario Golden's full-length play *One Less Queen* concerns itself with the themes of sexuality, desire, gender identity, and internalized homophobia. *One Less Queen* centers around the life and story of Alfonso, a gay Mexican immigrant and drag performer, and his best friend, Chuyis, a Chicana transsexual. In this play we are reminded, through the blending of fact and fiction, of the lives of women (especially transgendered women) who have been incarcerated while suffering from AIDS. The climactic confrontation between Alfonso and Chuyis' ex-lover Juan Gallo precedes Chuyis' dignified death and the ritual of her own transfiguration into the spiritual realm, manifesting as a surprising and hope-instilling form.

The Watermelon Factory, written by Alfonso Ramirez, situates itself around the journey of acceptance of a Mexican American adopted man, Gabriel Rios, and a middle-aged Mexican woman, Connie, who meet on the morning of Mother's Day in the park. The characters struggle between acceptance and denial, sorting through fact and fiction to understand their circumstances. This play delves into the themes of identity, sexuality, belonging, abandonment, isolation, and hidden realities often veiled within the Catholic Church. Ramirez unveils these issues through the intimate and private details shared by these two characters as they get to know each other.

Q.V. Atkins' monologue *Dolly: Old Lady, Love, and Life* is one of two excerpts in this anthology from the play script *Russian Roulette/Poison Places: Teens Living in the Age of AIDS*. Through the voice of her HIV-positive character Dolly, Atkins examines loss on multiple levels—loss of innocence, loss of love, loss of life, loss associated with being an invisible member of society due to drug use and homelessness. She also deals with the lack of education about HIV, such as the possibilities of superinfection and further transmission. Yet, Dolly still sees that her mission is to tell others about love and life. But many will not hear her—she remains invisible to them.

Like Mama Like Daughter, written by poet and writer Kulwa Apara, is another monologue from *Russian Roulette/Poison Places*. Through her depiction of a mother-daughter relationship, Apara highlights the patterns of abuse experienced by two different generations. Kneeling at her mother's grave, the daughter tells her mother that she too is HIV positive, following the path of her own mother in this and other ways. Apara offers a chilling and haunting picture of a young girl who longs for the mother she lost to AIDS and who, out of her own loneliness and need for love, stays in a relationship that is clearly bad for her.

Danger/Death: As Life Ends the Resurrection of Love Continues. The works in this section evoke the hidden and not-so-hidden emotions that accompany loss. They hallmark the importance and value of human relationships as they offer various reflections on how experience with HIV can actually push us toward a positive intimacy with self and with others. As we see characters finding ways to reclaim life and connection in the face of death and loss, these works show us how death is inevitably linked to renewal.

Zelma Brown's poem, "Numb," uses vivid imagery to paint one woman's existential journey of loneliness and isolation, rendering a glimpse of the impending mortality shadowing the consciousness of many with HIV. Although the speaker recounts her attempted suicide as an embrace of her own death, she ultimately finds the possibilities of survival through self-acceptance and acceptance of her disease, "these new friends called H, I and V."

Shay Youngblood's *Black Power Barbie* explores how childhood loss and grief affect two adult siblings, one of whom is dying of AIDS. Despite their love for each other and their shared childhood trauma, the main characters battle over power as they work with a therapist to understand their evolving gender identities, sexualities, and fates.

Joanne Bealy's *Elegy* reflects the narrator's impending thoughts about love and loss—how loss and grief are not separated by love. This consciousness unfolds as she reminisces about the way in which love stirs our most intense and passionate desires. We get a sense of longing, a desire to be touched and loved, and the yearning for intimate relationships.

Marijo's *Ashes to Ashes* reflects the failure of religious communities, in this case the black church, to embrace and care for members who are infected with HIV. With considerable linguistic flare, Marijo offers a humorous and moving account of a mother reclaiming the legacy of her son's life in the face of bigotry.

In *Nothing Forever*, Chiori Miyagawa explores the dynamic of the positive consciousness from yet another angle as she depicts the journey of an (unnamed) Asian woman whose thinking about her pregnancy is profoundly shaped by her close friendship with a man who is dying from AIDS. *Nothing Forever* is told as meta-memory, impressionistic and lyrical, using lighting, movement, poetry, dance, music, and time to move audiences through the experiences of the main character as they are filtered through a series of remembered encounters.

The closing piece of the anthology, V. Thandi Sule's *I Got You Under My Skin*, represents all that goes before touch, exploring a profound aspect of a positive consciousness that is often too difficult to confirm because it's so close to the "skin." In prose that reads as if it were written on the body, Sule closely examines the intricacies of desire, allowing readers to connect psychologically with both what has been lost and what has been gained: "So, I remain gasping for air, suffocating in my orgasmic juices. Shamed that I gave all of myself to you, yet overjoyed by my willingness to do so." She ultimately finds in her own ambivalent embodiment a sense of renewal: "It is the *maybe* that keeps life just below the surface of my skin—stirring things up."

The contributors in this anthology offer us a glimpse of hope and a reason to consider those signs of love to be had and gotten, even in the face of death. Certainly in that we can see a triumph of life over fear and dread. Thus, we are awakened by these narratives into consciousness, telling us that it is time, it is finally time to

reclaim
the
beauty once lost.

AMERICAN THEATER, WOMEN, AND THE PANDEMIC
Imani Harrington

In the early years of the pandemic, women's experiences—when they weren't ignored altogether—were often distorted by the media, creating a gap between what women were actually experiencing and how they saw themselves reflected (and not reflected) out in the world. In observing these missing aspects of women's experiences, I began to wonder: How do positive women feel about their bodies, their erotic selves? How do the representations they see of themselves—on the stage, in literature, in the news, in public policy debates—affect how they view themselves? How much of a role have blame, guilt, and shame played in shaping how they see themselves? How have social forces, especially via media and public policy, sought to control their personal agency? How do these experiences play out in shaping women's understanding of safety? And, how can *all* of these experiences and others be drawn out of imaginations, imaginations surely haunted by the experience of censorship, and rendered in dramatic forms? The very act of asking and answering these questions, of course, brings up a broader issue of value: What makes this kind of content and this process of making art more or less important than, let's say, a comedy on Broadway? I am not proposing that we banish one form of theater for the other. Rather I am asking us to consider whether it is possible for mainstream theater in the U.S. to create space for representing the full range of human experience, to allow real tensions, real differences at all levels, to occupy the stage of human thought.

With so much of the public discourse on HIV/AIDS focused either on men, or, especially when it comes to women, on questions of blame and responsibility, there has been little room for the personal voice and perspective of the positive woman to emerge in dramatic narrative. What has been missing from the stage, just as it has so often been missing from clinical trials and medical research, is the body of the positive woman, a body that has, perhaps, been considered too infectious to be offered up as aesthetic material for the public's imagination. In what way, then, could artists—especially women dramatists—articulate dimensions of how women have experienced the epidemic that American Theater (as an institution) has generally failed to capture? How can you see something when it's missing? As I considered this problem, I found myself having to go on a kind of archeological search, to borrow a metaphor from writer and dramaturg Sydné Mahone, a search for the missing body of women's experience in the epidemic. In this archeological dig, I uncovered in my own imagination aspects of positive women's history, fragmented bones from the body of women's experience left over from the early responses of the epidemic, buried by neglect and distortion. It was a body I needed to unearth, to reexamine, and to put back together again so that I could begin the work of representing the experience of the positive woman. And in order to do that, I needed to scrape off the labels attached to her, labels that called her bad, infector, and whore, labels that constructed an identity for her on behalf of a society bent on controlling the daily sphere of her positive existence. Having lived through the deaths of so many who were silenced and censored, and having fought for my own life, I know how little has been recognized of how positive women feel and have felt about their own bodies. Facing my own death in the context of this overwhelming silence, I was propelled by an emotional, sociopolitical, and intellectual response that led me both to write my own play, *Love & Danger*, and to compile this anthology of plays about women of color and HIV/AIDS.

When I wrote *Love & Danger*, the exclusion of the experience of positive women, especially positive women of color, from dramatic representation was nearly absolute, reflecting the social and cultural conservatism of American Theater and the pervasive denial of communities at large. And as Sydné Mahone observes in her work on African American women writers and playwrights, the "very act" of telling one's own story, of breaking forth into representation, is both an act of social and political empowerment, of "resistance to oppression," and an instrument of social change, of bringing forth "new attitudes and new worldviews" (Mahone, 1994). But Mahone also makes it clear that artists who create a tradition of their own are often rendered invisible anyway: the act of speaking doesn't guarantee that anyone will listen, let alone listen well. In fact, the act of representing oneself entails considerable risk, because it opens up the possibility for being misunderstood, for being attacked, or for having one's experience be appropriated. But that risk is necessary, because it is only through letting tensions emerge in real dialogue, with everyone present and speaking, that we can hope to move forward in our efforts to cope with this epidemic. That is why I forged ahead with *Love & Danger*, and that is why we have forged ahead with this collection.

It has not been until recently that the social realities and the voices of women and people of color have been reflected in social theater exploring the AIDS landscape. When I started writing *Love & Danger*, artists of color— in particular artists whose work was about advancing community awareness about HIV/AIDS—found themselves in a discouraging competition with the very few established playwrights whose work was given access to a wide audience. Theaters were generally reluctant to touch the work of new or emerging writers addressing political and social concerns about community and AIDS, at best out of a fear that the public wouldn't be interested in such work, and at worst out of fear of such work's possible contamination of the public's imagination. Thus, these plays were not given the same priority as work less directly interested in creating social change. It appeared that to move from the margin to the center would take revolutions. But by the time things seemed to be opening up in the theater, many artists had already died or had seroconverted, become depressed, exhausted, or weary. Many of my colleagues died while creating work that never made it to the stage or press. AIDS apathy saps the political will of artists, especially artists of color who are doubly marginalized, who seek to participate in the discourse on both HIV and AIDS.

The plays and poems in this anthology—and other works that carry out a similar mission—are credible and authentic aesthetic tools for transforming social thought and political imagination. One of our intentions in putting together *Positive/Negative* is to encourage artists writing with vision of community and to inspire new ones who may not have been afforded either the access or education (yet) to be a part of the American stage. Theater has enormous potential to help people, young and old, learn about dimensions of social and political life with which they are unfamiliar. We need a space and venue to present writing and performance about HIV/AIDS—and other underrepresented social experiences—that does that kind of teaching. For writers to create at their best, they require a nurturing environment, a space open enough and broad enough to reflect the vast array of human differences. *Positive/Negative: Women of Color and HIV/AIDS* was created to be that platform, to make that space. Welcome to this theater and its stage.

SECTION 1
LOVE/RELATIONSHIPS

Positive Women

1. DISCOVERY — Prologue: Loves That Kill
2. ANGER — Mariluz's Thanksgiving
3. FEAR — Delia's Race
4. HOPE — now and then
5. LOVE — Ilka: The Dream
6. LIFE — Epilogue: Elba's Birthday

Commissioned by the Latino Experimental Fantastic Theater (L.E.F.T.), Positive Women is based on a series of interviews of women with HIV conducted by Carmen Rivera and Cándido Tirado. It was first produced at LaMaMa ETC, New York.

Prologue: Loves That Kill

Sandra Rodríguez

Characters

ELBA

LALA

MYRNA

OLGA

[Bare stage, dimly lit. The lights should be placed to create four white spots that illuminate several areas onstage. On the sides there are three stools which will be used later. The scene will be played as a dance/movement scene with games, dance, songs, and isolated phrases spoken or sung by the cast.]

[The melody of "Verbena," a Spanish version of the "London Bridge" game/song, plays. Four women dressed with basic uniform-like costumes, preferably with flowing dresses or skirts, enter. Lights go up. They will sing as they play/dance.]

ALL: *[Singing]*
    Verbena, verbena.
    La Virgen de la cueva.
    Los pajaritos cantan.
    Las nubes se levantan.
    Pase misín, pase misán,
    por la puerta de San Juan.
    La de alante corre mucho
    y la de atrás se quedará.

[After performing "Verbena" a few times, their game transforms into "La Tablita" (a Spanish version of hopscotch). They play together, each taking one or two turns.]

ALL: *[singing]*
> Brinca la tablita
> Que yo la brinqué.
> Bríncala tu ahora
> Que yo me cansé.
> Dos y dos son cuatro.
> Cuatro y dos son seis.
> Seis y dos son ocho.
> Y ocho diez y seis.

["La Tablita" transforms into "La Señorita," which is danced as a circle of girls singing and clapping while one dances gracefully in the middle. At this point they start acting as young girls/pre-teens.]

[OLGA dances centerstage as the other women sing and clap.]

ALL: *[singing]*
> La Señorita Olga
> entrando en el baile.
> Que lo baile,
> que lo baile.
> Y si no lo baila,
> tendrá un castigo grande.
> Que lo baile,
> que lo baile.
>
> Saque usted.

[OLGA picks ELBA from the circle and dances with her.]

ALL: *[singing]*
> Que la quiero ver bailando.
> Buenos Aires,
> Buenos Aires.
> Lo bien que lo baila la niña bonita.
> Déjela sola, sola, solita.

[OLGA retreats, leaving ELBA dancing alone. The cycle is repeated once or twice, using the name of the character that is dancing alone. The women then hum the melody to "El Hijo del Conde" as they start to move around the stage as teenagers. Each one holds a white envelope with which she fans herself as she dances/moves.]

ALL: *[singing]*
>El hijo del Conde, caramba,
>me mandó un papel.
>Que si yo quería, caramba,
>casarme con él…

["El Hijo del Conde" is sung twice, the second time slowly and softly. As the women sing for the second time, they move around the stage, ending with each one standing in a spotlight. They look happy and excited about the white envelopes they are holding. Their expressions change as the next song is sung.]

FEMALE VOICE: *[sings from offstage]*
>Tengo una muñeca vestida de azul.
>Zapatitos blancos, camisón de tul.
>La llevé a paseo y se me enfermó.

[When "se me enfermó" is sung, the women open the envelopes, revealing another, red, envelope with a letter inside written on red paper, which obviously bears bad news. Women react.]

FEMALE VOICE: *[sings from offstage]*
>La acosté en la cama con mucho dolor.

[The women freeze for one intense second, holding their red envelopes as "El Hijo del Conde" is sung slowly and softly.]

OLGA: *[sings softly and slowly]*
>El hijo del Conde, caramba,
>me mandó un papel.
>Que si yo quería, caramba…

[Blackout. Total silence. Lights go up slowly.]

ELBA: I didn't know what was going on.

OLGA: I felt so guilty.

LALA: So dirty.

MYRNA: I didn't understand. It was just a cold.

ELBA: He loved me.

OLGA: El lo sabía y no me dijo nada.

LALA: I had nowhere to go. What was I supposed to do?

ELBA: We were married for so long. ¡Y por la iglesia!

MYRNA: I couldn't tell my family. Mis nenes…

LALA: I can't abandon him now that he's sick.

OLGA: I wish I had the courage to go and give it to everyone.

ELBA: Mis hijos. They don't let me touch my grandchildren.

OLGA: If my daughter would've not asked me to go and get checked, I would've never known.

[*"Tengo una Muñeca" is played slowly and softly for transition. The women freeze, and look intensely at the audience for a few seconds. Blackout. Three of the women exit, except for ELBA, who stays behind. Lights go up. Musak plays as stage hands set up the clinic: chairs, magazines, etc. ELBA puts on a light sweater and takes a small purse with a wallet inside and a magazine which holds the red envelope. She sits, trying nervously to read the magazine. She looks distressed but she seems to be trying very hard to conceal her emotions. The red envelope is sticking out of her magazine. She takes the envelope and reads the letter inside it several times. As she reads OLGA enters, holding a similar red envelope, and looks around. She doesn't notice ELBA right away. ELBA looks up and OLGA recognizes her. They hide their red envelopes at the same time and simultaneously greet each other.*]

OLGA: [*hiding the envelope*] Elba?

ELBA: [*hiding the envelope*] Olga!

[*Throughout the scene, ELBA will act slightly detached, sad, and weak.*]

OLGA: ¡Tanto tiempo!

[OLGA *kisses* ELBA, *who stays seated.*]

ELBA: Long time no see!

OLGA: To be exact, five years.

ELBA: Time surely flies.

OLGA: [*looking at her, complimentary*] Let me look at you. Oye, por fin te pusiste en la línea. Por que tu si que eras gordita. How many pounds…?

ELBA: [*uncomfortable*] I don't know.

OLGA: ¡No vayas a rebajar más! You've lost enough.

[As if realizing the possible reason for her friend's weight loss, OLGA *shuts up abruptly and sits.* ELBA *realizes it at the same time and also becomes very serious and uncomfortable, forcing a cordial smile.]*

ELBA: Just came for a checkup.

OLGA: *[not even letting* ELBA *finish]* Me too!

[Heavy silence.]

OLGA: *[as if trying to make conversation]* How are the kids?

ELBA: Fine.

OLGA: ¿Y tu marido? What's his name…Tito. How's he doing?

*[*ELBA *is about to answer when* LALA *enters, holding another red envelope. She sees the other two right away, and she hides her envelope quickly.]*

OLGA: No! Lala!

LALA: Olga. Oh my God! My God. Dios mío tanto tiempo. *[kissing* OLGA*]* How you been?

*[*LALA *doesn't recognize* ELBA *right away, but when she does, she screams in surprise.]*

LALA: Elba, Elba. Oh my goodness! Que sorpresa. I didn't even recognize you. Si estás flaquísima. Such a small world. Haven't seen you both in about eight years, and now I see you both…here…oh my God!

*[*LALA *embraces* ELBA, *who stays seated.]*

OLGA: Checkup.

ELBA: Checkup.

LALA: Checkup.

ELBA: *[without getting up]* Lala. I haven't seen you since you moved out of the block.

LALA: I know. I meant to stay in touch, but when you have a family, they take all your time.

OLGA: Dímelo a mí. Five, and two grandchildren de camino.

LALA: *[to* OLGA*]* ¿Tú? ¿Abuela? *[to* ELBA*]* You too?

ELBA: Four.

LALA: La hija mía dice que me siente a esperar para hacerme abuela. She is scared of marriage. I don't blame her.

[Throughout the scene ELBA has been slightly withdrawn and isolated, though cordial.]

OLGA: Hey Elba, I was beginning to ask you about your husband, Tito.

[ELBA reacts with discomfort. She is obviously distressed and tries to change the subject by opening her wallet and showing them some pictures. The other two women gather around her.]

ELBA: This is Tito Junior. He is in the army. This is Celia, my oldest, and these are her two kids. She married this Italian guy, very nice. *[getting a little worked up, nervous and teary]* This is Gina and her husband, and…

[As she shows the pictures, her red envelope slips and falls. Dead silence. She breaks down.]

ELBA: Tito died seven months ago.

[More silence. OLGA pulls out her envelope slowly. LALA does the same. They look at each other silently. A moment of intense silence. Then MYRNA enters, also holding a red envelope. She is surprised by what she sees.]

LALA, ELBA, OLGA: Myrna?

MYRNA: Checkup!

[Blackout.]

Mariluz's Thanksgiving

Migdalia Cruz

—for my cousin Tolo, who is singing with the angels now

Characters

MARILUZ: a petite, dignified, Guatemalan woman-girl of forty-five, with the wisdom of simplicity.

ANGELS: children with wings who still like to play.

FELIPE: MARILUZ's husband, who sleeps throughout the play.

Time: The present.

Place: A village in Guatemala which is also a dream place where songs are still sung; and an apartment in the South Bronx. The village is a piece of woven cloth which hangs in Mariluz's apartment and sometimes comes to life.

Author's Note: The ANGELS don't necessarily sing songs in their entirety.

[*As the lights come up, we see* MARILUZ *as a child playing with the* ANGELS. *They join arms and skip while they sing "Arroz Con Leche."*]

MARILUZ and ANGELS: *[Singing]*
> Arroz con leche se quiere casar con una vuidita de la capital,
> que sepa tejer, que sepa bordar, que ponga la aguja en el mismo lugar.
> Tilín, tilán, sopitas de pan, allá viene Juan, comiendo ese flan.
> Si no me lo dan, *[me como a Juan]* me pongo a llorar...

[MARILUZ *pulls herself away from the* ANGELS *and moves into her apartment.* MARILUZ *holds up a faded, once pink-and-blue satin rag. The piece of cloth is now more gray from age and use, but clean.* MARILUZ *holds the folded piece of cloth to her lips and kisses it, and then unfolds it to reveal a plastic mini-statue of the Virgin Mary. As* MARILUZ *begins to speak, the* ANGELS *may play and tease her in silence. When she feels their presence, she smiles.]*

MARILUZ: *[Speaking to the little statue of the Virgin Mary]* Remember how I lost you once? I was jumping over stones, pretending that each one was a beautiful boy who wanted to marry me.

ANGELS: *[Singing]*
Contigo sí, contigo no, contigo mi vida me casame yo.

MARILUZ: No, not you Mr. Greyrock-with-Stripes. Not you Mr. Redstone. Or especially you, Mr. Pebble. You fell out of my pocket and rolled under one of those loose pieces of mountain. But the Sun made me find you. It shined on your face and that special light that comes from you couldn't help but be seen.

[Pause]

I'm sorry I had to bring you so far from home. Mami would hate that I still have you. And I don't blame her. You're beautiful even though your hands aren't real. They're just painted on—not even carved—not even deep. That's strange for a virgin. I'd expect them to dig you in—nice and hard into the secret parts of this plastic that no one else ever touched before. And—excuse me, Mary—but you need a tan too. You're the palest Mary, whiter than the insides of my eyes…maybe you're sick too. If I'd been the one who made you, you'd be dark and beautiful. Your eyes would be black and your robe would be dark blue to make your eyes and hair shine. And your skin would glow.

[Pause]

My skin's all crazy now. You see these marks? They weren't there last week. Funny how quickly things happen.

ANGELS: *[Singing]*
Contigo sí, contigo no, contigo mi vida me casame yo.

[They all point at FELIPE.*]*

MARILUZ: Like my husband.

[Lights come up on the sleeping figure of FELIPE.*]*

MARILUZ: He came to me after forty years of my being just like you, Blessed Mary. Blessed Mary, my mother was so proud of that. Other girls in the village had children already—but not me. I waited to meet someone special. And I did—on Thanksgiving Day. Isn't that right, Felipe? You're lucky you can sleep so much. I almost never sleep. I sit up at night thinking about things that used to be. I remember how good you looked to me that day, Felipe. I knew I would marry you. You needed a wife—that's what I told myself, "That man needs a woman and it's going to be me." Cooked every meal for you from that day on. Cooked a turkey on the day we first met. My brother-in-law brought it home from the factory for me to cook for his family, but I brought it down to your apartment and we ate it together. Never left your side since then. *[Pause]* Since that day when Mami cursed me. *[Pause; returning to speak to the Virgin Mary statuette.]* Mami did not want me to marry Felipe. She told me, "I want to live just long enough to throw dirt on your grave." I think she'll get her wish.

[Pause]

I hear that curse in my head every time I have to go to the doctor. The doctors here have secrets. They do things and they don't tell you what they're doing. I try to speak English, but I can't. It's a tongue that's so thick it makes me choke. It makes no sense. It sounds like words from a children's game to me.

[The ANGELS *begin singing and playing the patty-cake game "I Have To The Teacher."* MARILUZ *joins in on the twist step. Or the* ANGELS *sing a reprise of "Arroz Con Leche."]*

ANGELS: *[Singing and playing patty-cake]*
   I have to *[curtsy]* the little donde empezar *[repeat]*
   Very good, ha, empezar. *[repeat]*
   I have to *[bolero step]* the little donde bolero *[repeat]*
   Very good, ha, bolero. *[repeat]*
   I have to *[twist step]* the teacher donde el twist *[repeat]*
   Very good, ha, el twist. *[repeat]*
   I have to *[pachanga step]* the teacher donde pachanga *[repeat]*
   Very good, ha, pachanga. *[repeat]*
   I have to *[freeform step]* the teacher donde pudín *[repeat]*
   Very good, ha, pudín. *[repeat]*
   I have to *[mashed step]* the teacher donde el mashed potato *[repeat]*
   Very good, ha, el mashed potato. *[repeat]*
   I have to *[turn around]* the teacher donde se acabó *[repeat]*
   Very good, ha, se acabó. *[repeat]*

MARILUZ: There's things I'd like to learn how to do. Like how to read and
write. People who can do that are lucky. People who can put letters
together to make words and sign their names can always prove what
belongs to them. That would help me fill out forms. You need to fill out
forms to get better in this country. Sometimes when they have different
colors on them, I can tell which one I need to bring to my case
worker—but sometimes they don't and another week passes by…or a
month…or two months…or two years.

[Pause]

I haven't seen my sister for at least that long. She threw me out of her
house 'cause I got the curse and she got scared of me, Mary. She was
pregnant then—I guess she's a mother now. And she didn't want me
near her baby. But that's not how you catch it, by being somebody's
aunt. And when I remember my sister and the baby she won't ever let
me see, I just want to cry. But tears don't help anybody. Especially
mine.

[Pause; it begins to snow.]

This is the worst for me. This weather. It hurts to open my eyes—I'm so
cold. Doesn't matter how much I put on. Doesn't matter if there's sun
between the snowflakes. Snow gets in my bones. Always has. I'm from a
warm place with mountains. This can never be that place…but my
body still thinks it's gonna go home one day.

[Pause]

I used to think that too.

[Pause]

I don't take my medicine anymore. I give it to Felipe. He don't like
going in to get his own, because he says they treat him like he's a
feather-dropper. And he isn't—that's what he always tells me. It was
playing with women got him sick—not men. He's a man who can't help
himself around women. Anyway, the medicines won't help me, because
I'm cursed. So what does it matter?

[Pause]

They're going to put me in a good program next week, but I don't
know if Felipe will let me go. He says I shouldn't go all the way to
Manhattan. There's hospitals right here in the Bronx. And that's true.
Why should I make him go all the way to Manhattan? It's probably not
even that much better. It's too far for him to go visit me and he's my
only family now.

[Pause]

Yeah. It's all the same.

[Pause]

My caseworker, Rosa, asked me last week if I was afraid to die. And I thought, what a crazy question to ask somebody who's dying. It's like asking me if I'm afraid to be Guatemalan or afraid to be dark skinned or afraid to be Mariluz. I am dying. I don't want to die, but I'm not scared of it. Not anymore. Not now that it's part of my life. When I wake up, I think, "I'm glad I'm not dead," not "I'm glad I'm still alive." When I sing a song, I think, "Will this be the last song I sing?" When I eat a piece of bread, I think, "Will this be the last thing I taste?" It's not about being sad or sorry for myself—no…it's about the truth. I always asked questions about everything, since I was a little girl. "Is this the last time I'll see the sun rise?" Even when I wasn't dying like I am now, I always planned to die. When I saw Felipe on my first Thanksgiving in this country, I should have asked, "Is this my last Thanksgiving?" A lot could have changed that day—if I hadn't fallen in love.

[Pause]

Is that what you were trying to tell me that day?

ANGELS and MARILUZ: *[Singing]*
Contigo si, contigo no, contigo mi vida me casame yo.

MARILUZ: I forgot the stones, when I saw the sunlight on your face, Mary. There's so much I would like to forget now.

[Pause]

Sometimes I dream about poisoning Felipe. I am always angry in my sleep.

[MARILUZ goes to FELIPE and strokes his hair gently, and then begins to write in a reading/writing primer as the ANGELS sing and lights slowly fade to black.]

MARILUZ: *[Writing in the primer]* "A" *[Pause]* ah-pull.

[She continues to go through the alphabet softly as the ANGELS sing.]

ANGELS: *[Singing "Arrullo"]*
Duérmete ya, mi niño Dios.
Te arrullaré cantando
un canto de amor tierno
y cuando estes durmiendo
un beso te daré.

Un beso en el alma
te entregaré todo entero
O, niño quien pudiera
Amarte hasta el morir.
Duérmete ya, duérmete ya.

Ven a la humilde cuna
de mis cansados brazos
no es raro, ni topazio
pero podrá dormir.
Duérmete ya, duérmete ya,
ya se duermió.

END

Delia's Race
Carmen Rivera

Characters

DELIA: late forties; AIDS patient; executive director of Mujer Positiva; very outgoing and gregarious.

DR. FELIX: her doctor.

ANGIE: DELIA's daughter; early twenties.

ROSA: mid-fifties; DELIA's best friend.

YOUNG WOMAN: late teens.

Time: Present

Place: Puerto Rico

Author's Note: *Delia's Race* is based on the life of Delia Rodriguez, AIDS activist and founder of Mujeres Positivas (Positive Women).

Scene 1

[A doctor's office, Friday afternoon.]

[DELIA enters DR. FELIX's office. They have been friends for many years but today he finds it difficult to speak to her.]

DR. FELIX: Delia, come on in.

DELIA: Hi Dr. Felix, how are you?

DR. FELIX: Fine. How are you doing?

DELIA: Great…I'm very excited! My daughter's wedding is coming up in a month. I just saw her new house in Bayamon and after I leave here I'm going to a fitting for my dress.

DR. FELIX: How's Angie doing?

DELIA: What do you think? Olvídate, she's going crazy. There are so many things to do. I don't remember weddings being so complicated when I got married. I'm trying to do as much as I can for her.

DR. FELIX: You know you have to slow down.

DELIA: She's my baby! I'll rest after the wedding. Oh I forgot to tell you, Mujer Positiva got accepted into the walk-a-thon.

DR. FELIX: I thought Mujer Positiva wasn't allowed to participate?

DELIA: I know, but I finally got through to the coordinator of the walk-a-thon. This great woman, Gina Tierney. And she said even though Mujer Positiva does not meet the one year minimum.

DR. FELIX: When did you start Mujer Positiva?

DELIA: Six months ago.

DR. FELIX: Six months already.

DELIA: Verdad, time goes so fast. *[Pause.]* Gina respects the work we've done in AIDS awareness and outreach around the island, SO...you know me, I told her "When do you want us there? Just say the word and we'll be there." Of course she said yes!

DR. FELIX: Very nice Delia.

DELIA: I'm really excited. It's been a long dream of mine to have a walk-a-thon right here in Puerto Rico like they have in New York. I can't wait. I even bought a new jogging suit for the occasion.

DR. FELIX: Great...Delia, we need to talk about your hectic schedule.

DELIA: You'll be attending the walk-a-thon, right?!

DR. FELIX: Delia, I'm serious.

DELIA: You can't say no?! It's the first annual AIDS walk-a-thon in Puerto Rico!

DR. FELIX: Don't change the subject, we spoke about your schedule the last time you were here.

DELIA: You can't miss it!

DR. FELIX: How are those headaches doing?

DELIA: I get them on and off, you know, just like anyone else gets the headaches.

DR. FELIX: You're not anyone else!

DELIA: I know that. *[Pause.]* Okay…don't you have test results for me?

DR. FELIX: Delia…

DELIA: Just say it, Doctor!

DR. FELIX: The test results show a change in…

DELIA: Just tell me. *[Pause.]*

DR. FELIX: Your T-cell count, it's…

DELIA: It went down again?

DR. FELIX: It's zero.

DELIA: Zero?

DR. FELIX: Yes.

DELIA: Last time you checked it was ninety-six.

DR. FELIX: I know.

DELIA: Zero?! *[Long pause.]*

DELIA: Are you sure?

DR. FELIX: Yes.

DELIA: Just like that? It's zero. I've only been infected for five years. How did it happen so fast?

DR. FELIX: Everybody is different. And you run around a lot—that stresses the immune system, even though you don't believe me.

DELIA: Nah…

DR. FELIX: And you may have been infected much earlier than when you tested positive.

[Pause. DELIA *gets her bearings.]*

DELIA: Actually this doesn't mean anything, right? What about that viral load test?

DR. FELIX: You definitely should take it.

DELIA: Schedule it as soon as possible. *[Pause]* Okay, our business is done for today. *[Checks her watch.]* Have to run.

DR. FELIX: Delia, wait—

DELIA: What? Do you have more information for me?

DR. FELIX: Not really, but…

DELIA: Well then, I have to go, I'm running late. The dress shop is going to close soon and I don't want to get caught in a traffic jam on the highway.

DR. FELIX: It's okay to get upset.

DELIA: I'm not upset. I knew this was going to happen. It's not like finding out you're HIV-positive.

DR. FELIX: I think you need to deal with this.

DELIA: What I need to do is go to my fitting for my dress for my daughter's wedding!

DR. FELIX: Delia, I think you should go to counseling.

DELIA: For what?

DR. FELIX: It's important for you to have a support group.

DELIA: I know all about support groups—that's why I started Mujer Positiva!

DR. FELIX: Delia, right now you don't need to lead any more groups, and as your friend I'm telling you, you need to be in a group. You can't do this alone. You need to receive support.

DELIA: Don't talk to me like I'm a little girl! I know what I need! I can take care of myself.

DR. FELIX: I don't doubt that…but I'm worried about you.

[DELIA gets up to leave.]

DR. FELIX: Delia, I'm serious about slowing down, you're full-blown now!

DELIA: Excuse me, I have a wedding to finish planning.

DR. FELIX: Delia?

DELIA: What?

DR. FELIX: I'm sorry.

DELIA: You don't have to be. Buenas tardes.

[DELIA *exits.*]

Scene 2

[DELIA'*s home, later that evening.*]

[DELIA *enters with her briefcase and her packages; she drops her bags on the floor.*]

DELIA: Support group…I don't understand…zero T-cells…how did that happen…? I take good care of myself.

[*Phone rings.* ROSA *enters.*]

DELIA: Hello.

ROSA: Delia, hi, it's Rosa.

DELIA: Rosa, what's up?

ROSA: Mira the T-shirt company called. They said you didn't pick up the T-shirts.

DELIA: Oh, um…the fitting for my dress for Angie's wedding took longer than I thought.

ROSA: Oh, don't worry about it. I picked them up.

DELIA: Okay, that's great. Thank you.

ROSA: Oh very important. Who do we call to organize the buses to bring the women who live far away to the walk-a-thon?

DELIA: I'll take care of it.

ROSA: It's okay, I'll take care of it; just tell me who to call.

DELIA: Rosa, I'll do it first thing in the morning, okay?

ROSA: Okay, esta bien. I'll see you tomorrow, bye.

DELIA: Bye.

[ROSA *exits.* DELIA *hangs up the phone. Long pause.*]

DELIA: I'm not even dead yet and she wants to take my company away from me…[*Pause.*] Ah Dios mío, I'm going to die before Rosa! Well then, I'm entitled to drink to my death. *[Laughs.]* Where is that bottle? *[*DELIA *takes out a bottle of vodka and drinks from it.]* AHHH! Yuck! How do people drink this stuff? It's terrible! *[She takes another drink and coughs.* DELIA *struggles to get her breath.]* AHHH! *[She sits on the sofa, staring downstage and shaking one leg. She is trying to hold back tears. She takes another drink with great difficulty. Again she coughs and struggles to regain her breath.]* What do I do now?

[Phone rings again.]

DELIA: Shut up! Leave me alone!

MACHINE: Hola, this is Mujer Positiva. For general information or if you are calling to sign up for the walk-a-thon please press one; for Delia Rodriguez, Executive Director, press two; for Rosa Sanchez, Administrative Assistant, press three.

ANGIE: Mami, mami are you there?

DELIA: Angie… *[Goes to pick up the phone, but decides not to.]*

ANGIE: Mami, mami, I thought you would be at home, Mom. What happened today? I waited at the dress shop for an hour. Anyway I hope you're okay. Don't worry about the dress, Crucita said you can stop by any time.

DELIA: Any time…I don't have any time, I have NO time…

ANGIE: Mami, I'm going to be late, I went to dinner with Mario in Carolina, and some of his co-workers want to be sponsors for the walk-a-thon. I told them no problem. See you later. Bye.

*[*DELIA *gets up from the sofa and starts to pace with the vodka bottle in her hand.]*

DELIA: What if I die before their wedding? Don't think negative thoughts…SO DON'T THINK NEGATIVE THOUGHTS… *[She tries to think.]* It doesn't work. Try again, DON'T THINK NEGATIVE THOUGHTS. *[She continues trying.]* Coño this is hard… *[She takes another drink from the bottle, then puts it down. The phone rings again.]* ¡VAYASE AL CARAJO! *[She picks up the phone and hangs it up.]* What the hell are you doing calling here anyway? *[She sits on the floor in front of the sofa and drinks from the vodka bottle. She is starting to get a little drunk.]*

Can you make it a magic pill to make it all go away? So many people drink to make their problems go away, so why shouldn't I start? Be just like everybody else. Can THIS *[gestures with the bottle]* make it all go away? Fly away like a bird. Fly in the sky, fly through the clouds, fly, fly…flapping my wings and going higher and higher, flying through the wind…leaving the ground behind.

[The phone rings again.]

DELIA: Hello, *[Laughs]* Mujer Positiva, hello, I'm dying…

[Answering machine begins to play recorded message in background as DELIA speaks.]

DELIA: An organization to create awareness in women that are dying. Do you know that thirty-three percent of Puerto Ricans on the island are HIV-positive, everybody is gonna be…*[Her index finger crosses her throat as if she were slitting it. She speaks to the answering machine.]* They're all going bye-bye. If you want to sign up to die press the star button. Yeah, yeah, yeah…

[YOUNG WOMAN enters.]

YOUNG WOMAN: Hello…hello…um…I…I…want some information about Mujer Positiva *[Pause.]* But I don't want to leave my name…do I have to? I mean can we talk without telling our names? I really need to talk to someone and I just want to talk, you know because…um…I think I'm sick, I mean I don't have AIDS or anything like that, but my boyfriend is really sick…um…and I want to ask you a question that's all…about, you know *[whispers]* sex. I can't ask my mother so I looked in the phone book and I found this number. Hello…hello…I'll call back.

[YOUNG WOMAN exits]

DELIA: No! *[She grabs the phone.]* Hello! Hello, are you there? *[She hits the receiver.]* Young lady…hello…ah dammit! *[She hangs up the phone.]* I'm sorry I didn't pick up, I'm sorry…

[Phone rings again.]

DELIA: Hello, young lady…hello, hello, is that you? *[No one answers. She abruptly hangs up.]* Oh God, you need to stop testing us and you need to wake up! *[She curls up in a fetal position and starts to fall asleep.]* Ah, no…I can't fall asleep. I might not wake up. *[She rocks herself.]* Can't fall asleep, can't fall asleep… *[She keeps repeating this to herself as she falls asleep on the floor.]*

Scene 3

[DELIA's home, close to midnight.]

[DELIA is sleeping on the floor in the living room. ANGIE enters.]

ANGIE: Mami…mami wake up.

[DELIA awakens, very startled.]

ANGIE: Mami, are you alright?

DELIA: How was your dinner with Mario?

ANGIE: Mami, what's wrong?

DELIA: Nothing.

ANGIE: Mami, you're sleeping on the floor.

DELIA: It's nothing, I was just reading and I fell asleep. SO, how was your dinner?

ANGIE: What were you reading?

DELIA: Angie, answer my question!

ANGIE: It was fine… *[ANGIE starts looking around the room and finds the empty bottle.]* Nice book, huh?

DELIA: Just give me that!

ANGIE: What's going on?!

DELIA: I told you I was okay! ALRIGHT?! Angie, you should go to sleep.

ANGIE: Not until you tell me what's going on with you.

DELIA: Angie!

ANGIE: Mami! I know something is wrong, you didn't meet me at the bridal shop. I'm not leaving until you tell me.

[ANGIE doesn't move and DELIA starts to cry.]

ANGIE: Mami, I'll stand here all night if I have to!

[Pause.]

DELIA: What if I were to tell you that I was going to die?

ANGIE: What?

DELIA: Angie, I'm gonna die.

ANGIE: Stop it! I know you've been through a lot but you survived ma...you're a survivor.

DELIA: I survived all that to get AIDS.

ANGIE: You don't have AIDS. You always say that HIV-positive doesn't mean AIDS.

DELIA: I don't have any T-cells left.

ANGIE: What?

DELIA: I don't have any T-cells left. My T-cell count is zero.

ANGIE: How do you know that?

DELIA: I saw Dr. Felix today. So you see...I'm gonna die.

[Pause.]

ANGIE: Didn't you tell me about some new tests that are given to AIDS patients?

DELIA: The viral load test.

ANGIE: You said it measures—

DELIA: How much virus you have in your body. I'm going to take it next week.

ANGIE: So, we can't jump into any conclusions.

DELIA: It's late, go to sleep. Vamos.

ANGIE: Do you want to talk to me about it?

DELIA: Angie I'm really tired, it's late mama.

ANGIE: We just have to get through this thing.

DELIA: I told you I didn't want to talk about it.

ANGIE: I just want to let you know I feel we'll get through this.

DELIA: That's very easy for you to say.

ANGIE: What is that supposed to mean?

DELIA: Never mind. Let's go to sleep.

ANGIE: Wait, you think because I don't have—

DELIA: AIDS?! Yes I have AIDS! Now go to bed!

ANGIE: Don't push me away…I'm part of this illness too. I live knowing that my mother is dying, I live knowing you might not see your grandchildren. [Pause.] I'm sad every day, I'm scared every day, sometimes I cry myself to sleep…

DELIA: I told you not to be scared—we have to be strong.

ANGIE: I am trying to be strong—I try to live every moment as if it was…

DELIA: You can say it…like the last one.

ANGIE: And dream of a cure.

DELIA: By the time they find a cure, I'll be dead.

ANGIE: Then why have a walk-a-thon, if you don't believe in a cure?

DELIA: I'm not going to the stupid walk-a-thon!

ANGIE: So you're giving up everything you've worked so hard for?

DELIA: Yes…I'm dying Angie, I can give up if I want to!

ANGIE: This is not my mother speaking—my mother is not a quitter, she's a fighter.

DELIA: What do you want from me? First you want me to tell you what happened—so I do—then you don't want me to be upset, you want me to fight! I'm tired of fighting…leave me alone and go to bed. I don't feel like speaking anymore.

ANGIE: Too bad, I feel like talking.

DELIA: Coño, this is not about you okay?!

ANGIE: Fine, forget it!

[ANGIE storms out.]

DELIA: That's right, forget it! [Pause.] People need to leave me alone.

[ANGIE re-enters.]

ANGIE: Why don't you let people help you?

DELIA: Ave Maria!

ANGIE: You help everybody, you make them talk about their feelings, you make them confront their fears, but you never open up! You don't let me in your life.

DELIA: I tell you everything.

ANGIE: You tell me things and facts, but you don't tell me how you feel.

DELIA: I just told you that I'm a quitter, verdad?!

ANGIE: How do you really feel?

DELIA: Angie, déjame ya! *[Pause]* Aqui esta—you want it, you really want it?!

ANGIE: Yeah!

DELIA: I'm scared, okay? I'm petrified. I check for my pulse every day, and when I feel it, I imagine the blood, as it goes through my body, and this blood is bad blood, my death is in that blood…I don't want to die, okay? Are you happy? I don't know what else to say. *[She starts to cry and holds out her arm.]* You see—look at this! How are you going to stop this?!

ANGIE: I'm here for you.

DELIA: I know, you're good to me. I don't remember feeling like this when I found out I was HIV-positive, I mean I thought I was gonna die. *[Pause.]* But then, I kept living and I took medicine and I even felt better. Now, with no T-cells, I feel like there's no hope. Like I am really falling out of a plane with no parachute. There's nothing that can save me. I'm sorry I'm crying…

ANGIE: Don't be sorry. You're always giving to everyone else, mami. Give me a chance to give to you.

[ANGIE takes DELIA in her arms and cradles her like a baby as she cries.]

ANGIE: Just let it out mami.

[ANGIE sings DELIA a lullaby.]

Scene 4

[A park in Puerto Rico, several weeks later.]

[A cheering crowd is heard. ANGIE *runs in. She is carrying flowers.]*

ANGIE: Do you see her?

*[*DR. FELIX *follows* ANGIE, *who waits upstage left.]*

DR. FELIX: She's making the turn...look, there she goes.

ANGIE: I see her! Mom, mami!

*[*DELIA *enters. She is walking slowly.* DELIA *is tired but she is also very elated.]*

ANGIE: Mami! Hi mami!

*[*ANGIE *takes a picture.* DELIA *waves to her daughter.]*

ANGIE: Just a little more, mami. Go mom!

DR. FELIX: Keep going, Delia.

ANGIE: Oh my God, she made it.

DR. FELIX: Delia!

*[*ANGIE *and* DR. FELIX *surround* DELIA *and congratulate her.* ANGIE *gives* DELIA *the flowers.* DELIA *hugs* ANGIE. *They exit together. Lights fade.]*

END

now and then

Michael John Garcés

Characters

MONICA
TANYA, her sister
ERIC
DAVID

Bronx, New York
scene   Monica

M: I am my name I am letter em letter oh I am my face letter en am my height my
weight letter ai letter cee my age letter ay sign here sign here sign here
who are you where born where live where registered
I am everything I've done am everything I've ever said ever thought I am all of
these things
why are you here fill this out check this in state your sex
am everything you think of me and everything I think of you I am my breath I am
what I eat who I love where I've been
last name first middle initial mother's maiden
what's keeping me going what's cutting me off
what I make and where I make it and what I can afford
am the wound and the skin am the drug the disease the hunger the thirst
sign where the ex and again on the line
everything and nothing at all…

scene   Monica, David   now

M: you know who I am.

    —

    what?

D: nothing.

M: then why you look at me like that?

D: no reason.

M: you know who I am.

D: sure.

M: who?

D: who?

M: who. who am I, David?

D: Monica.

M: yeah? Monica ever lie to you?

D: not that I know of. no.

M: nothing but straight with you.

D: sure.

M: so?

D: what?

M: so you think I'm gonna start lying now?

D: no, I just…

M: just what?

D: just…surprised, that's all.

M: so you gonna say you don't believe me?

D: believe it. I said I didn't believe it.

M: I don't lie.

D: I know.

M: tell you everything.

D: I know.

M: didn't I tell you everything about your cousin when he tried to get up on me?

D: yeah.

M: I lie about that?

D: no.

M: did he?

D: I guess. yeah.

M: didn't I tell you how it is with me before we done anything, before you even touched me, straight up?

D: we held hands, we touched, kissed, we—

M: don't be ignorant.

D: I'm not ignorant, if I was ignorant…

M: what? if you was ignorant what?

D: nothing.

M: before we did anything I said I was positive and you had to deal or walk, right?

D: yeah.

M: I ain't gonna have some guy come after me cause I lied to him, try to kill me cause I didn't tell him.

D: you told me, alright?

M: not that it ever stopped anybody. I had to bring the rubbers cause they would just—

D: I know you told me already.

M: I ever lie about who I been with?

D: no.

M: so how are you going to think I'm lying to you?

D: I don't.

M: how you gonna ask me that?

D: I just can't believe it, that's all.

M: what do you think I want from you?

—

I don't want you to marry me or nothing.

—

been there.

—

what, you think you got money?

D: I just don't think it's the right time.

—

M: when do you think the right time will be for me? huh? never, maybe? you think never would be the right time? would that be convenient for you?

—

D: I just…

M: you think I want your money.

D: no.

M: you think I'm not?

D: not what?

—

I think you are.

M: you think it's not yours?

D: I think it's mine.

—

M: that's right. cause I would tell you.

scene   Monica

M: there are some times and then there are other times
no ma'am I'm not on
but mostly it feels like no time at all to be who I am might be could maybe
become anything except bored except lost
I gave you that already I just need to pick up
but how can I feel like there's nothing to do with so little time to do nothing in?
yes I told you already I'm registered with
it's like the only time I'm anything but time passing doing nothing feeling empty
is when I get caught looking back at me
I can't come back later the doctor said
out of the brown in somebody else's angry eye
if you have the results why can't you just give me

or my own eyes angry in the mirror
how much longer am I supposed to wait?
or you sometimes saying something that isn't anything at all…

scene   **Monica, Tanya**   **then**

T: you should tell them.

M: what?

T: you should, they're your—

M: you better not say nothing.

       —

T: you been sick lately.

M: that's not why I went.

T: you had fever, throwing up, I saw you last night—

M: I went before that, alright?

T: then why did you go?

M: I was just curious…just…I don't know, I didn't think I had it.

T: then why did you go?

       —

       did you think Eric had it?

       —

M: I didn't think I had it.

T: girls get sick when they're pregnant.

M: I just wish that's what it was.

T: you been getting skinny anyway.

M: that could be anything.

T: were you scared?

M: no. I didn't think I—

T: you scared now?

       —

       why don't you tell them?

M: what? is that like a joke?

T: no. I just think—

M: what do you think they—

T: I just think—

M: I told you, alright?

T: yeah.

M: that's enough.

—

T: Tammy told her mom when she got pregnant. she got mad but…then she was alright.

M: yeah, but she lucky cause her dad left. her mom got cool since then.

T: yup.

—

he ain't even our dad.

—

M: he's your dad.

T: yeah, but…

—

he's a…I think he…I don't even—

M: forget about him right now, ok?

T: yeah.

—

M: they said no one back home gets things like that.

T: that's bullshit, lots of people on the island got—

M: that's not what they—

T: all kind of, they get pregnant there and they send them here—

M: mom allays says I'm like this since we came here, and—

T: so what do they all come here for? there are girls there who—

M: yeah, but those girls—

T: they get sick there.

M: not decent people. they're not like people here.

T: that's bullshit. I heard them talking, those ladies, and—

M: that's what mom said at dinner—

T: who cares? we ain't even from there.

M: that's true.

T: we from here.

M: yeah.

T: are you scared to tell them?

M: I ain't scared. what could they do? they can't do nothing.

T: will they freak out?

M: who cares?

T: will they throw you out?

M: I could be homeless. I don't care. I could get by.
—
nobody better hit me, cause…
—
it's not because of my friends. ok? it's not because of Eric. ok? it's not because of mom or my father. it's not because I'll get kicked out, I don't care if I get thrown out, I want to move out anyway when I can. and I'm tired of school anyway and don't have time for it. it's not because I'm scared that they won't touch or talk to me or eat and drink with me. I don't care. it's not because of what they'll think—they already do any way.

T: what, then?
—

M: what…then? I'm just…
—
I feel like…
—

T: what?

M: what if…what if they don't get mad?

T: they will.

M: but what if they don't?

T: I don't...what?

M: I'm...listen, don't...

———

I'm scared they just won't...care...won't...talk won't think won't kick me out won't...run or walk away won't anything. won't do anything. and nothing will have changed except for me. and nothing will go wrong and nothing will go right. and nothing will be dying except me.

———

like I can see kids playing and you on the phone and the basketball games on the corner and mom and your dad at the table arguing and all mad like they always are and the cars on the thruway and the ladies talk ing about back on the island and you sneaking ice cream and everything the same as now after I'm dead.

———

that's what'll happen if I say it. what if they don't get mad?

———

you see what I...

———

anyway, that's just it.

scene   **Monica, Eric**   **then**

M: if I got it you got it too.

E: I don't know where you been.

M: how can you say that?

E: I thought I did—you go and get all that dirt in you? you gonna tell me you was riding horse?

M: no.

E: good, cause I know you ain't. you don't know nothing about—

M: well, I ain't.

E: I'd just like to see you try to even buy—

M: I ain't.

E: I know. you wouldn't even know where to go.

M: I know where to go.

E: where? tell me where.

M: I ain't been doing that. I ain't ever even tried.

E: then I don't know where you been.

M: where you been?

E: well I thought I hadn't been with no one dirty. I guess I was wrong.

M: I guess you was.

E: I guess I was.

——

I was careful with you anyway. you didn't get it from me.

M: you got it.

E: yeah. from before.

M: you didn't tell me.

E: I had it for a while. I had it for a long time. I was careful with you. you should thank me. I don't know what you were doing.

M: careful how, Eric?

E: I know how to be careful.

M: so how'd you get it?

E: I was young, like…fifteen. it don't matter anyway. you can't even tell.

M: careful how?

E: they make a big deal about it, but you can't even tell.

M: how could you do this to me?

E: I didn't do nothing to you.

M: you can't be careful, in school they said—

E: that's bull what they tell you. they just want you to be scared. they always trying to scare you. I ain't scared of nothing.

M: we didn't use nothing, no rubbers, no…you didn't tell me—

E: hell no. I ain't using that.

M: you knew and you just—

E: I didn't do nothing to you. you better not say anything to anybody. you better shut up.

M: you shut up. I can tell whoever I—

E: you better shut up.

    ——

M: what am I supposed to do now?

E: don't ask me, I don't know.

    ——

M: we still together?

E: I don't know. I'm thinking about it.

    ——

    I don't know where you been.

scene   **Monica, Tanya**   **then**

T: you going back with Eric?

M: yeah, so? that's what I said.

T: yeah?

    ——

M: so?

T: nothing, he…

M: he what?

T: why?

M: you don't understand nothing.

T: I do.

M: you don't.

    ——

T: I do.

    ——

    he…

    ——

M: what?

—

T: he…did this…to you.

M: what? did what?

T: this.

M: what? he's good to me.

T: he killed you.

M: I'm not dead. do I look dead?

T: no.

M: you think I'm dead. how are you going to say that I'm—

T: no, I didn't mean—

M: then why you gonna say that?

T: he…he hurt you.

M: he loved me. he loves me.

nobody else does.

T: I do.

M: nobody else.

—

T: what if he hits you again.

M: he won't. he said.

T: what if he does?

—

M: he didn't think I could get it. they don't explain it to you right. it wasn't his fault. he was trying to be careful.

—

he's who I got, anyway.

—

he said he wouldn't. he promised. he's getting weak, anyway.

T: yeah?

M: yeah, he's like…sick.

T: yeah?

M: yeah.

T: how do you feel?

M: I'm fine. what do you mean?

T: nothing.

M: I'm fine. I'm not sick.

T: I know.

M: I'm fine.

———

T: you know…

M: what?

T: nothing…I love you.

M: yeah?

T: yeah.

scene   **Monica**

M: now and then I just want to look at a man and see just a man a man who might like me or might not but that's all feel a hand on my leg and just have it there want to look at my stomach and see nothing but growing see nothing but life see nothing other than love…

scene   **Monica, David**   **now**

M: I know you do. that's not the point.
———
   I'm sorry, but it isn't.

D: what is the point?

M: what are you going to do about it?

D: about loving you?

M: yeah.

D: take care of you.

M: good.
———

D: I don't think you should have it.

M: then you ain't taking care of me.

D: I don't think it's the best thing for you.

M: you don't think it's the best thing for you.

D: it isn't.

M: you said you wanted—

D: not now.

M: you said soon. you said before you got old.

D: I'm not old.

M: you're close.

D: I got enough taking care of you.

M: no one asked you to.

——

D: I know.

——

M: she doesn't have to be sick.

D: she?

M: yeah.

——

I hope so.

——

if I take care of myself, then it…she doesn't have to be sick.

D: you're not sick.

M: what do you think I am?

D: not sick.

——

M: she could be healthy, they told me—

D: how do you—

M: I read—

D: can't be sure that—

M: healthy, just like any other—

D: how's it—

M: she...she—

D: going to be like any other one without a mother?

—

how?

—

M: you said you take care of me, right?

—

right?

D: yeah.

M: you said you want to, right?

D: yeah.

M: for as long as it takes?

D: until you get—

M: until I get what? dead?

D: better.

M: ain't no better. for as long as it takes?

—

huh?

D: yeah. and I have.

M: so far. what if this ain't as long as it takes?

D: I'll keep on.

M: yeah?

D: for as long as it takes.

M: well it might be a long time.

D: I want it to—

M: good. because it might. long time.

—

that baby is me.

scene   **Monica**

M: here where I wake up in the morning where I stand here beside you
where I make you lunch where I kiss you good night see me here where I
sit watching tv here where I sew the rip in your jeans see me taking a
shower while you shave see me here where I am now and then and not
there where I'm going to be...

scene   **Monica, Eric**   **then**

E: I don't know what you're talking about.

M: me, talking about me.

E: I have no—

M: Eric.

E: I don't.

M: Eric.

——

E: what?

——

M: how you feeling today?

E: good. like always.

M: yeah?

E: yeah.

M: how come you ain't got dressed yet?

E: didn't feel like it.

M: no?

E: why you think you can ask what I—

M: just asking.

E: like you my mother or something since we got married you think—

M: I ain't got no ring.

E: city hall.

M: and your mother been saying things about me again I heard—

E: who told you?

M: she been saying that you ain't sick but if you are I gave it and you shouldn't be with me because I—

E: Tammy? you talking to her again?

M: she saying that I been with—

E: your sister?

M: your mother ain't doing nothing to help us here, ain't—

E: shut up about my family. I ain't seen your mother around.

M: she don't say nothing about you.

E: what she gonna say about me? ain't my fault.

M: what ain't your fault?

E: this.

M: what this?

E: you were the one who wanted to get married, you—

M: I wanted to be with you, I—

E: now you want to talk about babies—

M: wanted us to get through—

E: like I'm gonna sit here watch some baby just die, like I ain't got enough with—

M: ok, ok, ok…forget it. I'm sorry.

　　—

　　how you feeling?

　　—

　　Eric?

E: what?

M: why does your mother say I gave it to you?

E: ask her.

　　—

　　I don't know.

—

    maybe you did.

M: maybe I did?

E: you could of.

M: you already—

E: I don't want to talk about it.

—

M: you talk with the group. how come you talk there? you didn't even want to go, I had to make you, then—

E: what do I have to tell you to get you to—

M: I thought you got it from a girl.

—

    you never told me about…that…your father, he—

E: he ain't my father.

M: you never told me that.

—

E: I don't know what you're talking about.

M: I can't say nothing with that group, you can't say nothing with me.

E: ain't got nothing to talk about.

M: yeah…

—

E: I feel fine.

—

    fine.

scene   **Monica, Tanya**   **then**

T: well, you look good.

M: I don't feel so good.

T: you look good.

—

M: yeah?

T: yup.

M: Eric says—

T: why you gonna listen to him?

M: he's my husband.

T: I don't see no ring.

———

M: very funny.

T: I try…I try.

M: gonna have to watch what I say around you.

T: you don't need no husband anyway.

M: that's for sure.

———

T: don't even think about that test, your t-cell count can—

M: it's bad Tanya.

T: I been reading they got these cocktails now, they can—

M: they ain't gonna waste them on people like me, you gotta have money, gotta—

T: no, you gotta go to a center—

M: I been to—

T: you gotta try, gotta see people—

M: I'm doing my best.

T: I know you are.

———

we been praying for you. you should come.

M: no.

T: you should.

———

that's ok. I pray for you.

———

M: you been reading, huh?

T: yeah.

M: yeah. you know more about it than anyone.

T: I know a lot.

M: I know you do.

T: maybe I could help you. maybe I could go down there with you—

M: maybe.

—

its bad, Tanya…it's…god, I…

—

look at me, getting all…like I'm on tv, or…

—

probably be better if I could…

T: you can feel, ain't no reason—

M: I ain't got time.

T: how's Eric.

M: bad.

T: weak?

M: yeah. he kicked me out yesterday.

T: he hurt you?

M: he can't hurt nobody no more. cept himself.

T: where you staying?

M: I just went back. he didn't say nothing.

—

he needs me. his mother ain't gonna help him.

T: who's gonna help you?

M: I don't need no help.

T: you know—

M: I don't need no help. what do you think I am?

T: nothing, I just—

M: damn, Tanya.

—

T: you want me to say anything to mom?

M: I ain't got nothing to say to her.

T: I'll tell her you said hi.

M: I been making good money at the new job.

T: yeah?

M: not bad. I gotta stand for a long time, though.

T: you get tired?

M: it's ok.

T: you lucky to get that job.

M: yeah.

T: I wish you didn't have to work.

M: gets me out of the apartment.

T: still.
———
you should get your GED, you know, maybe you—

M: what for?
———

T: I'll see you soon?

M: I don't know, maybe…yeah.
———
you pray for me, ok?

T: yup.

M: cause I just can't.

T: you don't have to.

scene　　　　**Monica, Eric**　　　　**then**

M: yes you do.

E: I don't have to do anything I don't—

M: they said you should walk.

E: I went to the bathroom like—

M: that was two hours ago Eric—

E: well I'm tired.

M: you need to exercise—

E: that ain't exercise, walking ain't—

M: the doctors said—

E: they don't know nothing if they think that's exercise. I used to lift—

M: you can't lift nothing now.

    —

    sorry.

    —

E: you gonna help me or not?

M: yeah.

E: just a little bit. I'm tired.

M: yeah, just a little. it's good for you.

E: whatever.

    —

    you lost weight.

M: I been dieting.

E: some diet. my mother called. she's coming later.

M: now she's coming.

E: later.

M: she couldn't help us before and now she—

E: she called.

    —

    she said she wants to see me. she said she missed me.

M: yeah, well, that's good.

    —

    you want to see her?

E: I guess. damn you got skinny.

M: so?

E: how you gonna look like that?

M: like what?

E: all skinny.

M: yeah, well some guys think I look good.

E: who? who?

M: I don't know.

E: you don't know.

M: no…like on the street.

E: you been on the street.

M: I got to get here some way.

E: why don't you go be on the street where you belong anyway—

M: why don't I?

E: why don't you?

—

M: what are you doing?

E: I need to sit down.

M: no, you should—

E: let me sit down. damn.

—

be looking at me like that for?

M: I ain't looking at you.

E: good.

—

you hungry? I got some—

M: no.

E: be like that.

—

M: I'm leaving.

E: leaving?

M: yeah. leaving.

E: when you coming back?
—
when you coming back Monica?

M: I don't know.

E: take me with you, huh? I could walk if you—

M: I'm leaving.

E: then go.
—
go.

M: your mother's coming.

E: just go.
—
Monica?

M: yeah.

E: I…damn…I messed myself.

M: you supposed to go to the bathroom…you were just walking…you…Eric…
—

E: you ain't gonna leave me like this are you?
—
you could leave in a little while.
—
you still my girl, right?
—

M: yeah. I'm still your girl.

scene   **Monica**

M: *you know…you're mine…*
and I'm always gonna be
with you
I'm forever gonna care
that's true…
…cause you're mine

first step
I hold your hand
and catch you when you fall
and if your eyes
get filled with sand
you only have to call

I'm yours…it's fine…
and you only have to call
I'm there
no matter what you do
or dare…
…cause I'm yours…

scene   Monica, David   now

M: you know, I still feel…you know, I'm with you, and Eric died and all, and you treat me good, and I feel like my body is…is mine again…and I still feel like I got nothing and you gonna say you don't want this for me? for us?

D: I want us to be…I want to be able to…

M: how can there be an us if we don't got something together?
    —

D: we got each other.

M: yeah. you got me. great.

D: it is great.
    —

M: Eric didn't leave nothing…no one even remembers him.

D: you don't remember him?

M: not for long.

D: don't say that.

M: why, if it's true?

D: cause you are going to—

M: you ain't going to remember me.

D: going to be here for a long—

M: how you going to remember me without something to remind you?

—

it could be a boy.

D: a boy?

M: it don't have to be a girl.

D: a boy...a boy would be cool.

M: but you could play ball with a girl too.

D: a boy would be alright.

—

M: Tanya will help you out, after...she'll be real good to her, she promised.

D: her?

M: we'll see.

D: yeah.

—

I just don't...

M: don't what?

D: I just don't know.

M: you don't?

D: no.

M: you don't know?

D: no, I don't.

M: well, now you do, cause I'm having this baby. and it's yours.

D: ok.

M: ok?

D: ok.

M: ok.

—

don't say it. you say it too much. Eric never said it. I know you don't like to hear about him. but he did. and you do. you don't have to say it. save it for when I'm gonna need it. cause I'm gonna. and your baby's gonna.

don't waste it.

—

I love you.

—

I ain't got it to waste.

—

ok?

D: ok.

M: ok.

scene   **Monica**

M: *...there once was a girl*
who lived all alone
she didn't have an angel
or anyone at home

she didn't have a father
to help her on her way
but her mother left her three little words
to get her through the day...

scene   **Monica, Tanya**   **now**

T: you ok?

M: yeah.

T: I know how you hate hospitals and all.

M: yeah, but it was ok. this is a better reason to go.

T: you don't have to go through with it.

M: yes I do.

—

I have to.

—

T: I know you do.

M: it's all I want.

T: I know.

M: she's gonna need her aunt.

T: she?

M: I hope.

T: can they tell yet?

M: no.

T: a girl would be nice.

M: yeah.

T: you got a name for her?

M: I thought Monica.

T: I think so, too. what if it's a boy?

M: a boy? I haven't decided yet. I think…I don't know. David wants a boy. I thought maybe Eric, but David would—

T: you don't want to do that, you—

M: no, I just—

T: it'll be a girl.

M: yeah.

T: a beautiful, strong—

M: healthy—

T: healthy, strong, beautiful baby girl.

M: yeah.

T: just like her mom.

M: just like.

—

you think it could be a boy?

T: I don't know. it could be.

M: I hope he don't look like me.

T: I hope it don't look like him if it's a girl.

M: he'd be an ugly girl.

T: yeah he would.

M: he'd be an ugly boy.

T: why you saying that?

M: well he is.

T: is not.

M: I could do better.

T: than him?

M: I mean, you know, looks, and—

T: he's alright.

M: yeah, he's alright.

T: he treats you right.

M: he treats me good.

T: so what do you care what he looks like?

M: I don't see you out with no skinny ass ugly butt man.

T: well, no…but that's me.

M: yeah…you better laugh.

—

Eric was fine…before he…

—

T: Monica, you don't have to. I just want you to know.

M: I know.

T: matter what anybody say.

M: they all tell me not to. you gonna tell me that too.

T: no, no. I just—

M: I want to.

T: you're sure?

—

M: I'm positive.

Ilka: The Dream

Cándido Tirado

Characters

ILKA: Early forties

MANOLITO: Mid-forties

VICTOR: Mid-forties

GIGI: Early twenties

PAPO: Mid-thirties

[Two men, VICTOR and MANOLITO, walk around the stage wearing masks. ILKA sits downstage wearing a mask. One of the men rings a bell.]

MANOLITO: Are you ready Victor?

VICTOR: Yes, I am.

MANOLITO: So let's start the play. Ilka, are you ready to do Victor's new play?

ILKA: I don't want to play.

VICTOR: You don't want to play the play or you don't want to play-play?

[ILKA turns away from them.]

MANOLITO: I hate when she doesn't want to play.

VICTOR: Maybe she's been dreaming again. *[To ILKA]* Have you been dreaming? *[She doesn't answer.]* Are you going to answer me?

MANOLITO: Do you want us to tickle you?

ILKA: No. And yes, I've been dreaming.

MANOLITO: Don't worry, after a while you'll stop dreaming.

ILKA: I don't want to stop dreaming.

VICTOR: But it makes you feel miserable.

ILKA: I don't care. I don't want to stop dreaming. It's all I got left.

MANOLITO: Honey, dreaming is overrated!

VICTOR: She's very sentimental.

ILKA: What's wrong with sentimentality? No one wants to be sentimental but everyone is sentimental. Leave my sentimentality alone.

MANOLITO: I'm not going near your sentimentality.

[He elbows VICTOR.*]*

VICTOR: You can be as sentimental as you like and I won't say anything.

ILKA: ¡Coño, si ustedes joden!

MANOLITO: That's why you love us so much.

VICTOR: And when you're loved by Ilka, you know about it.

ILKA: There's only one way to love. One hundred percent! Any other way is a waste of time. *[Pause.]* I was dreaming I was alive again.

MANOLITO: ¡Ay, nena! Why are you refusing to let go?

ILKA: I don't know. I want to, but it's as if I forgot to do something. But I don't remember what it is.

VICTOR: It's too late now.

MANOLITO: Don't tell her that. Maybe you need to get busy and it'll come to you. It'll jar your memories and you'll remember what you forgot!

ILKA: I could almost touch it.

VICTOR: Instead of doing my play why don't we act out your life?

ILKA: Oh, please!

MANOLITO: It's a great idea. Maybe it'll jar your memories and help you remember what you forgot.

VICTOR: We've done that for every one of our friends.

MANOLITO: We'll put on a show like we used to in La Tertulia.

VICTOR: Or in Intar Two.

ILKA: That's where we did your last play. You were already sick.

VICTOR: I was directing but I couldn't finish it. *[To* MANOLITO*]* Do you know that she would come to the hospital every day and sit with me for hours?

MANOLITO: She did the same with me.

ILKA: Don't you start getting sentimental on me. What are friends for?

MANOLITO: So are we going to do the play or what?

ILKA: Let's do it. You already have me thinking about my life anyway.

*[*MANOLITO *and* VICTOR *cheer.* MANOLITO *rings a bell.]*

MANOLITO: Here ye, here ye! Today we'll be performing Ilka's life.

ILKA: Oh, please.

VICTOR: We are performing your life. Don't be so modest.

ILKA: We are performing excerpts. A life cannot be performed—only lived. Excerpts can be performed.

MANOLITO: *[A bit annoyed]* Today we'll be performing excerpts from Ilka's life. I don't like the word "excerpts."

*[*ILKA *gives him an evil look.]*

VICTOR: Ay, mijo, just go on.

MANOLITO: Okay, okay! Excerpts it is! Ilka was born—

ILKA: You can't say when I was born.

MANOLITO AND VICTOR: Why not?

ILKA: The audience will put it together with the day of my death and they'll figure out how old I was. A true lady doesn't let anyone know her age.

MANOLITO: *[To* VICTOR*]* If I'm going to narrate this story, I have to do it my way.

VICTOR: It's her life.

ILKA: Are we telling my story or not?

MANOLITO: Yes, yes we are. Ilka knew how to live life. As a little girl she wanted to be a performer.

ILKA: You can skip past that. And skip the middle, too. Except the part of my daughter being born. Jump to the last part—that's where I'm having this memory gap.

MANOLITO: Am I narrating the story or you?

ILKA: You are, of course. Don't be so sensitive. Start after I became a lawyer.

[MANOLITO *clears his throat.*]

ILKA: Okay! Go on.

MANOLITO: Then the eighties came. Ilka, now a lawyer, still acts in plays, movies and TV.

VICTOR: But the eighties also brought a disease that was very angry at humanity.

MANOLITO: Who, Reagan?

ILKA: The dark years!

MANOLITO: From what I hear those dark years are still there.

VICTOR: Is Reagan still in office?

ILKA: He wasn't when I was alive.

VICTOR: I was the first one in the Hispanic theater community to die from it.

ILKA: I was so angry. How did this disease take you away so quickly? You had so many plays to write. So many poems inside you. Back in '81 no one knew what AIDS was or how it was contracted.

MANOLITO: Ladies and gentlemen, the first scene you'll see today will be Ilka visiting Victor at the hospital.

[*Lights up on* VICTOR *wearing pajamas, sitting on a chair.* ILKA *enters with a container of soup.*]

ILKA: How are you feeling?

MANOLITO: Ensorrao. How is my play doing?

ILKA: Manuel took over the direction.

VICTOR: Is he keeping my vision?

ILKA: Yeah. I bought you soup.

VICTOR: I'm not hungry.

ILKA: Victor you have to eat—you've lost a lot of weight.

VICTOR: I want to finish writing my new play…but I can't hold the pen in my hand.

ILKA: Dictate it to me, I'll write it.

VICTOR: Will you do that for me?

ILKA: Of course.

VICTOR: You're so good.

ILKA: We're friends and I love you.

VICTOR: I love you, too.

ILKA: If you love me, you'll eat the soup.

VICTOR: I don't love you that much.

ILKA: You can't take it back. Now, open your mouth.

VICTOR: It tastes good. When I leave the hospital I'm going to write a play about you.

ILKA: What will you write about?

VICTOR: About your dirty secrets.

ILKA: ¡Mira! Be careful.

VICTOR: I would write about how you come to see me every day here at the hospital when you could be doing more important things.

ILKA: The critics won't like a play like that. Not enough drama for them.

VICTOR: Fuck the critics. They wouldn't know a good play if it bit them in the ass. They are just like those so-called good friends who don't come to see me. I'm not a leper or anything.

ILKA: People are scared. They don't know how you catch this disease.

VICTOR: Are you afraid?

ILKA: Of course, but I'm not deserting you.

VICTOR: That's why you deserve a play. I'll call it "Mother Teresa meets Ilka Tanya Payan."

ILKA: You're pushing it.

VICTOR: I'm scared, too. I don't want to give what I got to anyone. The doctors don't even know what it is. I guess I'm a guinea pig for them. Trial and error is how they're treating me. I could die tomorrow and I got so much unfinished work. [Cries.]

ILKA: Victor, dictate the play to me.

VICTOR: I can't right now.

ILKA: Yes, you can. Look, I'm holding a pad and a pencil. Start. Okay?

VICTOR: I know what you're trying to do.

ILKA: You're so perceptive. You could always see through me. How does your play begin?

VICTOR: I love you so much. [Pause.] The play begins in—

[ILKA steps away.]

MANOLITO: Scene two. Victor got worse. One day Ilka goes to see him to find him dressed and packing. He was released. His doctor told Ilka there wasn't anything they could do for him, so they sent him home to die.

VICTOR: They're letting me go. I'm going to be fine. I feel much better. I'm going to finish a new play and I'm writing a book of poetry. Being sick has been a blessing in disguise. It has shown me that life is but a blink of an eye and we have to take advantage of that blink because once the eyes close it's over. Every second is precious. When are we going to produce my new play?

ILKA: As soon as you finish it and we raise the money.

VICTOR: We don't need money. Let's just do it! Okay?

ILKA: Okay...

MANOLITO: A week later Victor passed away. He was the first in the Hispanic theater community to pass away from AIDS and he certainly wasn't the last. Along with his mother and four friends, Ilka traveled with his body to Puerto Rico, where he was buried at the Caquas cemetery. That day she met his nephew, who was destined to become her second husband for seven years.

ILKA: And my friend for life.

[The wedding march is heard.]

VICTOR: Scene three, Ilka's house. The dreaded disease attacks another of Ilka's friends, Manolito.

*[*ILKA *joins* MANOLITO *and* GIGI.*]*

GIGI: Let's do it again. I think I got it now.

MANOLITO: Nena, you're going to kill me. *[He sits.]*

GIGI: Come on. I'll start. *[Sings and dances.]* "Me and my shadow." Come on!

ILKA: Leave him alone. You know he's getting old.

MANOLITO: Look who's talking.

ILKA: Yo estoy mejor que nunca. Better than ever, baby!

MANOLITO: I'm not.

ILKA: What's the matter?

MANOLITO: I don't know how to tell you this.

ILKA: Spit it out.

GIGI: What's the matter, tío?

MANOLITO: I don't want you to freak out, Ilka. Promise me you won't freak out. Promise me.

ILKA: You're freaking me out already. What is it?

MANOLITO: Sit down.

ILKA: This must be really bad. I can't sit. Tell me. *[She sits.]*

MANOLITO: I got AIDS.

ILKA: You mean HIV.

MANOLITO: No...no...no...I got AIDS. Full blown.

ILKA: Oh my God! Why didn't you tell me before?

MANOLITO: I was afraid of how you'd react.

ILKA: I love you like my brother.

GIGI: We're going to take care of you.

ILKA: That's right. Honey, can you get me a glass of water?

GIGI: Sure. You want one too, tío?

MANOLITO: Yes, sweetheart.

[GIGI *exits.*]

What's the matter?

ILKA: I'm going to take the HIV test.

MANOLITO: What for?

ILKA: Manolito, everything that happened in your life has happened to me. We have this connection.

MANOLITO: Connection?! Connection?! Please!

ILKA: It's a cosmic connection. We're both Capricorns, right? Born four days apart. We were hired for similar jobs at the same time. Hear me out! Remember when I was dating the Assyrian Christian Arab, and no sooner you started dating an Assyrian Christian Arab, my boyfriend's brother. And when your boyfriend bought you a dog, that same day my Gilberto bought me one, too. Events in our lives have always coincided.

MANOLITO: Nena, this is different. You have no signs. And you're married to a wonderful man. What is he going to say when you tell him you're going to take an HIV test?

ILKA: I have nothing to hide.

MANOLITO: I hope this is when our connection gets broken.

ILKA: Gilberto took it as well as any man could and we both got tested.

VICTOR: Two weeks later she got her result. It was a test she was hoping to fail.

[ILKA *is sitting. She's in another world.* GIGI *enters with Walkman. She's singing.* GIGI *looks at* ILKA*'s face and turns off Walkman.*]

GIGI: Mom, What's the matter?...Ma!

ILKA: I can't talk right now.

GIGI: Mom, whatever it is. I want to know.

[ILKA *goes into her pocketbook and takes out two envelopes.*]

GIGI: What is it?

ILKA: The HIV test result. *[She hands the envelopes to* GIGI.*]*

GIGI: *[She opens one of the envelopes and pulls out a blue card.]* It's negative.

ILKA: That's Gilberto's result.

GIGI: *[She opens the other envelope and takes out a red card.]* Noooooo! *[Cries.]* Mommy. Noooo!

*[*ILKA *embraces* GIGI.*]*

VICTOR: Ilka racked her brains and finally realized how she contracted it.

ILKA: Papo.

MANOLITO: The writer from Puerto Rico?

ILKA: I met him at a party.

[Flashback. PAPO *appears holding a drink.]*

PAPO: Nice party.

ILKA: What have *you* been drinking?

PAPO: *[Laughs.]* It is boring. You're an actress. A very good actress. I've seen your work.

ILKA: And you're a writer.

PAPO: How do you know?

ILKA: Word gets around. I've read a couple of your plays.

PAPO: Don't tell me what you think…Okay, what do you think?

ILKA: I like them very much.

PAPO: Are you trying to be nice?

ILKA: No, my theater group is having a reading series. I'd like to submit one of your pieces.

PAPO: You can submit one if you act in it.

ILKA: If you want me to.

PAPO: I do.

ILKA: How long have you been in New York?

PAPO: A week.

ILKA: Have you been taken around the city?

PAPO: Not really.

ILKA: Come on.

PAPO: Where are we going?

ILKA: I'm going to take you on a New York City night tour…

[End of flashback. PAPO exits. ILKA goes to MANOLITO.]

MANOLITO: When was the last time you saw him?

ILKA: About four years ago. I have to see him.

MANOLITO: Are you going to Puerto Rico?

ILKA: I need to take some of that Puerto Rican tropical sun anyway.

[PAPO appears. MANOLITO exits.]

ILKA: How are you doing?

PAPO: Up and down like a yo-yo. One day I think I'm okay, the next I can't get up from the bed. I'm sorry. I'm really sorry. I was shooting up drugs. It wasn't sexually transmitted. Who knew AIDS would be transmitted like that?

ILKA: Why didn't you called me to let me know?

PAPO: I didn't know when I contracted it. I should've called. I can't believe I did this to you.

ILKA: I don't know how to think about it. I'm angry. I'm confused. I'm scared. I don't want to die, you know.

PAPO: I know. I know. What the hell is this AIDS, ah? What the hell is it?

ILKA: I don't know.

PAPO: I've seen so many of my friends drop dead in their prime.

ILKA: I've lost a lot, too.

PAPO: It's crazy!

ILKA: Yeah…I wanted to see you, you know? Just wanted to see you.

PAPO: I've always loved you.

ILKA: Me too.

VICTOR: Papo died a couple of years later. Ilka returned to New York.

[PAPO *exits.* GIGI *enters.*]

GIGI: Mommy, Manolito is worse.

[MANOLITO *enters wrapped up in a blanket.*]

ILKA: Manolito, ¿como te sientes?

MANOLITO: Ay nena. Not very good. How do you feel?

ILKA: My body feels fine, but my heart is breaking.

MANOLITO: Don't be so sentimental.

ILKA: I'll be sentimental if I want to.

MANOLITO: Ilka, could you take care of my matters when I die?

ILKA: Don't say you're going to die.

MANOLITO: The writing is on the wall. Take care of my mother.

ILKA: I'll take care of everything. Don't you worry.

MANOLITO: I love you.

ILKA: I love you, too.

VICTOR: Manolito died a few weeks later. This left Ilka without her cosmic twin. She and Gilberto divorced.

ILKA: Amicably.

VICTOR: Amicably.

ILKA: Gilberto and I became lifelong friends.

MANOLITO: Ilka became an AIDS activist.

ILKA: Someone had to fight for Latinos with AIDS.

VICTOR: That someone was you.

ILKA: Gigi became a singer, moved out of my house, then moved back in when the AIDS symptoms started appearing. She wanted to take care of me.

GIGI: Did you take your vitamins?

ILKA: Yes.

GIGI: Ma, do you want me to give you a massage?

ILKA: Ay, sí nena. That would be so nice.

[ILKA *lays down.* GIGI *massages her and hums a song.*]

ILKA: You should be a masseuse. You have great hands.

GIGI: Shhh! [*She begins to apply pressure.*]

ILKA: I don't need it there today. Try the lower back. That's better. Yeah, that's it.

GIGI: You've lost some weight.

ILKA: Not really…some. But I feel good. I look good, right?

GIGI: Yeah…How's your energy level?

ILKA: Energy comes and goes. [*Changing the topic.*] Did I tell you I met a nice man? Handsome, classy. A jewel!

GIGI: Really?

ILKA: I took a walk in the park. I sat on a bench to watch the sunset. And this attractive man sat next to me. He said he goes there every day to watch the sunset. He said the sunset belongs to him and he offered it to me.

GIGI: He offered to give you the sunset? What did you say?

ILKA: My apartment was too small to have a sunset.

GIGI: That was rude.

ILKA: In that moment, as the sun was setting and we talked, I saw myself growing old with that man. Taking long walks. Even dying with him.

GIGI: Did you at least get his name?

ILKA: He gave me his card. I threw it in the river. I watched it flow on top of the water until it disappeared.

GIGI: You should've kept it.

ILKA: And do what with it? You tell a man you are HIV-positive and they run faster than if you told them you had fifteen kids. God, he was beautiful! I went there to think about the press conference I'm being forced to give about my condition because I'm a public persona. This is a private matter but I have to share it with the whole world. My family in Santo Domingo is going to freak out. Are you going to go with me to the press conference?

GIGI: Of course!

ILKA: I don't see death as an ending. Death is a transition from one state into another. I could accept it. Could you accept it?

GIGI: I don't want to talk about it.

ILKA: You have to accept it, Gigi, and go on.

GIGI: When the time comes, I'll deal with it. Right now, I want to look at you. To do things for you. To talk to you. Just to do living things with you. To love you.

[ILKA *joins* VICTOR *and* MANOLITO.]

VICTOR: Three years later, Ilka passed away.

ILKA: Wait!

MANOLITO: What is it?

ILKA: I didn't tell her I loved her.

VICTOR: But she knew it.

ILKA: But I told both of you I loved you before you passed away.

MANOLITO: Now I know why you're clinging to life.

ILKA: I can't go on until I tell her.

VICTOR: But you told her. You just didn't use words. Let's go back to the last scene.

[ILKA *joins* GIGI.]

GIGI: Right now, I want to look at you. To do things for you. To talk to you. To do living things with you. To love you.

[ILKA, *full of love, caresses* GIGI's *hair.* GIGI *then leans her head on* ILKA, *who kisses her head. This image lasts a few moments.* VICTOR *and* MANOLITO *go over to them.*]

VICTOR: Words couldn't have said it better.

MANOLITO: And he's a poet. He must know what he's talking about.

ILKA: I want this moment to last forever.

VICTOR: It will!

MANOLITO: Are you ready to do my play now?

ILKA: Yeah…I'm ready.

[ILKA *stands, kissing* GIGI*'s face, who feels the kiss and touches her cheek.* VICTOR, MANOLITO *and* ILKA *get their masks and cover their faces.* GIGI *sings a lullaby.* ILKA *takes off her mask for a second to look at* GIGI, *then puts the mask back on, joining* VICTOR *and* MANOLITO.]

END

Epilogue: Elba's Birthday

Louis Delgado

Characters

ELBA

LALA

MYRNA

OLGA

These four women are HIV-infected grandmothers. They are the same women who appear in the Prologue.

Place: AIDS clinic in the Bronx.

[*A women's AIDS support group. There are three women present. They are getting ready for a party.*]

OLGA: [*Looks at her watch*] What time do you have, Myrna?

MYRNA: I want to make sure I've got the right time.

LALA: What time does your watch say?

OLGA: It says eight-fifteen!

LALA: That's the time alright!

OLGA: Are you sure?

LALA: Of course I'm sure, my watch says eight-fifteen too! No, no, now it says eight-sixteen.

OLGA: My watch is still on eight-fifteen!

MYRNA: Will you two stop it! What's the matter with you?

OLGA: I'm just worried. Elba should have been here by now. It's her birthday.

LALA: She'll be here.

OLGA: What if something's wrong? You know, she wasn't feeling so good last week. Damn it, I should have called her.

MYRNA: She would have called us if there was something wrong.

OLGA: What if she couldn't get to the phone?

LALA: Oh my God! ¡Ay Dios mío!

MYRNA: She lives with her mother. If there was something wrong, her mother would have called us.

OLGA: Do you know her mother?

LALA: No.

OLGA: Do you, Myrna?

MYRNA: No, but I'm sure—

OLGA: Sure of what? Why should her mother call us?

LALA: ¡Bendito! What if she needs our help? She's been through so much.

MYRNA: I don't know how she's held on so long. Damn it, she doesn't deserve this shit.

OLGA: Who deserves it? I get so mad at times, she is such a good woman. ¡Ese pendejo!

LALA: What's that all about?

OLGA: Her old man goes out and fools around and then comes home, damaged goods!

MYRNA: Ella es una Santa. She took care of that man until his last breath.

LALA: I would have killed the bastard if I were her!

OLGA: That's just the type of woman she is. Maybe this wasn't such a good idea.

MYRNA: What?

OLGA: You know, making such a big deal out of our birthdays. Big deal! So we've lived long enough to have another birthday.

LALA: I remember when I never wanted to celebrate my birthday. Once I got over thirty, that was it. It was nobody's business but mine. Now we're celebrating—this is crazy.

MYRNA: It's not that crazy!

LALA: It's not, eh? Look at us, we're waiting to die. And we're celebrating birthdays.

OLGA: Lala, maybe you're right! What the hell is it all for?

MYRNA: Don't say that! It means something, it's another year.

LALA: Who cares?

MYRNA: I do!

OLGA: You know something, so do I!

LALA: Ah shit! So do I! I wish Elba were here.

[ELBA *enters.*]

ELBA: Hey, what is this, a funeral?

MYRNA: Elba, you're here!

OLGA: Oh baby, you don't know how happy I am to see you!

LALA: Don't do that shit no more!

ELBA: What, what did I do?

MYRNA: You were late! We were worried. We thought something was wrong.

ELBA: There was something wrong!

MYRNA: What happened?

ELBA: I'm all dressed and ready to leave the house…

LALA: AND…

ELBA: And just as I am opening the door, she starts to scream…

ALL: WHO?

ELBA: My mother!

LALA: What was she yelling about?

OLGA: Don't tell me, she didn't want you to go out, right?

ELBA: You know how she is. She worries. But that wasn't what she was yelling about.

MYRNA: What was she yelling about?

ELBA: That damn dog! She was yelling about the dog. She wanted me to walk him.

OLGA: That's why you were late? Oh my God, I thought—

MYRNA: Sh!...

ELBA: What, you thought I died? Baby don't count me out yet. I'm not ready to go. Although sometimes I feel it would be easier…but I'm not a quitter. And besides, what would all of you do without me? You know what? I promise to be on time next year!

[They all sing "Happy Birthday" and "La Señorita Elba" (the song from the Prologue) as lights fade.]

END

Love & Danger
a play in two journeys and fourteen scenes

Imani Harrington

Characters

PLAYER A /SALOME: African and Latin descent, mid-thirties. Well-composed with a strong desire to love.

PLAYER B /SELENA WEBB: Asian, late twenties. A dancer with a bag of tricks.

PLAYER C /CANDICE MAR: European and Native American descent, late thirties. Sharp and witty.

PLAYER D /WINTER MARK: African American, late thirties. A mother on the edge.

PLAYER E: early twenties. A changeling and a ghostly curious student.

AGENTS 1 and 2: any PLAYER except PLAYER E.

AGENTS A, B, C and D: PLAYERS A, B, C and D.

SOCIAL CHORUS: ALL except PLAYER E.

Time: In the past, present and maybe the future.

Place: A clinical trial site and beneath a city street.

Author's Note: Depending on individual productions, the role of SOCIAL CHORUS may be played by three additional female actors; however, the role may also be doubled. The role of PLAYER E should be cast as a woman of color from anywhere in the world; and if casting roles of dual heritage presents itself as a problem, then the role of SALOME should be played by either an African woman or a Latina and the role of CANDICE may be played by either a Caucasian or Native American woman.

Production Note: The S.F. Art Commission/Culture Equity Program funded this play for development through its 1995 Individual Artist Commissions. First showcased for development at New Conservatory

Theatre, San Francisco, 1995, with director and dramaturg Abraham Celaya. In 1996, it was also in development at the San Francisco AIDS Theater Festival and Cable Car Theatre, with director and dramaturg Alice Elliot-Smith, choreographed by Richelle Donigan; and later developed at the Cleveland Health Museum Theater, 1997, with director and dramaturg Abraham Celaya.

Prologue

[At a clinical trial site, the AGENTS *are lining up* PLAYERS. *There is a sense of chaos and confusion. Shadowed lighting gives the sense that there are women everywhere. One of the* AGENTS *speaks into a bullhorn in a monotone voice.]*

AGENT 1: Attention all registers, attention all registers: You have been recruited to the trial site because you failed to register your health status. You must be screened for infection and other possibilities.

AGENT 2: If you are pregnant stand in line one. If you are not certain of your status stand in between line one and two. For all others stand in line three.

AGENT 1: Those who have not been assigned to any trial must stand behind the yellow line.

AGENT 2: If you are negative you must at all times stand at least five feet away from those who are positive.

AGENTS 1 AND 2: If you are positive you must not sit, spit, sweat, touch, kiss, flirt, talk nor have sex with those who are negative.

*[*PLAYERS *join* AGENTS 1 AND 2. *The lighting makes it difficult to see their faces.]*

ALL: Remember, under no circumstances are you to have sex. We will not bend this rule, or any rule, for any one person. If you break any of these rules, you will be arrested and prosecuted—and your treatment could fail. Your treatment could fail.

[A siren goes off in the background]

ALL: *[Whispered breath]*
  Desire is hot sweat!
  Huh! Huh! Huh!
  Desire is hot sweat!
  Run. Run. Run.
  Huh! Huh! Huh!

JOURNEY ONE
The Oral Interrogation

[PLAYERS appear on the stage. When they get to a landing, they freeze into a tableau. ALL are watching PLAYER A, but she can't see them. Lights dim on the faces in the background and up on PLAYER A in the foreground. A pool of light circles her, and a thin and shadowy effect seems to loom around her. She is perhaps caged behind a structure of some kind. She is wearing a white full slip. The interrogation has been going on for some time. In the background is the distinct sound of dripping water that never stops.]

PLAYER A: Something's terribly wrong in the state…of affairs. And I don't know how to fix it…No, I told the other agent the same. The light is too bright…I'm wearing this because I was trying to get dressed… before you entered. I see these questions are taking a turn from the last agent…Yes; it depends on what I am going through, and right now I'm going through a lot. I don't think you noticed. I'm wet…Because I'm hot…I'm sweating… Because I'm wet…Yes, of course. I make and want love like anybody else… No, but it should be artistic…don't you think? I have hormones too and physical needs that happen to be attracted to a certain species of humankind which requires a certain connection to gentle love and if I were not I don't think I'd be interested…No I didn't! Someone infected me and someone infected them and someone infected them…I'd like to know too. All my lovers said they were safe, and their lovers said they were safe and their lovers said they were safe. Then one day I learned I was not safe, and so perhaps we should teach the meaning of masturbation in schools. *[a beat]* Can you turn that off? *[Covering her ears with frustration]* The noise! The drip! The light, it's too bright. *[Shielding the light from her eyes]* The water. *[Hands to her mouth]* I'm thirsty. *[a beat]* Can I have some water? Yes, no, yes…Love of semen. Blood. Sex. Vaginal Fluids. *[a beat]* Vaginal fluids, what the hell is that?…How can I answer a question that doesn't appear to have an answer, except results? Look, if you want to control me and my hormones you're doing a bad job. You might want to change your field…Yes, that's the part that's dangerous, besides ignorant lovers…You can have the best intentions and the wrong thing can happen. It's like marrying the wrong person…Yes, so what does love have to do with any of this?…If you want to control my movement you should start…Yes right there…Yes, I was married twice, I left the ring on the table both times, and I see that you have one—you're playing danger with your left love hand…Look…wait, don't. I can't…I want you…to…Yes, um…Here…right. Let me show you how to adjust…to…wait! No…you shouldn't *[a beat]* stop.

II. The Verbal Interrogation

[In the interrogation room at the trial site, we see one PLAYER *after another in profile as snapshots are being taken. After one* PLAYER *speaks, lights quickly go down and then up on next* PLAYER. *Each light change is accompanied by a loud and spectacular flash. Each* PLAYER, *except for* PLAYER E, *wears a white full or half-slip.]*

PLAYER D: No, I didn't infect anyone, have you? Do I look like somebody who would? Actually, I'd like to live longer, like anybody else, wouldn't you? Why did I have a child? I wanted one.

[Lights down on PLAYER D *and up on B]*

PLAYER B: I don't know how it all came to be. Maybe it's just that I don't want to know what happened. How would you cope? I never said I wanted to be tested and I never said I wanted the results. Would you? I don't want to talk about it!

[Lights down on PLAYER B *and up on* PLAYER E.]*

PLAYER E: You're trying to confuse me. No, I was not in that trial. I wasn't in any trial. No, you've mistaken me for someone else. I'm not positive. I'm not pregnant. I'm negative.

[Lights down on PLAYER E *and up on* PLAYER C.]*

PLAYER C: I've got stomach pains, gynecological complications, blurred vision and bad taste for fucked-up people. I didn't have any place to go. I was looking for someone, a friend I couldn't find. We were together right before they jumped me.

AGENTS 1 AND 2: Clinical trials for women *come here.*

ALL: *[Whispered breath]*
Huh! Huh! Huh!
Run! Run! Run!
FROM! FROM! FROM!
YOUR LOVE.

III. When Positive Meets Negative

[Below a city street; the underground.]

[PLAYER D is mumbling to herself as she searches the grounds. PLAYER B enters, toting a large bag of goods. There is an awkward moment of silence.]

PLAYER D: Who are you?

PLAYER B: And who are you?

PLAYER D: Identify yourself.

PLAYER B: How?

PLAYER D: Your status.

PLAYER B: Which one?

PLAYER D: Your health status.

PLAYER B: *[a beat]* I'm not certain, and you?

[PLAYER D gives no verbal response, but studies her]

PLAYER B: *[a beat]* It's cold out there, cold enough to kill you.

[PLAYER D still looking at her]

PLAYER B: I saw two agents running after you. *[Searches the grounds]*

PLAYER D: *[a beat]* Yeah. They took my child.

PLAYER B: *[To herself]* They don't know what they're doing. There was an open clinical trial for negatives.

PLAYER D: Yes, how positive.

PLAYER B: In the open trials they say you can do what you will.

PLAYER D: And if it's closed?

PLAYER B: You do what they say. They persuaded me to get tested, but I didn't stay for the results.

PLAYER D: Well, I don't have the answer for you.

PLAYER B: No, you don't. And I don't have one for you.

PLAYER D: It's funny how things tap at the spine, makes you wanna holler, and once you've hollered it turns into relief.

PLAYER B: I'd call that aggravation. But rain…that sounds like music. When I was a little girl I would go to the window and press my ear against the pane. I'd separate the drops from the splatters. Then when the lights and bolts came, I'd scurry underneath my bed, waiting until my mother would come and find me there. That was my peace.

[PLAYER A *enters. She is wearing a full slip. At times she is preoccupied and at other times engages with other* PLAYERS.]

PLAYER A: I saw you both near the trial site.

PLAYER B: [*To* PLAYER A] It's raining hard as ice out there, huh?

PLAYER A: Yes, so hard that it can cut you to hell.

PLAYER B: Yes, you're right.

[PLAYER D *stares* PLAYER A *down*]

[PLAYER A *begins searching the grounds.*]

PLAYER B: [*To* A] There's nothing over there. I've already looked.

PLAYER A: Traffic control.

PLAYER B: That's what they say.

PLAYER A: Everywhere I go I feel as though I'm being watched

PLAYER B: You are being watched.

PLAYER D: I wonder why?

[*A noise is heard*]

PLAYER A: It feels as though the walls have eyes. I bet you they hid one over here.

[*Resumes her search*]

PLAYER B: [*To* PLAYER A] Well, when you find one just smile and say cheese. You must be cold.

[PLAYER B *digs into her bag, pulls out a jacket, and offers it to* A.]

PLAYER A: No. I'm hot.

PLAYER C: [*From offstage*] Elizabeth! Elizabeth! [PLAYER C *enters; bumps into* PLAYER A] Oh, hi there. I was looking for a friend.

PLAYER A: [*Curious*] Can't you see?

PLAYER C: I thought you were her.

PLAYER D: But we're not, or are we?

PLAYER B: *[To* PLAYER C*]* You're bleeding.

PLAYER C: Am I? Those dogs!

PLAYER B: *[To* A*]* You're trembling.

PLAYER A: Yes, I am.

PLAYER C: *[To* A*]* You *must* be cold.

PLAYERS B AND D: No, she's hot.

PLAYER B: When the clock strikes another woman will die.

PLAYER D: And where did you learn to keep time?

PLAYER B: My mother taught me.

PLAYER C: Oh really? What did she teach you?

PLAYER B: How to play.

PLAYER C: With?

PLAYER B: Dice.

PLAYER D: *[To* B*]* Oh I see. So when you play do you *win* when you play?

PLAYER A: Not if they're *dying.*

PLAYER C: Yeah, you're right. OK! *[To* B*]* Then can you throw them to make them not die?

PLAYER B: I don't know. Guess we'll have to see, won't we?

[No verbal response from A, C *and* D*]*

PLAYER A: *[a beat]* Agents! They're everywhere.

PLAYER C: Yes, they are, aren't they? Gives me the jitters. They kept me separated from everyone else while they scrambled around like little tiny mice in fur coats. Get this: in red ink they wrote, "She is the other."

PLAYER A: *[To* C*]* The other what?

PLAYER C: Exactly my point. *[To* A*]* Does that make you feel protected?

PLAYER A: Yes, it does. *[Clutches her cross]*

PLAYER C: The last time I wore one of those I ended up at a trial site. Bleeding!

PLAYER A: *[a beat]* They're keeping busy up there, aren't they?

PLAYER C: Yes, just think of it. What sense does it make to register if you're positive? I'll tell you, it doesn't.

PLAYER A: No, you got it wrong. You're suppose to turn in the names of those you've been with—if you're positive.

PLAYER C: No, no, no. You're suppose to tell before you kiss, like this.

[Jumps in front of her]

PLAYER A: Ridiculous!

PLAYER D: No it's not.

PLAYER B: *[To D]* Then go back out there. Go on.

PLAYER D: *[To B]* In my own time.

PLAYER B: What would they do if there were no more negatives?

PLAYER A: *[Laughing]* They'd turn positive.

[PLAYERS A and B share laughter]

PLAYER B: They're tracking the movement of all past lives.

PLAYER A: Yes, and loves.

PLAYER C: Yes. One of the rules was broken in the trial.

PLAYER B: No, all of the rules were broken.

PLAYER D: And whoever she is she got away with it. They blamed me.

[Rapid tempo]

PLAYER B: Someone said it was a man.

PLAYER C: A woman.

PLAYER B: A man.

PLAYER D: A woman.

PLAYER A: A man.

PLAYER D: They stamped her infector!

PLAYER C: She's marked on the forearm.

PLAYER D: No, on the breast.

PLAYER A: I hear below the navel.

PLAYER C: Well she won't get far, will she?

PLAYER B: So if I were positive I could look you in the eye and I could lie, couldn't I?

PLAYER D: Yes, but not if one witnesses your mark.

PLAYER B: You mean stamp?

PLAYER A: No, curse.

PLAYER C: Oh, what a shame.

[A noise is heard from offstage]

PLAYER A: *[To ALL]* Did you hear that?

PLAYER C: *[To A]* Yes I did, and let's make certain that...

[PLAYER E enters. She looks extremely troubled and anxious. Her bag is full of books and papers.]

PLAYER E: There was someone following me. But when I turned they were gone. I thought it was an agent.

PLAYER C: And how do we know you're not one?

PLAYER D: We don't.

PLAYER E: I'm not. *[a beat]* Where are all of you from?

PLAYER C: I'm from the mid part of the city.

PLAYER B: The lower region.

PLAYER C: *[To A]* And you?

PLAYER A: *[To C]* I'm from the heart of the city where nothing stops pulsing. *[To D]* And you?

PLAYER D: The bowels.

PLAYER C: We know what that means, huh?

PLAYER E: I'm from the upper region. *[New thought]* Vertical transmission. They kept saying, "vertical vaginal transmission."

PLAYER C: *[To ALL]* I can tell she's not going to get any of this.

[Rapid tempo.]

PLAYER D: *[To E]* Why did you come here?

PLAYER B: She just told you.

PLAYER D: Well tell me again.

PLAYER E: *[To D]* I said someone was following me and I thought it was an agent.

PLAYER C: *[To E]* Are you positive?

PLAYER E: No!

[PLAYER A moves away from the group and watches]

PLAYER B: *[To D]* Well I'm here because I'm not certain if I'm positive or negative.

PLAYER E: *[To ALL]* I'm negative! *[To D]* Are you?

PLAYER D: What?

PLAYER E: You know, positive?

PLAYER D: *[Sarcastic]* No! I'm totally pessimistic, and you?

PLAYER E: What do you think?

PLAYER C: *[To E]* I think you have a real problem.

PLAYER E: *[To C]* No, you have a problem.

PLAYER B: We all have a problem.

PLAYER D: No. *[To B]* I don't have a problem. *[To E]* I'm aware of my problem.

PLAYER E: Are you?

PLAYER D: Yes! That's my point.

PLAYER B: *[To D]* Lay off her.

PLAYER C: *[To E]* She's not untouchable.

PLAYER E: I can speak for myself.

PLAYER C: Then speak.

PLAYER E: *[To* PLAYERS C *and* D*]* I really don't have to indulge in conversation with either of you.

PLAYER B: No. You don't.

PLAYER D: *[To* ALL*]* That's the problem.

PLAYER C: Banter! Banter! Do I need to call an agent?

PLAYER B: No, let's progress. *[To* ALL*]* This is absurd. I'm not positive. I'm not negative. I'm not angry and I'm not happy. OK everyone! Anger *[Gestures to* PLAYERS C *and* D*]* meets *[Gestures to* PLAYER E*]* peace.

PLAYER D: You think I'm angry, wait till I'm happy.

PLAYER C: She's in denial, I'm positive.

PLAYER B: I don't know.

PLAYER C: *[To* E*]* Then show us your navel.

PLAYER E: I'm not showing you my *navel.*

PLAYER C: She's not going to show us her navel. What a pity.

PLAYER B: *[To* C*]* You don't mean that?

PLAYER D: Of course she means that.

PLAYER B: She's hardly an agent.

PLAYER C: A virgin maybe, but not an agent.

PLAYER E: You're right. I'm not an agent.

PLAYER D: But she could be the one who fled.

PLAYER B: *[To* D*]* And so could you.

PLAYER D: *[To* B*]* That's where you're wrong.

PLAYER B: It could be any one of us.

*[*PLAYER A *moves back to group]*

PLAYER A: *[To* D*]* Yes, she's right. It could be any one of us.

[Short silence]

PLAYER D: I can tell.

PLAYER B: How?

PLAYER D: Just look at her.

[ALL look at E]

PLAYER C: Oh I see.

PLAYER D: *[To E]* Why did you come here?

PLAYER B: *[To D]* Maybe for the same reason you came here, to get away from that up there.

PLAYER A: *[To D]* Except you're so reasoned that you want one of us to be her?

PLAYER D: *[To A]* She is the reason I'm suspect. I should not have to pay for her stupid behavior.

PLAYER C: Well, now that I think of it I don't know how stupid it could be if they've stamped her just below the navel. She must have been doing something right. You know, to put a chokehold on something that close to your labia.

PLAYER D: *[To C]* You accept her behavior?

PLAYER C: No, I just would love to meet her.

PLAYER D: Really?

PLAYER C: Yes, I mean I'd like to meet her and show her how to use her navel. I mean…scratch that.

PLAYER E: *[a beat]* They're skilled.

PLAYER B: They're agents, they're supposed to be skilled.

PLAYER E: They're so calculating that I actually got confused. For a minute I was thinking that I had done something wrong, but I haven't done anything.

PLAYER B: Maybe that's it.

PLAYER E: What?

PLAYER B: That you haven't done anything—can't you see the logic in it? No action leads to some other kind of action due to in-action.

PLAYER E: *[To B]* I don't quite see it that way. What they call logic seems confusing to me. *[To ALL]* They said, "We understand that you believe you're negative. Well, we believe you're negative too, but you should be tested." One of them had a strange looking mustache. He walked like this *[Mockingly]* "Are you pregnant?" I said, "I'm not positive. I'm not pregnant. I'm negative." They said that if I didn't get tested and start medication that my infant would be at risk and that I could be charged for intentional, vertical, vaginal transmission. Sounds like a car doesn't it?

PLAYER C: *[To* ALL, *taunting]* Yes, maybe it's a VULVA.

*[*PLAYER E *takes a newspaper out of her bag]*

PLAYER D: *[To* E*]* What do you have there?

PLAYER E: I didn't tell you this before because you all seemed so upset. I think you should know about this. There's a warrant for her arrest and a list of names of those who they believe are positive.

PLAYER D: *[curious]* Let me see that. *[Receives newspaper from* E *and reads aloud]* "If you have seen this woman or have come in contact with her you must notify us immediately. If you give us any information we will gladly pay a $50,000 reward."

*[*PLAYER D *hands the newspaper back to* PLAYER E*]*

PLAYER E: I like the part that reads "Beware, she likes human contact."

*[*PLAYER E *offers the newspaper to* PLAYER B, *who takes it and reviews it.* PLAYERS C *and* A *stand at a distance watching the other* PLAYERS*]*

PLAYER E: *[To* PLAYERS C *and* A*]* Would you like to see it?

*[*PLAYERS C *and* A *take turns looking at the newspaper ad. They give no verbal response.]*

PLAYER B: There's no picture of her.

PLAYER E: No, because someone broke into their lab and stole all the most recent pictures.

PLAYER D: How do you know that?

PLAYER E: I heard someone talking about it right before I came here. *[Reads aloud]* "The following names are those who need to come forth." Want to hear who they are?

ALL: NO!

[Short silence]

PLAYER B: So that's how they record registers and non-registers.

PLAYER E: *[To B]* Yes, exactly.

PLAYER C: Fifty thousand!

PLAYER B: It's dirty money.

PLAYER D: For a dirty woman. *[a beat]* So, they're looking for this woman they want to question—

PLAYER C: Actually, I'm looking for one too.

PLAYER B: *[To C]* Please let her finish.

PLAYER D: *[To B]* No, let her rot.

PLAYER A: What kind of hope is that?

PLAYER C: It's the kind that decays.

PLAYER B: Or is it just foul?

PLAYER E: She got away.

PLAYER A: What a good woman.

PLAYER D: What else?

PLAYER E: I don't know.

PLAYER D: Young child.

PLAYER E: Don't call me child.

PLAYER D: OK. Then what are you if not a young—

PLAYER C: Woman.

PLAYER E: I'm a student.

PLAYER D: And what exactly do you study?

PLAYER E: Statistics.

PLAYER D: I see.

PLAYER C: She has radar and she studies stats on a list but she doesn't know anything else.

PLAYER E: Oh, but I do, and they don't have a clue.

PLAYER A: You're right.

PLAYER C: She's implicating. No, speculating. How titillating. *[a beat]* Or is that irritating?

PLAYER E: I know more than you think.

PLAYER C: That's irritating.

PLAYER E: They examined my hair, skin, forearms and hands. They even looked at my thighs and feet. One of them said, "She isn't marked!" Then they asked me at what hour was I last with someone.

PLAYER C: And?

PLAYER E: I said I wasn't with anyone.

PLAYER C: I told you she was a virgin.

PLAYER D: This woman—is there anything else about her you learned?

PLAYER E: Yes, they showed me a series of photographs, images of a woman on a large screen. They showed her face at different angles, with different features, short hair, long hair and even with different skin colors. They know everything about her. You're not going to like this, but she looked like all of you *[To* ALL*]* It's really confusing. They said she called herself Autumn Wine.

ALL: Couldn't she be you?

PLAYER E: Who me? I'm negative.

*[*PLAYER E *stands at a distance watching]*

ALL: *[Whispered breath]*
Huh! Huh! Huh!
Desire is hot sweat!
Desire is hot sweat!
Huh! Huh! Huh!

IV. When Love Motions: The Chance for Real Love

*[*PLAYERS A, B, C *and* D *play* AGENTS A, B, C *and* D, *but are subtly disguised.* AGENTS *move and speak softly.]*

AGENT D:
They called her Autumn Wine
it soaked her pores
naturally reading as the prose of her memory

the lyric missives of her heart
nothing in the world
can kill love when you need it
into her hazy memory
where the dust remained in the air
until it would decide
to settle as words might in a dictionary
those grains in
her mind
she would never forget what was left on the bed
the shadow of a ghost, a wet ring left on the table
a picture without a frame
a mere reminder that she'd try
to forget those scars of love that had pierced her body
how love spoke to her body and her mind
thought as negative
certainly she was not positive
that's what she kept telling her friends
"I know I'm safe
I'm not positive"

Even though she had had some of the greatest
love affairs with some of the City's
finest and accomplished and as supple
and refined as they were they knew
and had the means to live, to love and eat well
Oddly so
this had helped to make
them feel safe too
plus never seeing any
image of who they were in the world
provided a strange and
awkward sense of security
something like female bravado
Like when an image mirrors who you can be
without mirroring who you really are
is a very lethal reality
She had never seen anything like herself
become infected
never seen an image

or the words in print that could convince her
Hey sister
did you know
you too can get infected?
The contours of her love space
and the daily desire
the want of it pacified the texture
of life and sense of self

She thought herself
indifferent to those other girls
the ones who survived off
the luxury of corporate men
and the home girls from the projects
of which she came
knew that
without a financial backing
she was just like them

AGENT A:
So she pushed the last love affair
she had into that memory space
and like an insect it kept coming back

She had lain with this one like she
might a queen or how a
a gentle man might stroke
her sculptured grooves
holding her bronze
brown
body in place
with gravity and then contracting with the
sacred treasure that lay below her steady palms
she delightfully took the nectar
from the sweet
succulent
ripened
cones where milk came
abundant as ever
with this gentle consent of peace love
she straddled her raspberry

amber
chocolate
legs over bronze iron
like she might
a well-loved horse and they rode
into the next morning
while the sun broke
itself into microscopic needles
in the sky
turning those particles into wasted love
There were no real pauses in their thoughts
or movement
until there was a moment
without air

AGENT B: *[begins a subtle dance]*
She had enjoyed the fullness of that night's
nourishment
an affirmation of her womanesque
this lovemaking could not have happened
any other way
by now even if it could have
been different
it was too late
they had already made love

She remembered
that night her body took all the things
that love can give of your soul
a mere sense of connectedness
something
she had always felt without
Then something flashed before her
but she buried it like the dead
and when it came back
she remembered
the awkward moment in the dance
of love
as though she were a dark
Salome *[Pause]* and neither bothered
to ask the particular, detailed,
love stories of their past

ALL: *[Ad libitum]*
> Where have you been?
> Who have you been with and how?
> And where are you going?

AGENT C:
> To do that she said,
> "It would take the fun out of the moment"
> her understanding was that
> it's difficult for a woman to pass it on to a man
> but easy for a man to pass it on to a woman
>
> And what about another woman?
> She thought how men who loved men
> were doing it
> the men who had wives
> that traveled well kept in the night
> there were signs everywhere for them
> but not for her
> she couldn't conceive
> of any possibility

AGENTS A AND B:
> She was not a man

AGENT C:
> She was a woman
> She had been seduced by a
> history of false reasoning
> images that equate to lies
> this
> peculiarity
> how could a woman give
> it to another
> woman or man

AGENT A:
> She thought it completely safe
> and in that invincible moment
> where love's passion unfolded
> as it always does
> it had turned blind

and the particular and singular
details of that moment
What was that?
We don't know.

AGENT C:

She got up that morning
and prepared her bronze lover
slices of kiwi and strawberry fruit
feeding her lover's rounded voluptuous
mouth until a fullness of love
came and the savvy musical
notes of love
inspiring juices
of her own creation lived
while the juice ran down her
fingers
the thought of love came
into that memory space

AGENT D:

She tried to push it away like
the dead
but it kept coming back
When the lover left closing the door behind
she turned in the nude and went back
stood watching
and like a silhouette
her lean hung over
the bed
she stared at its frame and
thought about the wet ring she would never part
where they had lain she was left to study
the sheets that rippled love waves
And like the tide of an ocean
it soon came back to the forefront of her mind

AGENT C:

Whatever could they have done wrong?

AGENT D:

Soon she was left to justify her love.

AGENT A:
> "All the lovers I have ever been with were safe."

AGENT B:
> They were as safe as they
> thought they could be
> and one day when she realized that the lover
> had left for good, a surprisingly frightened thought
> presented itself to her
> She could be infected
> and something had been
> happening to her body but by this time it was too late.
> A strong notion overcame her:
> Every time you sleep with anyone
> you lie with all the lovers they have ever had
> And that was the beginning of her trial

ALL: *[Whispered breath]*
> Huh! Huh! Huh!
> Desire is hot sweat!
> Desire is hot!
> Sweat!

V. The Art of Play: It's More Like Who Are You

PLAYER E: *[To C]* If the agents find you will you tell them what they want to know?

PLAYER C: You mean have I told them what they wanted to know? No. Will I tell them? No.

PLAYER E: *[To B]* Will you tell them?

PLAYER B: What is there to tell? I don't think there's much left to tell. They seem to know everything.

PLAYER A: Not much to hide, except your body—and she can't hide that.

PLAYER C: No she can't, not with that mark. There's nothing invisible about that. Is there?

PLAYER B: *[Takes dice out of bag]* I have an idea. Let's play a simple game and give ourselves new names.

PLAYER E: I don't need to play. But I think we're safe here, and I'm negative.

ALL: We know.

PLAYER E: They can't stop me from being who I am.

PLAYER D: If they ask you your name what will you say?

PLAYER E: I don't need a name.

[PLAYER B *throws dice*]

PLAYER B: Call me Selena.

PLAYER C: Candice.

PLAYER D: Winter.

PLAYER A: Salome.

[ALL *look to* PLAYER E]

PLAYER E: I don't need a name!

PLAYER B: Let the dice determine the possibilities.

[SELENA *throws dice.* PLAYER E *watches*]

ALL: *[Whispered breath]*
　　Huh! Huh! Huh!
　　Desire is hot sweat!
　　Sweat! Sweat!

VI. The Law Of Desire: I Don't Want to Talk About It

[Rapid tempo]
[Seriocomic]

PLAYER E: It's my turn. I want to play now. I want to talk about—

CANDICE: Sex?

PLAYER E: No love. What was the most daring thing you ever did when you were a little girl? I mean, did you ever fall in love?

SALOME: Yes.

[*From a distance,* WINTER *studies* SALOME]

CANDICE: *[To E]* To tell the truth, I really don't think so. But, oh yes, I did.

PLAYER E: Did you...you know?

CANDICE: Well, I once let little Tommy…you know…have it there. I'm afraid I suddenly discovered there was nothing loving about that. Let's see, but there was Joie and Bobbi—they were both girls. Bobbi was my first love.

PLAYER E: *[To* CANDICE*]* Well I don't see it like that.

CANDICE: It's more about how you play with your thoughts of love. Love, my friends, is the most bourgeois conceit there ever was. It doesn't seem to be for those who really love.

SELENA: *[To* CANDICE*]* Love is like the art of dance; unlike the sport of men, it doesn't have a place in this world.

CANDICE: *[To* SALOME*]* What was your love about?

SALOME: I don't think you want to know about my love.

ALL: *[To* SALOME*]* Yes, yes. We want to know about your love.

PLAYER E: *[To* ALL*]* What is love?

SELENA: My love is—

CANDICE: Wait! If I remain celibate any longer, I'll have to join a monastery.

SELENA: My love is—

SALOME: Supreme.

WINTER: *[To* SALOME*]* You think your love is supreme?

SELENA: It's to praise your self first.

SALOME: Love is free.

WINTER: *[To* SALOME*]* Really? I don't have time for love. I don't want it knocking at my door any time it wants to. I can't stand the thought of love. Yes, I despise love.

SALOME: *[To* WINTER*]* I know, and love tries to despise me.

SELENA: My love is positively electric.

CANDICE: You got that right, shocks me all the time.

PLAYER E: What is love?

ALL: Love! Love! Life! Death! Freedom! Sex and War!

PLAYER E: And peace.

SELENA: LOVE! LOVE!

WINTER: Love is when the food comes.

CANDICE: When water stays and the man goes.

SALOME: When the man stays and when the woman comes—

PLAYER E: Home. So what did you say to your love?

SALOME: I'll call him Old Lover. I did what I could to make him love me and love me well.

CANDICE: Go on. So what did you say?

SALOME: I looked into the depth of his eyes and said: I am a luminous landscape of love. I am a gentle flower standing before you, the gem of your iris, why do I distract you? Do you think you can see through my love or float on top of it like something that can't go deep? You can't bury me as wasted love. What does my ability to turn you on equate to if I happen to stimulate your moves? [To ALL] I asked him if this was just a phase in his life. He said, no, it isn't. I want to love you dearly, let me show you. I said, wait, stop, you're moving near my mucosa, simply adjust your mind to this. You have two, no three options, but that really depends on your position. No, not like that but like this. Yes you found it. It's artistic don't you think? I asked Old Lover, can you see my horizon, I want you to touch my margins like vertical discussions you have with your eggs in the morning—know who I am? He loved me everywhere except there. So I said, wait, you're near my feet and making geographic mistakes. You can't love me that way. By now he had gotten up to get dressed and was on his way out the door. I was numb. He stood there half naked with his back to me facing the door. I asked him if he knew the color and flavor of my skin's history. Is it written on my body or in your mind as negative, positive? I don't need your love that bad and I will no longer be your peacock—blue, black, turquoise and green camouflage, the one you once plucked feathers off. I will no longer be that love and the goddess you could've had. We could have loved, had you not changed your concept of love, had you not written positive on my body. By now, all I could hear was the hollow noise of footsteps patterning down the stairs—that was the last time I ever saw him.

WINTER: [To SALOME] So that's how you love?

SELENA: How do you love?

SALOME:

> Let me tell you
> I will love you sun up
> sun down
> At eight in the morning while turning around
> With loyalty and praise
> not to possess
> my love
> is central and cannot exist alone.

CANDICE: *[To* SELENA*]* How will you love?

SELENA:

> Let me tell you
> I will let you be free
> To imagine all possibilities of love
> Like when the chickens come and when the rooster
> runs after the hen
> I will love your back
> front
> history
> color shape and size
> twirl your locks
> curls
> naps
> plaits
> My love is so necessary to provide.

CANDICE: Well, there are five things that once appealed to me.

SELENA: What?

CANDICE: The battles of great women, the valor of music, love, poetry and titillating sex and—

WINTER: *[To* SALOME*]* Rules, secrets and lies.

SELENA: *[To* WINTER*]* Yes then, how about the rules of desire?

SALOME: Yes, let's talk about that.

SELENA: As in safe?

SALOME: Yes, that one. I have always played safe.

SELENA: Really? How do you know that?

SALOME: I think of it as one hundred percent safe.

SELENA: There's a difference between the idea of security and real safety. I think of it as though I were driving a car through a green light that suddenly turns yellow. At this moment you're not one hundred percent safe because you're at the point of no return. You don't mean that kind of safety, do you?

SALOME: Obviously, we measure safety differently. But go on, it sounds good.

SELENA: Yes, let's back up.

SALOME: And do what?

PLAYER E: Don't try it.

SELENA: You're at the deciding point before departure where you either put your seat belt on or you don't.

PLAYER E: Oh I must hear this.

SALOME: Well, I didn't exactly get mine on yet but go on anyway.

SELENA: Whether you put it on or not, you can never ascertain the when of someone colliding into you or you them, right?

WINTER: Right. Yes! Go on.

SALOME: This might be getting good.

SELENA: So, where am I?

SALOME: You're in the middle of a yellow light.

CANDICE: Right!

SELENA: OK! So I made it through yellow, but without my noticing, it turns green. So I motion myself through green. Now it feels good, right? But there's a curve in time, motion and space. And I came, I mean I *come*, round again, but this time I get to another yellow light that turns red. And even though I stop, I notice that I am almost hit from behind. I make it without collision. At this point I've witnessed how close fractions of seconds could have been to taking my life. But the irony is that I'll never really know when another passerby might come speeding through.

PLAYER E: Wait! What does this have to do with sex?

SELENA: *[To* PLAYER E*]* Oh, it's there. The difference is that you're not driving a car, but passionate heat. Get it?

SALOME: *[Rapid delivery.]* I got it! You're fucking a cheap, red-hot Volvo.

SELENA: *[a beat]* No, loving. It's the element of heat, the chemistry of passion. Love! You can't learn passion; you experience it. It's the law of desire.

PLAYER E: Now it's my turn again. Let's play another game. If the agents come here what will you do? What will you say?

SELENA: Now the game will turn serious. *[Takes an object out of her bag and throws it to one of the* PLAYERS*]*

PLAYER E: Forget it. I don't want to play.

WINTER: Then who's on first?

CANDICE: Yes, who?

SALOME: Who's going to be the first to get tested?

WINTER: And which one of you will talk of lies?

SALOME: No, who lives and why?

CANDICE: Who will be the first to return to the city streets just as you are?

SELENA: Or someone else and afraid to think or say—

CANDICE: Positive!

SELENA: No, negative.

[The object is finally thrown to PLAYER E. *She stands at distance.]*

PLAYER E: Something is going to happen, isn't it?

SELENA: Something has already happened, hasn't it?

PLAYER E: What?

SELENA: I don't want to talk about it.

[Short silence]

PLAYER E: *[To* SELENA*]* Why? Please tell me, what happened?

SELENA: *[Hesitates. Then to* E*]* I just had an image of it. I'm afraid to say what. If I say it, you will have to also tell. I don't want to talk about it, do you?

*[*PLAYER E *studies* ALL*]*

PLAYER E: *[To* WINTER*]* What's wrong? *[To* SALOME*]* You're sweating. *[To* CANDICE*]* Your color has changed. *[To* SELENA*]* You're trembling. *[To* ALL*]* What's wrong?

SELENA: I don't know.

[Light fades on PLAYER E. *She stands alone.]*

SELENA: When the clock strikes eleven who will lie?

PLAYER E: What time is it? *[To* SELENA*]* You're trembling, what's wrong?

SELENA: I don't know.

ALL: *[Whispered breath]*
Huh! Huh! Huh!
Desire is hot.
Sweat!

VII. Loveless Lovenotes: How We Cope

*[*ALL *move in tandem. Their isolation is made apparent by the direction. This entire scene is rapidly spoken, and is performed relentlessly. At various points they stop to subtly inhale and then exhale.]*

SALOME: In the trial I kept wondering, if there were a cure, would it have feeling, smell, taste? A sound of silent love? Or is this all in my head?

ALL: *[to audience]*
IS ANYTHING TACTILE ENOUGH TO BE LOVED?
WE ARE HUMAN PLAYERS WHO ARE CONSIDERED POSITIVE,
BUT AT THE OPPOSITE END OF THE SPECTRUM, YOU ARE
THOUGHT OF AS NEGATIVE.

*[*PLAYER E *hesitates, and then, after watching for a few moments, decides to join. Each line is spoken with increasing distortion.]*

Oh Mary mack, mack, mack all dressed in
black, black, black, waiting for love
LOVE

> She asked her mother, mother, mother
> If she was worth, worth
> More than fifteen cents, cents
> Now even her mother, mother
> Could not answer, ANSWER!

*[*PLAYER E *drops out and then looks on from a distance. Her isolation is made apparent by the direction. She watches the group.]*

[Rapid tempo]

PLAYER E: *[anxious]* How did you survive? What did you say, do, think, when you found out? Will you tell me? Will one of you tell me?

SALOME: I kept those thoughts to myself...

CANDICE: I was afraid to say what I thought...

SALOME: Afraid I'd be left alone...

SELENA: The words live inside my head...

SALOME: Choked by my own desire...

SELENA: I don't know if I'm positive or negative. What will I do if I am? What would I say? What would you say?

CANDICE: I've been fucked by ignorance, maimed by shame and battered by another person's reality.

PLAYER E: I have thoughts about mine...

SELENA: Tell me what it means...

SALOME: What is the meaning of being negative...?

SELENA: What's the meaning of being positive...?

CANDICE: Who are the others...?

SALOME: I've got to find love...

SELENA: I've got to find a peace of mind...

WINTER: My lover is gone...where is my baby?

SELENA: After I was tested, my body froze...

CANDICE: I slid under ice...afraid to speak...

WINTER: I could not move...

CANDICE: I went in search of my lover...

SALOME: I could not breathe...

[ALL *stop their movement at the same moment. They subtly but quickly inhale and exhale. Then, as though in a dream, they resume their movement with lines spoken relentlessly.* PLAYER E *looks on from the outside and attempts to connect with them, but they do not notice her.*]

SELENA: I could not speak...

WINTER: Guilt swells inside me...

CANDICE: I was shocked...

SALOME: My mind went numb. So I went in search of love...

WINTER: Where is the Holy Ghost I once saw in myself...?

CANDICE: Where is Elizabeth...?

SELENA: What if I'm positive...?

SALOME: I had images of a dead river flowing through me...

WINTER: Dreams of my home and baby flow through my mind...

SALOME: I remember love on a rooftop...

WINTER: I had thought to hate myself fiercely. I exiled into shame...

CANDICE: Bashed for loving...

SALOME: I wanted to jump out a window. I stood on the ledge waiting to exhale...

PLAYER E: *[Overlapping]* Agents were following me.

SELENA: I lost control. I could not eat, walk or think...

CANDICE: I was still fucked by ignorance. There is a constant stab at my pain...

SALOME: When I stopped kissing, was it a sacrifice or my disaster...?

WINTER: A natural disaster...

SALOME: Between my thighs is the memory where canals once opened. A riverbed now closed...

CANDICE: Damn...

SALOME: The terror of my mind…

SELENA: Even though my bone sets in pain…

CANDICE: The outside seems to fail me…

PLAYER E: *[Overlapping]* I need some air…

CANDICE: Because I can't find the other inside me…

WINTER: They took my baby. I couldn't tell nobody, how could I…?

PLAYER E: *[Overlapping]* I am not infected. Do you hear me? I am not infected.

ALL: She couldn't tell nobody, how could she?

WINTER: *[To audience]* Could you?

SELENA: This feels like a dream…

PLAYER E: *[Overlapping]* I'm negative.

WINTER: I'm positive…

SELENA: I'm not certain…I don't know…

SALOME: Night after night I dragged my body over the kitchen floor. My head held down like the pendulum's swing, the glass hour of despair…

SELENA: I tremble in the island of my dreams. Am I positive or negative?

WINTER: I paced back and forth while my head continued to nod in shame. How did this happen…?

SALOME: I tried to love myself…

CANDICE: I'm not certain, am I the other…?

PLAYER E: *[Overlapping]* What if they come for you? What will you say?

WINTER: I remain alone in my silence…

SELENA: If I am I will not want to tell the story. Why should I have to? *[To audience]* Would you?

WINTER: They told me I was dying…

PLAYER E: *[Overlapping]* I need some air. I've got to get air. What time is it?

[ALL, except for PLAYER E, subtly inhale and exhale in unison and then begin moving and rapidly speaking again.]

SALOME: Nightmares about my love…

CANDICE: I remember the blood pulsing…

SALOME: Heat rages through me…

CANDICE: Where is she…?

SELENA: I kept dancing at odd hours of the night…

WINTER: I feel cursed, am I?

CANDICE: I've got to find her…

WINTER: I need to revive my soul.

[As though in a dream dance, ALL move about the stage in tandem, speaking to the audience with a gradual build. The last line of the final stanza is spoken when they arrive at the fourth wall and stop.]

ALL: THE NEED TO CLEANSE OUR BODIES
AND THE HISTORY FILLED WITH YOUR SHAME
A NEED TO FIND OUR OWN
AND THE SUBTLE INDIFFERENCE
THAT GOES UNNOTICED

WHO DO YOU LOVE? WHO CAN YOU LOVE? WHO WILL YOU
LOVE? WHEN YOU LOOK AT HER, DO YOU SEE A LEPER? A
VAMPIRE BANISHED WITH THE PLAGUE? A DREAM OF YOUR
HUMAN POSSIBILITIES? OR A FUTURE NIGHTMARE OF
YOUR PAST?

PLAYER E: *[Anxious. Moves about the stage. As usual, stands at a distance from the others.]* I need to get out of here. I can't find the exit. There' s no air. Will you show me the way out? Which way should I go?

ALL: I HAVE COME TO PAY ALLEGIANCE TO LOVE
AND THE DEAD, TO UNBURY THE DEAD WITH MY VOICE
I MUST PULL THEM OUT OF SILENCE
I WAIT LIKE A SUCCULENT CACTUS FOR WATER TO COME
IN THE MERE ABSENCE OF SOLACE, WHERE ARE WE TO SEEK A
PLACE OF REFUGE AND AIR? IF WE MUST DIE—THEN WE WILL
DIE SPEAKING OUR TRUTHS

[Lights change]

[Whispered breath]

> Huh! Huh! Huh!
> Desire is hot.

[Breath]

> Huh!

JOURNEY TWO
VIII. The Inquisition

WINTER: *[To* SALOME*]* If there's nothing to hide then you have nothing to be concerned about. Which trial were you in?

SELENA: *[To* WINTER*]* What are you trying to do?

WINTER: Maybe it's what I'm not doing.

SALOME: I don't have to tell you anything. You are not my gatekeeper.

SELENA: *[To* WINTER*]* My mother once had a keeper, that was right before she died. The keeper didn't keep her safe. Neither of them trusted the other, they couldn't understand why they had each other in their lives. Both wanted to feel safe, but they could never do so, because they were always in each other's face. *[To* WINTER*]* Just like you are doing now to her.

WINTER: Unless there is something to hide, she should have no reason for fear, nor think of me as her keeper.

SALOME: *[a beat]* They asked me who did I love.

WINTER: What did you say?

SALOME: What could I say? What would you say?

PLAYER E: *[To* SALOME*]* What did you say?

CANDICE: Will you get back to the point?

SELENA: I thought that was where we were at. I guess that's the comedy of this tragedy.

[Rapid tempo]

WINTER: So, which trial were you in?

SALOME: The third one.

WINTER: For how long?

SALOME: I don't remember.

CANDICE: You're cringing.

SALOME: You're pressing.

WINTER: You're hiding.

[faint sound of heartbeats]

WINTER: Who were your agents?

SALOME: I don't remember.

CANDICE: How long were you in there?

SALOME: Why?

CANDICE: I want to know, who was your agent?

SALOME: It was a man, a woman.

WINTER: What were their titles?

SALOME: I don't remember.

WINTER: What did he do?

SALOME: I don't remember.

CANDICE: What did she do?

SALOME: I don't remember.

WINTER: Was he an analyst?

SALOME: I don't remember.

CANDICE: Was she an ethicist?

SALOME: I don't know.

WINTER: Were they from the state?

SALOME: I don't know.

CANDICE: The church?

SALOME: I don't know.

WINTER: What was the nature of your trial?

SALOME: I don't know.

CANDICE: Was it private?

SALOME: No.

WINTER: Public?

SALOME: Yes!

WINTER: Did you have unprotected sex?

[SALOME *gives no verbal response*]

CANDICE: Did you use barriers?

SALOME: Have you?

WINTER: Are you illogical?

CANDICE: Suicidal?

SALOME: No!

CANDICE: Why did you come here?

SALOME: For the same reason you came here.

WINTER: Have you told others your status?

SALOME: Have you?

CANDICE: Who was your last lover?

SALOME: Who was yours?

WINTER: Who was your first lover?

SALOME: Who was yours?

CANDICE: How many lovers have you had?

[SALOME *gives no verbal response*]

WINTER: How does it feel to be positive?

SALOME: Negative!

WINTER: How does it feel to be negative?

SALOME: Positive!

WINTER: What do you do?

SALOME: I live!

WINTER: Who are you?

SALOME: I am a woman!

[Heartbeat stops]

IX. The Judgement

CANDICE: She's guilty!

SALOME: I thought the same about you.

SELENA: *[To* CANDICE *and* WINTER*]* You're both offensive.

WINTER: *[To* SELENA*]* Do you have something to hide too?

SELENA: *[To* CANDICE *and* WINTER*]* Do either of you? Why would I want to tell you?
*[*CANDICE *and* WINTER *give no verbal response]*

*[*SALOME *makes a decision]*

SALOME: They gave me medication.

SELENA: Everybody received medication.

CANDICE: There were those who couldn't take the medication.

SALOME: Yes, and those who didn't get the right kind of medication.

WINTER: *[To* SALOME*]* What kind did they give you?

SALOME: It certainly wasn't a cure. *[Makes a decision]* They gave me medicine to suppress my libido.

[As though suspicious, WINTER *and* CANDICE *move in silence and study* SALOME. SELENA *studies* WINTER *and* CANDICE, *while* PLAYER E *studies every move* ALL *make.]*

SALOME: *[Hesitates]* They wanted to know about everything I ever did. *[laughs]* They wanted to know about my relationships. I said I'd like to know about them too.

WINTER: And?

SALOME: They wanted to know how I loved, when I loved and why I loved. They said they were measuring the meaning of safety. Then the woman, she laughed in my face.

CANDICE: What else?

SALOME: What else do you want from me?

WINTER AND CANDICE: ANSWERS!

SALOME: You think I have them? I don't. I suppose they wanted me. That's the answer. You really want to know what it was like in there? You can't think what it's like in your own mind. *[a beat]* It was torture. *[To* WINTER*]* What happened to you?

WINTER: You don't want to know about my trial.

SALOME: Tell me something so I can feel normal about what is happening.

PLAYER E: *[To* SALOME*]* She's trying to understand what happened to you in your trial.

SALOME: What if I tell her about my trial and she still wants more, then what? What are you going to do, because they're not letting up? *[a beat]* They tried to take control over my thoughts. They asked me over and over, who had I been with and how? They told me I was disposable waste, inferior quality. You can't touch her. For a moment I wondered, maybe I am inferior. I was trapped between worlds. There was water coming from pipes. I thought I was hallucinating. Was I an animal? What had I done? Where had I been and with whom? I wasn't certain which was safe, to tell them the truth or to lie, or should I just be the animal? I saw two agents making out. Bone and flesh was their measure of safety. I can hear the faint sound of an almost breathless chant: desire is hot, sweat, sweat. They used no barriers. On the other side of the glass I watched her strip. There she was, her body standing like some shadow. When I closed my eyes I saw part of myself that once knew someone. All I could see was Old Lover who desired me. She strapped her legs round his waist and while he cupped her breast she held onto his backside and she entered. It was my nightmare. What was I supposed to learn from watching them? How could they be so cruel to make me remember? How could they make love when I'm not supposed to? They finished like dinner, got up, dressed, and left me with a memory. After that, another agent came into the room and that was my trial.

[Short silence]

WINTER: You work against yourself.

CANDICE: You're lying.

SELENA: Maybe she's telling the truth.

CANDICE: You're trying to save her?

SELENA: [To WINTER and CANDICE] Why not?

WINTER: [To SALOME] You're the one they're looking for.

SELENA: [To CANDICE and WINTER] You're both acting as though you have no feelings.

[PLAYER E stands alone, watching from the outside.]

WINTER: [To SELENA] You stand there and applaud her negative and solicitous acts. [To CANDICE] Damn it, you're bleeding again.

CANDICE: Am I?

PLAYER E: [To SALOME] You're sweating.

SALOME: Yes, I am. [To SELENA] You're sweating too.

SELENA: Really?

WINTER: [To SALOME] I'm convinced that you're talking about the agent who fucked you. I've been watching you. [To the others] That sounds great, doesn't it? What did you say to Old Lover earlier? "I can no longer be your peacock—blue, black, turquoise and green camouflage, the one you once plucked feathers off. I will no longer be that love and the goddess you could've had. We could have loved, had you not changed your concept of love, had you not written positive on my body."

SOCIAL CHORUS: [sotto voce] Look at her. She uses her body like she owns the world, as if it's hers.

SALOME: I said that and I'd say it again.

WINTER: That is a very important line, I will no longer be that love you could've had. And the goddamn goddess you could've had, had you changed your concept of love—

SALOME: I did not say goddamn.

WINTER: No, I did. You don't expect us to believe that that is what you told the agent? [To others] She told us that she saw someone making love in front of her and that they had suppressed her sexual appetite—

SALOME: Libido! That's true!

WINTER: It was you. You were the one. You were the one that broke the rule in the trial.

[SALOME *retreats to a place of safety, her mind. When the voices get too much for her, she tries to hide but finds that she can't go anywhere*]

SOCIAL CHORUS: [*sotto voce*] You had sex, you touched and you kissed an agent.

WINTER: If you had not broken the rule none of us would be where we are now—it's people like you that make us look bad.

SOCIAL CHORUS: [*sotto voce*] Bad! Bad! She's bad! She's a bad girl.

[SALOME *attempts to strike out at* WINTER. PLAYER E *continues looking in from the outside.*]

WINTER: Go ahead. *Touch me.* You didn't witness any agents making love, because it was you. It's all in your mind.

[*Lights fade on* SALOME]

SOCIAL CHORUS: What did you do? Was it safe?

SALOME: To us it was.

SOCIAL CHORUS: Did you use protection with Old Lover?

SALOME: No.

SOCIAL CHORUS: You wanted skin. You wanted to touch. You wanted to be loved.

SALOME: Yes, and so did he.

SOCIAL CHORUS: You will be charged. She's reckless.

SALOME: What about him?

SOCIAL CHORUS: What about him? Who cares?

SALOME: Go away and leave me alone.

WINTER: No! I'm not going away because what you did won't go away.

SOCIAL CHORUS: [*Sotto voce*] LOVE! SEX! TOUCH! You're the accused. You're the one to blame. Shame! You had sex. You touched. You kissed

[SALOME *buckles. It is as if the* SOCIAL CHORUS *is drowning her. She struggles to defy its force.*]

WINTER: She's ahead of us because while we struggled in our trials, she was being pleasured. What we do for love. Tell the truth. There was no one making love in front of you, it was you yourself.

SELENA: Why are you doing this to her?

WINTER: What we do for love, sex. We hate love, we disown love, disrespect love and we leave love. She was abandoned, rejected, RAPED! The killing hearts of love—

SELENA: You're railing with your own bitterness.

WINTER: [To SELENA] There's a lot to be bitter about.

[SELENA makes a decision]

SELENA: Stop it. Stop it. Stop! I didn't want to remember but I have to. We were all in the same trial. [To CANDICE] You weren't in the second trial. [To WINTER] And you weren't in the first one. [To SALOME] The intercom was on. They made us listen to you. There was an echo, a voice of laughter, someone being pleasured. I hear it now. [To CANDICE and WINTER] But there's more that took place in that trial and neither of you will say what that was.

[ALL remain uncomfortably silent.]

CANDICE: [To SALOME] If you're not her, show us that you're not marked.

[CANDICE and WINTER go after SALOME. SELENA goes after CANDICE and WINTER.]

SALOME: Stay away from me.

[SALOME cries out in pain. CANDICE and WINTER apprehend her and examine her body.]

SALOME: Keep your hands off me. Leave me alone. We only wanted to love each other.

SOCIAL CHORUS: [sotto voce] She's marked!

X. What Are You Going to Do?

[ALL stand alone, contemplating their options. PLAYER E studies them from a great distance. They do not notice her.]

PLAYER E: What are you going to do now?

SELENA: *[To* WINTER *and* CANDICE*]* She's right. What are you two going to do? What have you gained from this?

PLAYER E: Information!

SALOME: *[To* WINTER *and* CANDICE*]* More or less.

SELENA: Less. *[To* WINTER *and* CANDICE*].* I told you I was there. I'm the one who took the photos from the lab. *[Reaches into her bag and pulls out photos]* You can't hide.

SALOME: And if you do, who will you be? Look at me!

*[*ALL *look at* SALOME*]*

SELENA: If you want to give her up, then set the ghost free.

[Long silence]

CANDICE: *[To* SALOME, WINTER *and* SELENA*]* No, I can't hide. Can I?

SELENA: While she was in the trial, so were we. And every moment you thought to touch someone or even thought about it, so did she and everyone else.

SALOME: In that sense, I'm no different than either of you.

*[*WINTER *stands all to herself.* PLAYER E *continues looking on anxiously, with heightened curiosity.]*

CANDICE: Out there, it was so easy to hide, because they didn't see me. I was the other! And as long as I was *that,* I didn't have to be positive, nor did I want to be. That's how I lived my life—negative.

*[*SELENA *makes a decision. She takes a marker out of her bag, walks near* SALOME *and draws an outline of a heart around her.* SELENA *steps inside the heart next to* SALOME. *The others watch but remain separate.]*

SELENA: If I turn her in, I have to turn in myself and everybody else out there. Every night when I lay my head down to sleep, I wake up afraid, afraid to go to sleep, afraid to stay awake. My dreams are filled with those moments of my past. Each night, when I lay my head down on my pillow, I see their faces, staring at me. Those lovers—so many I can't count. Except there's one…I can't forget. You see, I had an Old Lover too. That night we lay in each other's arms, cajoling ourselves into mad oblivion—it was heaven. We lost all sense of time and place and then, at the height of my feeling love for him, was the moment of feeling hate for him, because, you see, I knew I could die. Yet I stayed.

CANDICE: I was trained to believe that there is no difference between fucking and loving. Now I realize there is a difference because I've been fucked by ignorance, maimed by shame around the fear that others have because of who I am. I should have remained alone in the darkness of my mind. I wonder, should I have shielded my eyes and known about the consequences of loving a woman? Maybe I should have screamed like a man that day I heard what felt like metal clash against my skull. All I could hear them say was, "This isn't your world. You can't do what you want with your body." Maybe I should have let the blood that ran down my head get into their eyes. Should I have let my menses choke them to death? Strangled them with that night's air? Maybe I should have just realized that my woman destiny was crossed long before I came to be the woman I thought I was. Am I not the other?

[CANDICE *gradually reveals herself by taking off her garments and wig, and showing her skin.* ALL *take notice of her bruises and the person she now appears to be.*]

CANDICE: I dressed like this, and does it matter? They told me that because there was nothing to penetrate I had nothing to worry about. I believed it. I made love to her not knowing. It's what I believed. They kept saying, you have nothing to worry about, you don't have sex with men. What do they know?

SELENA: What happened?

CANDICE: It happened the first day I arrived at the trial site. When they first announced they were conducting the trials. Elizabeth, my lover, she has some rare blood disease. I decided to go to the trial site to see if she could get into one of the new trials for liver transplants. Someone reported to them that I needed to be in one of the trials and that's when they ran a check on my status. The last time I saw her was right after we held each other and kissed. She left me. I stood watching her until she turned the corner. Two large shadows hovered over me with cigarettes dangling off the corners of their mouths. They asked me, do you want a puff? No, I want Elizabeth. You want who? Elizabeth. They stabbed their cigarettes into my skin and told me I better not say a word. No one came, no one looked out their window, no one stopped to say, hey, you all right? Ever since then I've been afraid to be who I am. At the trial site I stole one of the agent's clothes from out of their locker room. I put them on and escaped. Elizabeth's somewhere out there waiting for me. All I want now is to see her and to go back out there wearing my favorite blue sequined dress she bought me with my black patent leather shoes. *[a beat]* *[To* SALOME*]* I'm sorry I treated you the way I did.

*[*CANDICE *makes a decision and joins* SALOME *and* SELENA *inside the heart while* WINTER *and* PLAYER E *remain outside it, looking in.]*

[Lights change]

ALL: *[Sotto voce]*
   Tell us what happened to you, Winter. Tell us.
   What did you tell them in the trial?
   What happened in your trial?
   Could you take the medications?
   Did you take the medications?
   Did your body accept them or reject them?
   What happened to your child?
   What did you tell them in the trial?
   Who are you Winter, who are you?

[Lights fade out on ALL *and up on* WINTER, *who stands alone.]*

WINTER: I couldn't tell anybody. I couldn't tell a soul. Where is my baby? *[*WINTER *is back at the trial site, remembering. She is on the edge. She begins pounding on a door.]* I'm not crazy, give me my baby. What about my baby? My body? I have a sense of love for my own. You can't tell me how to love my child. Open up, let me out of here. I am a mother, you can't take that from me. I don't want to feel any more pain creeping into my body. If there is something wrong with my body, then there is something wrong with my body. I am the one who says there is something wrong with my body, not any of you. You didn't hear me when I was gagging on my own blood! My menses would not stop. I screamed during the night. I found myself crawling, searching for God. My baby—I gave her the taste of a mother's love that was given to me. Nobody knew the trouble I had while I was vomiting out all the shit and lies fed to me about being a no-good mother. I am a good mother. Why are you offering me a trial when I am damn near dead? My baby, I want my baby, my rights. I come from four hundred generations of mothers. I am a descendant of slaves and have even mothered you. You can't tell me that I am nothing, because I am somebody.

[Lights change. ALL *suddenly reappear.]*

WINTER: *[To* ALL*]* In the trial they said I was dying. What happened to you?

CANDICE: They said I was losing my vision.

WINTER: Are you?

CANDICE: Yes.

SALOME: I'm going to live!

SELENA: I don't know.

WINTER: *[To* ALL*]* I can't tolerate the medication. How do you take something you can't take? But isn't that what this is all about? Taking what you can't take? *[To* SALOME*]* You said you wanted to know something different. I need to know something different so I can understand. *[To* SALOME *and* SELENA*]* I didn't tell you about my love—I couldn't tell myself. In my trial they kept asking me questions about motherhood and infection. By the time they got to me it was too late. How did my baby get infected? It was a mistake. In that moment of need, I put her sweet gentle lips to my…why, I forgot—what it felt like to have something alive, dear, loving you, nearby. I fed her. I put her to sleep. They told me I should be sterilized. I hate myself for that, all of it. And now it's too late to love anything. *[To* PLAYER E*]* Every time I look at you, I see her. All my life, I've taken the blame. There's no damn love left, only trials. *[To* SALOME*]* Who wants blame?

*[*WINTER *makes a decision and joins* SALOME, SELENA *and* CANDICE *inside the heart.]*

[Lights fade]

ALL: *[Spoken with distortion]*
    She asked her mother, mother
    Who am I?
    Her mother told her
    Who she is, is
    What do elephants, elephants, elephants
    Look, look, look,

Like, like,
When they love, love, love
When they die, die, and live, live
They could not, not
give her the answer
for her
child, child

XI. I Don't Want to Play This Game Anymore

PLAYER E: *[To* ALL*]* What are you saying? *[To* CANDICE*]* Someone reported you? You were bashed? *[To* WINTER*]* They took your baby? *[To* SELENA*]* You didn't want to remember? I was beginning to think that it was safe here. I don't want to play anymore. I'm not infected. I can be who I am. I don't have to deal with this kind of thinking. This was all a game. Wasn't it?

*[*PLAYER E *goes to* ALL, *however directed. She is beginning to panic.]*

PLAYER E: Look at all of you. What's happening here? Your face, your skin, your size. You've all changed. Are you dying? Are you living? Yes, you're dying aren't you? Is it the medication they gave you? Did that change your body? *[To* SELENA*]* Tell me, what time is it? I feel like you're playing tricks. You're trying to frighten me, aren't you?

SELENA: You said you wanted to pretend, but now we're being real.

PLAYER E: What time is it? Did you hear me? What are they doing up there? I need some air. I've got to get out of here. *[To* SELENA*]* Will you tell me what time it is?

SELENA: *[To* E*]* I think you know what time it is.

ALL: *[sotto voce]* Do you want to live? Do you want to die? Do you want to love?

*[*PLAYER E *exits without the others noticing.]*

WINTER: *[To* CANDICE*]* You're bleeding.

CANDICE: Yes, I am.

SELENA: *[To* WINTER*]* You're not sweating.

WINTER: No, I'm not. *[To* SALOME*]* You look calm.

SALOME: Yes, I am.

XII. The Inevitable That Couldn't Happen...Or Could It?

SELENA: Where is she?

SALOME: She was just here.

CANDICE: I don't know, what do you think?

WINTER: What happened?

SELENA: We told her not go out there until she was prepared. Let's see where that gets her.

[PLAYER E enters, walking slowly. She is wearing a ripped white slip that has bloodstains on it. She is near-faint and in an obvious state of shock. She falls onto the stage. When ALL notice her, they recognize what has happened and attempt to respond appropriately.]

PLAYER E: NO! DON'T TOUCH ME. PLEASE DON'T TOUCH. It... it...was...was a dark...dark hallway. I sensed someone was there. I couldn't breathe, all I could do was gaze against the wall. I couldn't move from that force. I tried to get out of that place. They took me like I was a prize, there was a blow to my head, I was left with the blood, I was left for dead, I crawled into my mind, it was the safest place to be. Something's in me. I don't know what's in me, but I know something happened, their palms were stamped. You can't go out there. Somebody tried to lock me up in a van, but I laid myself under the body of another woman with a child. *[She struggles]* It doesn't matter anymore if I am tested. I had no choice. They said that it couldn't happen this way. Not to ever worry about someone trying to take something from you, that doesn't belong to them. I never thought that this could happen to me. I never had the chance in any of this. I wasn't the student you thought I was. I'm not her. I'm somebody else. I wanted to be pure, now waste runs through me. I thought it was safe. You told me. Somebody promised me that I would be safe. I believed I was safe. I feel so dirty. Ollie, Ollie, Oxen Free! Free!

[ALL attempt to console PLAYER E]

PLAYER E: No, don't *touch* me. *[To herself]* There was never any real choice. I never had the choice or the chance.

WINTER: We're just like you.

CANDICE: Show her the reality.

[ALL *stand watching over* PLAYER E. *They reveal the stamp of a cross on their palms. The others crowd around and stand watching over* PLAYER E]

WINTER: *[To* PLAYER E] Let me help you.

SELENA: Now you know the story.

PLAYER E: Yes, I do.

ALL: *[Sotto voce]* Is she alive or is she dead? Who is she? She's the woman in the trial.

[Lights gradually fade with rhyme]

ALL: This ole agent
    they play one
    they play nic nac on my...love...No. No.

    This ole agent
    they play one
    they play nic nac on my...mind...No. No.

    This ole agent
    it play me
    it play nic nac
    on my bodi with a nic nac patty wac
    give a dog a bone this ole child came
    crawling home

XIII. The Edge of Isolation

SALOME:
    She lived in a constant state of fear
    terror always seemed to follow her
    through strange streets and
    dark
    stench alleyways

    She was paranoid
    about how others
    deemed her crazy
    she knew she wasn't crazy
    even though she was on medication
    she neglected to take or
    perhaps forgot

She knew that when the voices
became too much for her
she would think that it didn't
necessarily have to do with what
THEY had called a chemical imbalance
but there were other things
that had gone wrong
other than herself
long before her state of mind came and went
she looked out the corner of half-cast
eyes from under the blankets that
once blurred her vision and saw that
there was something really
wrong outside of her
that she simply
had no control over

SELENA:
She had only known
she was positive for six months
and the day that she learned
she completely disappeared into
the landscape
under cars and in between
the cracks of buildings and when that
got too cold she found refuge under
the lethal arms of brazen and
shadowy thin men who were so
deprived of love
so worn
beaten
tried
and treacherous that they would eat her love raw
there was no love

ALL: *[Ad libitum]*
There was no love

WINTER:
The streets kept her insanity on the edge
her nights filled with bad people and things
that were always out to harm her

succeeded at every opportunity
She was easy prey
there was no love

ALL:

There was no love

WINTER:

Ever since she was a little
precious girl
someone had probed her mind
never realizing when she was a woman or
when she was a child
A constant state of confusion
said the neighbor who had
tried to tell her mother
but who couldn't understand
why her child was such a problem at home
and in school
she acted so bizarre
No one knew her name
there was no love

CANDICE:

Now at the age of twenty-one
walking through the streets
barefoot over
shards of glass
stripped veins
and no name
the damaged soles of her tiny feet
that would never grow
all in a daze
and mute as ever
that night

ALL:

They raped her
and that was not her love
it was her body

SALOME:

> There was no love
> the streets made music to the silence of her pain
> there was no love there was no love

WINTER:

> She found a doorway and
> while lying asleep
> the only thing she could do
> was to moan soft screams and the residue
> of death
> she could not breathe
> but the wet murmurs of blood
> pulsed beneath her feet
> making her scream out her history of pain
> and we did not hear her shame
> we did not respond to her name

SALOME:

> When the numbness wore off she noticed
> the only thing that seemed efficient enough
> to offer her solace was a respiratory machine
> technologically engaged
> infused into her screams
> leaving her tangled in between tubes and cotton sheets
> was terror and the whispers of a child
> who never had a chance to grow up
> there was no love

> And now it did not matter that she was positive
> she didn't have a chance
> because you see she could no longer breathe

> No one knew her name
> no one tried to save her
> no one knew her name

ALL:

> All they could do at the end
> was to tie a tag to her
> and say

"she is dead and gone"
And that, that was the end of that trial.

[PLAYER E *rises and exits as a ghost*]

XIV. The Possibilities of the Return

WINTER: Are you going back?

CANDICE: I don't know, are you?

SELENA: I hear something. I think they're coming.

WINTER: Then they'll have to come.

SELENA: There's nowhere to go.

CANDICE: No there isn't, is there?

SELENA: You can't escape your past.

WINTER: It will only come back as if in a dream.

CANDICE: [*To* SELENA *and* WINTER] What are your dreams?

SELENA: That maybe there's something better out there for us. I see it. You
have to imagine it. Can you see? Look out there. Look!

[ALL *look up and out towards the fourth wall to try and see what* SELENA *is
seeing.*]

CANDICE: What does it look like? What does it sound like?

SALOME: Is it love or is it danger?

SELENA: It's who you are. Close your eyes and imagine that person, the possibilities of being who you are. I see love and respect while everybody's
singing and smiling with joy and pain. My body is what it is. For I am
the same, no one is positive and no one is negative. I am young, vibrant
and unknowing.

SALOME: I love my body and my body is mine.

SELENA: It's as if it never happened.

WINTER: Yes, there's medicine.

CANDICE: A cure?

SELENA: A dream. It's just a dream and the possibilities of that dream.

WINTER: There's a child.

SELENA: Yes, there is.

CANDICE: I see Elizabeth! She is waiting for me.

SELENA: Yes, she's waiting. In the trial they told us to look at the woman
behind the glass. I see the other woman. Do you see her? She is not
afraid to be or to love.

ALL: Yes, I see her.

[They look to SALOME*]*

Epilogue

*[*PLAYER E *returns and, as before, appears ghostly and alive.]*

PLAYER E:
I pay allegiance to the dead. My skin translucent
ephemeral as ever
I will grieve shadows that roam

SALOME:
I close my eyes and envision a land of loss and survival
some will nod in mourning
some will dream of flesh
and connection
I watch my fingers turn into red dust
I can
no longer feel the sense of touch
yet I feel the sense of love
my tongue is numb
my limbs are stunted
but I have
grown
I am a cactus
an open wound festering
I wait for water to come

SELENA:
I have conversations with the dead. I dance with the dead
watch the dead
clash into the living searching for the complicity of peace that one may

never find
some will find, lovers who have fled
lovers who will stay,
today is gone and the ghost in the wind is here
to stay

WINTER:

I will sleep with the dead
blanket of bone and ash
milk splattered
covering spirits that pulse to flutter
in the wind
like butterflies
we may not know
we may not see
who they are until it's too late

CANDICE:

I will study the palms of my hands
the indentations of identity and time
the lines
of ancestry
the ones that turn into short road maps
of a forbidden future

WINTER:

Our children's future.

ALL:

And we rise with the living and take lessons from the dead, to live and
to love.

SALOME:

And on this plateau we must ask ourselves, what will our movement
be?

CANDICE:

Where to now?

WINTER:

What hour is this?

END

Allah appears as an eyelash in brooklyn

Dorinda L. Welle

This poem is part of a family of poems that emerged from a decade of voices and stories told to me by African American women affected by HIV/AIDS. In the tradition of ethnopoetics, which values the music and mystery, power and politics of storytelling, the poem honors the spirit of survival which African-descended women have shared with me, and the spirit which sustains me—a white woman, an anthropologist, a poet—in solidarity with women survivors of various oppressions and erasures. In this poem, "allah" means "all of," alive in ordinary language, a name for all that I love.

> allah i remember is how it was
> way past midnight & dark as yr eyes
> when somethin curled &
> soft shook me outta my
> semi-precious sleep.
>
> allah once there it was,
> one a yr killer eyelashes
> catchin moonlight & all hell
> layin there w/o my explicit permission
> on yr side a the bed.
>
> "i spoze you think yr so big
> just showin up like that
> when i just happen
> to be dreamin me some new vision
> a loveliness."
> but it just bat itself
> & look at me
> all dewy & shy.
> "the way yr actin
> you'd think you belong
> to damn bambi!"

well, i mustah riled it up
cause w/o warning
it start growin long-wise
& get to twistin around
till it take up allah yr space
& some a mine.

then it pull an AT&T
& reach out & touch me
& next thing my eyelashes
turn into a flock a fantastical birds
each eye a night sky full a swans
all green & gold & blue
makin they way south
where everything's warm
& the church ladies
gotta cool they selves
with fans made outta allah they lovers'
eyelashes
can i get an amen.

When i came to, allah i saw
was that sliver a you
catchin a little more light than before.
well, i said, bein just one
makes anything kinda unique
so i plucked it up
and with no voudou intention whatsoever
pressed the lengtha that lash into the soft wax
a my mango candle
& let it burn down real slow.

it was still goin next mornin
& it's still goin tonight
throwin slivers a light
allah cross my sight

which goes to show
one eyelash can go a long ways
from yr eye to my bed
& allah way
to wherever yr restin
yr head

these days
it's a world a lost eyelashes
left behind in intimate places
but when the night sky open its extra eye
allah i see
are yr sacred traces.

I'se Married

Sweet Potato Pie

(Ernest Andrews and Ntombi Howell, with music by the late Peter Barclay)

FEMALE VOICE: This poem is dedicated to all the lovers who in spite of the epidemic have the courage to enter into the space of love and who strive, despite the possibility of loss, to be fully present, alive, caring, spontaneous and able to express the rainbow of emotions.

MALE VOICE: Lying here recovering from yet another assault from this thing I endure—called AIDS. My mind drifts to the future, and today I'd like to feel wanted, not rejected because some think I've got the plague. I'd like to find peace of mind in the arms of another once again. I'd like to say SEE I'SE MARRIED NOW like the jazz singer in *The Color Purple*. I'SE MARRIED NOW, TILL DEATH DO US PART.

FEMALE VOICE: It's all the things before death: the testing of viral loads, the counting of T-cells, the offering of cocktails—and this is not happy hour, because every two hours the timer goes off, the doctor visits continue, and I wonder if she'll still be there for me tomorrow…the fear, oh my God the fear.

MALE VOICE: Oh! The fear, I dance it out. When it threatens to drown me, I dance—even if I can't get on the floor—I chair dance, letting the music run through me. As my body sways from side to side sometimes in the middle of the night, I curl up into his chest, letting his heartbeat lull me and soothe me.

FEMALE VOICE: We met at a party—dancing, we watched each other, asking questions with our eyes. We met and loved and moved in. Then I tested positive and everything changed. She held me through the tears and the trembling.

MALE VOICE: I met him at an AIDS benefit. I spoke, sharing my story, the pain and the possibilities of being positive—he came up to thank me, stayed to talk. He's everything I ever wanted and I'm grateful that he is

in my life, but I get pissed that it's now when I may have so little time—
I know that sounds ungrateful, pessimistic, but you know what, it's real,
cause I get angry—angry that I have the virus, angry that I get sick,
angry that I'm afraid and that I may lose the man who finally makes
my heart sing.

FEMALE VOICE: Her eyes are full of love and sometimes the fear of loss.
The fear that makes us fight, tearing at each other with words and attitudes, but our love overcomes our anger. There are times I want to plan
for our tomorrows, create in words and images the vision of what we
might become. I dream of us growing older together but we don't talk
about tomorrow, we don't plan for the years to come, for us each day
must be enough. But still I'd like to do what all lovers do and talk in
terms of forever.

MALE VOICE: I'd like to feel rice bounce upon my head, sneak its way down
past the cloth, sliding down my back, touching the rim of my
underwear—tap dancing in celebration of my union in spite of AIDS.

FEMALE VOICE: Sometimes when I forget things, can't find things, or find
myself standing and staring, I worry about dementia, worry that I have
said or done something awful, worry that it's the end coming near.
Then I pull myself together, and figure out I'm just suffering from CRS:
Can't Remember Shit.

MALE VOICE: I get tired easily, sometimes I just want to lay in bed, not
bother to get up—but then he's there tickling me or just snatching off
the covers, especially when it's cold, and when I'm really feeling sorry
for myself he tells me, "Your name is Ernest, not AIDS Patient" and so I
deal with it and my life, knowing that there is someone there beside
me. Each day I get a little lighter, less full of stuff, each day I get a little
lighter—and have more room for love.

FEMALE VOICE: She used to take pictures all the time, then she stopped, I
asked her why, she replied, I now take mind pictures and store them in
my heart/our love no longer needs a lot of words, we live it/our love,
this flame against the night of possible loss and pain.

FEMALE AND MALE VOICE: [in unison]
SEE I'SE MARRIED
I'SE MARRIED
I'SE MARRIED NOW
TILL DEATH DO US PART.

SECTION 2
SEX/SEXUALITY

So...

Migdalia Cruz

Characters

A WOMAN: thirties, African American, beautiful in a robust way, a hopeless romantic.

A MAN: thirties, white, beautiful in a sculpted way, a tender fatalist.

ANOTHER WOMAN: twenties, Latina, wasted looking though once beautiful, a grounded realist.

ANOTHER MAN: twenties, Latino, beautiful in a brutal way, a scared pragmatist.

Time: The present

Place: A place of worship where one kneels before one's God. Each character speaks to God in his or her own way. God is a shaft of light that slowly fades.

Production Note: A commission by Sean San Jose Blackman for the Names Project, an AIDS benefit sponsored by Bay Package Productions and the Magic Theatre, San Francisco.

[In a place of worship, four people are caught in separate shafts of light. The light comes on as each one begins to speak, then stays on. Each one speaks to the light as if it were God.]

A WOMAN: So...finally...I'm in love.

A MAN: So...I'll always love him.

ANOTHER WOMAN: So? I'm still in love with the son-of-a-bitch.

ANOTHER MAN: So, of course I still love him.

A WOMAN: He has blondish hair—what's left of it. And a bald spot suitable for kissing.

A MAN: He has brownish hair—what's left of it. And a bald spot suitable for licking.

ANOTHER WOMAN: He has black hair and a hardass heart let me tell you.

ANOTHER MAN: He has my same mouth and nose and looks just like me when he smiles.

[As A WOMAN continues, the others are lost in thought and prayer.]

A WOMAN: There's too much hair on his back and shoulders—but that's part of his charm. Too much and too little of something or other. His eyes are blue—not scary shark blue, but azure like the sky, like the sky on a good day. His fingers are long and good for giving people the finger—not that he does, he wouldn't, I mean, not so they could see him do it anyway. He's what we used to call a pushover—now we'd say a wuss or a pussy. And what's that about?! Pussies are good things—as far as I'm concerned anyway. I know I like and admire my own. But it's no good without the proper stroking. The cajoling of my inner thighs is simple for the loved one to master. The object of my desire has a really goofy laugh. I think it must be genetic. A Midwestern "I find really stupid things funny" kind of laugh. A laugh that's not afraid to be laughed at. A laugh that registers on the Richter scale a full four-point-oh kind of laugh. We have walked through cemeteries together, admiring the flowers which grow wild over the most forgotten graves. I will write him a beautiful eulogy—because girls always live longer than boys. So I'm told.

A MAN: He has so much hair on his legs and inner thighs. I have a made a porridge of his fluids on that nest of his hair. And boy do I have a thirst for his breakfast cereal. It is composed of tears and pain. But I'm strong for him. He knows this, so he tortures me. He sends me away from him when he needs me the most. "Get used it," he whispers. "Get used to life without me." But I don't want to. I still smell him on me wherever I go. I haven't washed my pillowcases in six months because he lingers there like a new scent by Nina Ricci—too many flowers and not enough herbs. In its faintness, it grows sweeter and easier to remember. In its faintness, I am reminded of how soon he will leave me. I ask for just one thing. He offers something else…his collection of North African pop on vinyl. He thinks I crave the exotic. I just crave him. A hand in mine, a head on my shoulder, a walk to the toilet in the middle of the night because he can't hold it in anymore. "You don't have to hold it in around me, baby. I love every bit of you." This he will not believe. He is embarrassed by his own weakness as I could never be. This he cannot believe. So he sends me away.

ANOTHER WOMAN: He's killed eighteen people. He said he kilt them because they were white and whites don't have no feelings—not like the rest of us. I think he had to kill the thing he most wanned to be. And anyway, he was killing himself the whole time same as them. I don't shoot up anymore. Without him it's not the same. I did it for him and with him. And now he's alone in there. I know he's dying in prison because I'm dying out here and that's how it works. I tried to see him, got as far as the bus. Turned around. I'm too ugly anymore for anybody to love me. My daughter, Lizzie, says I got number eleven legs because they so skinny, like sticks. I used to be fine. We loved to go out dancing—all dressed and looking sharp. But then the killing started and I couldn't go there with him. I had Lizzie to keep those bad things out of my mind. I could still see the good in people with Lizzie to show me how. He never liked her—from the day she was born all he wanned was for her to be quiet. I think it's because she reminded him of good things too. Things he thought he didn't deserve to feel. That's what I think. I think the State will kill him before it does. I hope I don't go before him. I don't got nobody to care for Lizzie. But I'm looking. So maybe I'll find somebody soon.

ANOTHER MAN: What's that stupid social worker think? That a man don't love his brother just because he's dying? I can't help it that I can't see him. I don't want to remember a crazy faggot in a bed hooked up to a machine. Don't get me wrong—I mean, he's not a real faggot, that's just a figure of speech. Sure he used drugs, but that's all. He got hooked in the army when he was in Germany. They give you drugs to stay in the army. That's what he told me anyway. People assume you're a faggot because you got it but that's not the truth—not in this case. I just wanned to be clear on that with you. Anyway, I want to remember the guy I went out and picked up girls with. The guy I took trick-or-treating. He always wanned to be a ghost. I made him all his costumes. One Halloween we got a real good one when our sister Wandi got her period and we used her sheet—boy, we grossed a lot of people out that year. It was a good year. And I hate to say it but I guess he got his wish now, huh? That's like a joke but it's not a joke because I bet he looks dead already—and why would I need to see that? I know he doesn't want me to see him like that. She said he's been asking for me, but I say she's lying. How can somebody who's already dead ask for anything? She just thinks a family member or some shit needs to be there to see him die. I don't gotta see that because I see it already in my head. So what would you do?

A WOMAN: I know what I'm going to do. I'm going to declare myself to him. He's stopped drinking so I know he can hear me now. I heard him all those times he declared himself to me in his drunkenness. He'd grab for a body part and say he could hold me so good like nobody else ever could. But I didn't believe it coming out of those vodka scented lips that have kissed more mouths than I could count—more mustaches too. That's the sad part.

ANOTHER WOMAN: I'm gonna go see him next week. It's my birthday present to myself. Might be a good time—might be the only time. But I don' know, he's jus' gonna look at me and scream. I've never looked so bad that a little make-up didn't help. But make-up just ain't working no more. I keep smearing my lipstick when I cough and then I look like a clown. Lizzie tells me that too. "Ma, you're looking like Bozo today," she says. I wish I looked as good as Bozo these days…

A MAN: I'm going to go and buy myself some new pillowcases. The ones with his smell on them, I'll sew them up at the end like a secret and put them inside my new cases and I'll sleep there on them and only I will know what's on the inside.

ANOTHER MAN: I'm just not going to go. That's why I came here. I wanned to explain myself to someone who'd listen.

[The lights begin to fade slowly.]

ALL FOUR: Hey, don't go.

[The lights stay on at their lower level.]

ANOTHER MAN: Are you mad at me now? I'm just being honest. Men shouldn't see other men looking weak. Brings the strong ones down. Let the girls go see that—they like to cry. I got no use for that. He'd feel the same about me. I wouldn't want him anywhere near me.

A MAN: I tried real hard the last time I saw him—I tried to give him a kiss but he turned away from me and started coughing. I think it was on purpose. He thought I'd get all grossed out by his mucus and blood, but I just wished I could suck it all out of him and make him better. I would do anything to kiss him. I kept trying but he kept coughing and motioned me out the door. I rested my lips on the other side of that door and left a kiss for him anyway. In my head I see him kissing me back.

ANOTHER WOMAN: You think they let people on death row get kissed by other people? I'd have to kiss him if I got in to see him but I bet I'd have to kiss him through plastic or somefin. Oh, it's okay to kiss. My doctor tole me it's okay with Lizzie and everyfin. I would die if I couldn't kiss her. Right now, right here, I would jus' die.

A WOMAN: I wish for a sweet, four-minute-long, open-mouthed kiss. That's all. Then I could die happy. I know it's four minutes because I practiced with his picture and that's how long I could keep his face in my head without opening my eyes. Four minutes in heaven. The only thing is, he won't let me kiss him, because he thinks he's diseased—but that's not how you get it, right? By kissing? I know you don't get it like that. But still he won't let me.

ANOTHER MAN: I think about his hands sometimes. They were so delicate. I would tease him about those hands all the time. Sweet, faggoty hands. And then I'd chase him and kiss those hands if I caught him. I'd kiss them now if I could. He knows I would if I could. But I can't...

ALL FOUR: So...what's a kiss?

[The lights fade slowly out.]

ALL FOUR: Don't go.

END OF PLAY FOR NOW...

One Less Queen
Mario Golden

Characters (in order of appearance)

JUAN ROQUE/JUAN GALLO: Early twenties, raised in the U.S. Involved in a street gang.

EDGAR ROQUE: Fourteen, raised in the U.S. Brother of JUAN GALLO.

ALFONSO MATA/ALMA: Late twenties, born and raised in Mexico. Considered one of the best drag performers in San Francisco. As ALFONSO, wears mostly male drag; as ALMA, full female drag.

MARÍA DE JESÚS GARZA/"LA CHUYIS": Early twenties, Chicana transsexual, born and raised in South Texas. ALMA's close friend, also a drag performer.

A PRIESTESS

TWO SPIRITS

EDGAR'S SPIRIT (EDGAR'S BODY): A teenage Black woman.

SALVADOR ARTEAGA: Early to mid-thirties, mixed Chilean and Anglo, raised in both countries. AIDS educator and Marxist activist.

LUZ PALOMA CASTILLO: Thirty-six, of Caribbean/African descent. A lawyer, loving partner of CELIA.

DOÑA IRENE: Early fifties, Latina immigrant. Widowed mother of JUAN and EDGAR ROQUE.

CELIA JURY: Mid- to late thirties, of Afro-Latin descent. Teacher and spiritual guide. Loving partner of LUZ PALOMA.

ALEXIS: A transsexual.

A JUDGE

MR. GONZALEZ: A prosecutor.

CHUYIS' SPIRIT (CHUYIS' BODY): Young boy.

The Setting: The play takes place in the San Francisco Mission District, early 1990s, during the fall and winter months. "The Mish" is a lively neighborhood, especially along Mission Street, between 16th and 24th Streets, and down 24th Street. Spanish and other non-English languages can be heard everywhere. Women shop at the tiendas and do laundry. Children attend school and play in the side streets. Bohemians and intellectuals contemplate the meaning of life at cafes and bookstores. Teenagers cruise the entire "hood." Homeless people "park" by the subway stations. Many men hang out in the traffic-filled streets, some as (undocumented) day laborers waiting for employers to drive by and pick them up at known corners. Patrons frequent restaurants and taquerías serving food from all over Latin America, the Caribbean, and the rest of the world. At night, while most people go home and rest in preparation for the new day, loud music can be heard from crowded bars in the vicinity of 16th Street, where bar patrons, prostitutes, drug dealers, homeless people, and gang members, among others, parade and interact.

Like many other inner city neighborhoods in the U.S. during this period, the Mission breathes the tensions of the times: the economic impact of free trade and the global market; the end of the Gulf War; racial divisions and the aftermath of the Rodney King uprisings; increased attacks on immigrants, women, the poor, and the homeless; the "war on drugs" and violent crime; restrictions on youth; gang warfare; anti-gay violence and homophobia; the AIDS pandemic; and gentrification alongside growing decay. None of this stops Mission residents from nurturing their families and communities, creating culturally, and organizing politically, even across borders. Yet there is a general sense of a sort of heaviness, of collective exhaustion, of accumulated damage and deep isolation and losses which have not been sufficiently (or at all) grieved, and which can surface all too easily in the form of explosive anger, abuse, and misdirected violence.

Production Notes: The stage is used flexibly to recreate different spaces, both material and spiritual. Before the play, in between acts, and at the end, music from Luis Miguel's *Romance* and *Romance II*, CHUYIS' favorite albums, is played. The song "Te Extraño" closes the play.

ACT I

Scene One

[Lights on CHUYIS, *positioned centerstage in full drag.]*

CHUYIS: Good evening everyone. Welcome to the staging of the play *One Less Queen* by Mario Golden. My name is María de Jesús Garza, also known as "La Chuyis." I'm one of the characters in this play. In fact, this play is all about me. Well, not really, it's also about a lot of other people, but you'll see—Mario always has to make things so darn complicated. Anyway, I just wanted to say that I am very happy you are joining us this evening, and I hope you enjoy the play. Buenas noches a todas y todos ustedes. Mi nombre es María de Jesús Garza, pero de cariño me dicen "La Chuyis." Soy uno de los personajes de esta obra, del autor Mario Golden...Ay, bueno, dejemos el rollo para después y ya verán que relajo se arma. ¡Que se diviertan!

[Lights down on CHUYIS, *then up downstage for a brief moment.* JUAN GALLO *and* EDGAR *enter, walking across. Stereotypical cholos, they are exact replicas of one another: baggy pants, oversized shirts, straddling walk.* EDGAR *carries a baseball bat. He walks a few steps behind* JUAN GALLO, *who seems to be headed somewhere. At one point,* EDGAR *stops and looks towards centerstage as if trying to look through a window, caught by loud music and laughter.]*

JUAN GALLO: Come on, Edgar.

*[*EDGAR *quickly catches up.]*

[Lights fade as they exit, then rise at Las Cariñosas, a gay dance club near the 16th Street subway station. Las Cariñosas operates in the best of the fichera tradition, whereby customers purchase tokens and exchange them for a dance with their favorite "girls," who in turn try to get the customers to buy drinks and more tokens. It has a reputation of being a rowdy place, where one can always find a good lay or, at the very least, enjoy a great show and dance to the best salsa. The clientele is almost entirely working-class Latino, notably men who give no impression of being gay at all and actually consider themselves heterosexual, but also a good number who seem comfortably openly gay, and some women, primarily, but not exclusively, "butch" lesbians. Las Cariñosas is best known for its mesmerizing drag shows—which draw the most creative and best-trained drag performers—as well as fabulous salsa contests held every other month to raise funds for people living with HIV.]

[The night is lively. At rise, ALMA *and* CHUYIS *dance a plena sisterly. Both are*

dressed seductively and made up to perfection. Halfway through the plena,
ALMA *is signaled to get ready to perform. She mouths the words "I gotta go,
honey."* CHUYIS *responds by wishing her good luck and kissing her on the
cheek.* ALMA *exits and* CHUYIS *goes to sit at a table, joining other patrons.
Music fades. A voice is heard over the loudspeaker.]*

VOICE: Good eeveening, laydees and gent-la-mens. Las Cariñosas welcomes
   jue to or fabulos Friday night cho. Bienvenidos sean ustedes, señoras y
   señores, a nuestro fabuloso chou de los viernes, aquí en Las Cariñosas,
   su club preferido. Antes de empezar, no olviden apuntarse para nuestro
   concurso mensual de salsa el próximo trece de octubre, en el que ten-
   dremos premios fabulosos y como siempre, se donarán las entradas
   para personas que viven con el VIH. Don't forget or fabulos salsa contest in October tear-teent. Donations will be made to peepl leevin whit
   HIV. Tonight we begin or cho whit a true star, a whoman we all love
   and feer, who does not have a singl rivl in all of San Francisco. Jue kno
   who I an talking aboat. Empezamos nuestro chou con una estrella con-
   sagrada, mujer que amamos y a la vez tememos y que no tiene rival
   alguna en toda la Bahía de San Francisco. Saben ustedes a quién me
   refiero. Se trata de la ingeniosa, la profesionalísima, la brutal, Alma!
   Recibámosla con un fuerte y caluroso aplauso.

*[Lights out momentarily. Two tables with memorabilia (a framed picture, a
stuffed animal, letters in envelopes, etc.) are placed at opposite sides of the stage.
The song "Mala" by Liliana Felipe rises followed immediately by bright lights.*
ALMA *enters grandiosely and walks confidently, beginning her performance of
an embittered, evil woman. As the song progresses, she destroys the memorabilia in a farce of rage, tenderly caressing an assortment of weapons, including a
knife and a toy gun which she pulls from under her dress. A master of improvi-
sation, her lip-synching is flawless, her attitude invitingly tough, and her
expressions unforgettably outrageous.* CHUYIS *watches her in delight and walks
up to give her a five-dollar bill. A couple of minutes later, the song ends with
roaring applause as patrons chant "¡Otra! ¡Otra!" demanding another song.*
ALMA *takes a bow. Music rises again, this time "Amor Eterno," by Rocío
Durcal. Suddenly, two gunshots are heard, followed by a shrieking voice holler-
ing "¡Auxilio! ¡Mataron a la Chuyis! ¡Mataron a la Chuyis! Chuyis is dead!"
Music stops abruptly.]*

[Lights fade to black.]

Scene Two

[In full darkness, the sound of seashells pierces the silence. Rattles shake, then drums pound with increased volume and speed, first allusive to the rhythm of an Indigenous ritual dance, blending swiftly into Asian, then African rhythms. A PRIESTESS *wearing a large African mask appears, dressed in a dark cloak and holding a lit candle on each palm. She walks ceremoniously towards the center, then downstage, raising the candle holders as a way of making an offering, placing them close to one another on the floor. The candlelight reveals the presence of the club patrons, frozen at their tables. The* PRIESTESS *dances around the stage, creating an imaginary circle which she closes with a gesture at the point where she placed the candles. Just then two* SPIRITS *enter. They're also dressed in dark cloaks, one wearing an Indigenous mask, the other an Asian mask. Taking slow steps, following the initial path of the* PRIESTESS, *they carry* EDGAR'S SPIRIT, *covered with a white mantle, high above their heads. While the* PRIESTESS *continues to dance, they place the body centerstage, in the middle of the imaginary circle, then exit at opposite sides. The* PRIESTESS *blesses the body in a trance, inspired by the drums in crescendo. As she passes her hand over* EDGAR'S SPIRIT, *she removes the mantle. The drums stop. Quickly, she exits, mimicking a flight for which she uses the mantle as wings.* EDGAR'S SPIRIT *is revealed in the form of a Black teenage girl in a traditional African dress. For a moment, she remains still, her hands crossed over her chest; then she begins to come to life, as if waking from a deep sleep. As she awakens, she utters the word "mama," like a child in distress. She repeats the word, a little louder, this time accentuated at the end: "Mamá. Mamá. ¡Mamá!" Embracing herself, she becomes restless and begins to weep, curled in fetal position, finally screaming the word "¡Mamita!" The* PRIESTESS *and the two* SPIRITS *re-enter and sit around* EDGAR'S SPIRIT, *extending their hands out to her.]*

[Blackout.]

Scene Three

*[*LUZ PALOMA'S *office, represented by a desk and chair with two additional chairs facing it.* ALMA, *as* ALFONSO, *sits next to* SALVADOR, *whom* ALFONSO *knows through his involvement with the fundraisers at Las Cariñosas. It's an unusually hot day.* ALFONSO *flips through a magazine while* SALVADOR *rummages through his backpack.* ALFONSO *sets the magazine down and looks in a heavy book positioned close to the edge of the desk.* EDGAR'S SPIRIT *enters, playing with a balero (a Mexican toy) nonchalantly.* SALVADOR *and* ALFONSO *freeze.]*

EDGAR'S SPIRIT: *[stopping, then noticing the audience]* If you're confused by what you see, it's probably because you've made the wrong assumption. It's natural. I used to assume a lot of things myself, until I came back and remembered. You can't help but remember after you've died many times. *[Pause. Playing with the balero.]* But let's not go into that heavy stuff. You're probably wondering who I am. Well, I'm Edgar's spirit. I know that sounds to you like I should look like a boy, but spirits come in many shapes and sizes, and colors too. Actually, we don't, it all depends on how others want to see you. Anyway, in this past life that I just went through I died from a gunshot. Right en el corazón. It hurt like a motherfucker…excuse me, like crazy. None of my other deaths hurt so bad. It made me think I don't wanna die again, at least not soon. But of course, none of us can control that. *[Pause.]* When I arrived here I started searching for my last dad. We died in pretty much the same way. But he's not around, he's gone back to live. I may have to wait until he dies again to talk to him. Mi papá y yo, we've got some unfinished business to take care of. *[Pause.]* So…back to the present…you know how we gotta always stay in the moment. Can you tell why these two are frozen? It's because time has stopped. It happens whenever a spirit interacts with a human. Humans don't really notice it, not a whole lot, 'cuz it usually happens in their dreams, and they almost never remember. Alfonso and Salvador, they remember me alright, but not as a spirit. Not yet.

[At this moment the book falls on the floor, making a loud hollow sound. EDGAR'S SPIRIT *exits on impulse. Instantly* ALFONSO *comes to life. He picks up the book, grabs the magazine again, and flips through it with a single move of the hand, fanning himself with it.]*

ALFONSO: I hate this heat. It hasn't been this hot in years. I hope the fog rolls in soon. ¿Qué te pasa? ¿Te comieron la lengua los ratones?

SALVADOR: Huh?

ALFONSO: You haven't said a word in the last ten minutes.

SALVADOR: *[in perfect standard English]* Sorry, I'm a little distracted.

ALFONSO: Yeah…para variar. So is she all that good?

SALVADOR: One of the best.

ALFONSO: I feel like I'm at the doctor's office. They take you into the examination room and then you have to wait for an hour because some emergency came up.

[SALVADOR *ignores him.* ALFONSO *takes out a small make-up case. He stares at his reflection, puts on a little powder, and puts the case away.*]

ALFONSO: Why should she wanna help Chuyis?

SALVADOR: I've already told you. She takes up battered women's cases.

ALFONSO: But Chuyis ain't really a woman.

SALVADOR: You know, you're being a little difficult.

ALFONSO: And you're making me nervous. What the hell are you looking for?

SALVADOR: A leaflet.

ALFONSO: You carry leaflets in your backpack? That is so weird.

SALVADOR: It's my backpack.

[LUZ PALOMA *enters abruptly, carrying a pile of files. She seems a bit frazzled yet has a flair of earthy elegance, partly from her striking beauty and partly from the pride with which she naturally carries herself. Like a mother, or perhaps an older sister, she commands instant respect and, at the same time, endearment.*]

LUZ PALOMA: [*speaking rapidly with a heavy South Bronx Puerto Rican accent, as she walks across the stage with matching speed*] Honey, would you puh-lease take care of mailing the copies of the depositions? I'd do it myself but I have to rush outta here, pick up Celia to take her to her appointment with the acupuncturist and stop by the pet shop to get food for the parakeets before going home to cook some dinner. ¡Ay! I'm already exhausted and it's not even lunch time. [*Turning to* ALFONSO *and* SALVADOR.] Hel-lo! I'm sorry I'm a little late, I got caught in one of those silly meetings that eat up all your precious time, planchando nalgas. How are you? I'm Luz Paloma. [*She extends her hand.*]

SALVADOR: How do you do, Ms. —

LUZ PALOMA: Castillo. But must you be so formal?

SALVADOR: I'm sorry. I'm Salvador Arteaga.

LUZ PALOMA: It's okay, honey, nothing to be sorry about. And you are...?

ALFONSO: Alfonso Mata, but you can call me Alma.

LUZ PALOMA: ¡Alma! ¡Ay, qué nombre tan precioso! Pues muy bien, Alma, nice to meet you, sweetheart. And Don Arteaga. You American?

SALVADOR: From Chile.

LUZ PALOMA: ¡Chileno! You sure you're not a relative of Salvador Allende? Both of you's got the same first name. Just kidding. *[She plops the files on the desk.]* Oh, my god, you won't believe this is the first time in years that my desk looks so clean. Thanks to my wonderful new secretary. She's New York hyper-productive, absolutely heaven-sent. Would you care for some café con leche or anything else with caffeine? I'd be happy to get you some tea, or just water if you don't have that kind of an addiction.

SALVADOR: I'm fine, thanks.

ALFONSO: No, gracias.

LUZ PALOMA: Cheverísimo. ¡Pues! I just had a cup of coffee as you can probably tell. So how can I be of help to you today?

SALVADOR: Well, my friend Concha Estela recommended that we speak with you.

LUZ PALOMA: Oh, how nice. How's homegirl doing? I've been so busy I haven't had a chance to catch up with her.

SALVADOR: She's doing fine. Anyway, we have a difficult case on our hands. A murder case.

LUZ PALOMA: A murder case!

SALVADOR: It involves a battered woman.

LUZ PALOMA: She was murdered?

SALVADOR: No, fortunately not.

LUZ PALOMA: Oh, that's good.

SALVADOR: But unfortunately—

LUZ PALOMA: She's the one being accused of murder.

ALFONSO: She ain't a Luz Paloma woman either. She got the equipment done and everything, pero no nació mujer.

LUZ PALOMA: Well, honey, I guess that makes her as much of a woman as anyone else. None of us chose the equipment, nor the label, nor the hassles that come with it, I might add. So she's being accused of murdering who?

ALFONSO: She didn't murder nobody. I know her like a sister. She's not that type of a girl.

LUZ PALOMA: Right. So, who was the victim?

SALVADOR: Not the guy she was with.

ALFONSO: His brother.

LUZ PALOMA: Was this a love triangle?

ALFONSO: No, he was just a kid! God!

SALVADOR: He was in his early teens, fifteen maybe.

ALFONSO: Fourteen.

LUZ PALOMA: Lord almighty. What happened?

ALFONSO: That's what we want you to help us figure out. But I know she didn't kill him on purpose. She had nothing against him.

LUZ PALOMA: Wait a minute. Did she or did she not kill him?

ALFONSO: She...shot the gun. But she wasn't trying to kill him.

LUZ PALOMA: Look, you got to relax a little, okay? I'm just trying to get some information here. What is your friend's name?

ALFONSO: María de Jesús Garza. Pero de cariño le decimos Chuyis, la Chuyis.

LUZ PALOMA: Did you know the victim?

ALFONSO: Not really. Se llamaba Edgar.

LUZ PALOMA: How did he die?

ALFONSO: I told you, from a gunshot.

LUZ PALOMA: Were there any drugs involved that you know of?

ALFONSO: No, Chuyis drinks sometimes, but she don't do drugs.

LUZ PALOMA: Mmmm...I have to tell you, this is a tough one. Do you know if she entered a plea?

ALFONSO: What?

LUZ PALOMA: Did she admit to killing the boy?

ALFONSO: We don't know. Anyway, we ain't got no money so you don't have to defend her.

SALVADOR: We can find money, Alfonso.

ALFONSO: How? She's probably gonna charge us shitloads. Todos los abogados son unos rateros.

SALVADOR: We'll find a way, the main thing is we can't waste any time.

LUZ PALOMA: *[looking at* ALFONSO *straight in the eyes]* Mira, honey, cógelo con take it easy. I know this is very hard for you, but if you give me a chance, I can at least figure out if I can help you or if someone else can. Do you trust me to do that much?

*[*ALFONSO *breaks down crying.]*

LUZ PALOMA: Bendito…

Scene Four

[Crossfade to CHUYIS' *prison cell, two days later. The heat has given way to San Francisco's traditional coolness.* CHUYIS *lies in a cot, huddled up against the wall. She wears a jail uniform. Curled into a ball, her hair completely disheveled, she mutters unintelligible sounds, having intermittent spasms.]*

CHUYIS: I didn't mean to kill him. He was just a kid. Ay, Dios mío, what am I gonna do? I'm so scared. They're gonna kill me.

[Crossfade to a cemetery. Loud church bells ring ominously. DOÑA IRENE, *on her knees next to Edgar's tomb, weeps inconsolably. She continually holds her rebozo—wrapped around her head and shoulders—up against her chest. Her son,* JUAN GALLO, *stands soldier-like to her left with a stern expression, dressed in black oversized clothing and dark glasses. His left arm is in a cast. The sun is beginning to set. A cold fog clouds the view of the ocean over the hills.]*

DOÑA IRENE: Hijito. Mi Edgar. ¿Por qué te fuiste? ¿Por qué me dejaste? ¡Ay, Dios mío, me voy a morir de dolor! ¡Ay, Jesús bendito! ¿Por qué te lo llevaste de mi lado? ¿Por qué de esa manera Diosito? ¿Por qué si era tan joven? ¡Ay, qué dolor tan grande! Primero Pedro y ahora Edgar. ¿Por qué no mejor me llevaste a mí que estoy vieja y maltrecha? ¿Por qué a él si apenas era un niño? ¡Ay, virgen santísima! Yo tuve la culpa. Si lo hubiera cuidado más de cerca esto no hubiera pasado. ¿Por qué lo dejé crecer tan solo? ¿Por qué no me fijé más en él?

JUAN GALLO: It wasn't your fault, mom.

DOÑA IRENE: ¡Perdóname señor! ¡Perdóname Edgar!

[A male voice is heard in the distance, chanting eerily "¡Flores! ¡Flores para los muertos!" The chant fades, followed by loud church bells. EDGAR'S SPIRIT *enters (if possible from within the audience), carrying a bundle of red carnations. Instantly, the scene freezes. She walks slowly towards* DOÑA IRENE, *and around* JUAN GALLO *without looking at him. She stops a few feet away from her.]*

EDGAR'S SPIRIT: Mami…Mamita…Le traje claveles, sus flores predilectas. *[She carefully places the flowers on the tomb in front of* DOÑA IRENE *without touching her.]* They smell so beautiful. *[Kneels down at her side, speaking tenderly.]* Mami, I had to return to look for him. The heaviness was weighing on me. All those years drinking, despising himself. And the violence. It was a heaviness of centuries, across the oceans. I needed to look for him so I could release it. *[Pause.]* Mami, I understand now. We would have stayed home, but there was no sacred place left anywhere. We were bound to leave sooner or later. It's been a very long journey. I was tired!

*[*EDGAR'S SPIRIT *caresses the flowers, stands up, and exits slowly. The scene unfreezes.* DOÑA IRENE *looks up. She notices the flowers and crosses herself.* JUAN GALLO *cannot see what she sees.]*

Scene Five

[Lights on at the prison's visiting room. ALFONSO, *waiting anxiously, sits at a desk divided by glass in the middle. There is a telephone on each side of the glass. After a few moments,* CHUYIS *enters, looking haggard. She walks very slowly towards the desk, like a child trying to avoid being punished. Upon reaching the desk, she picks up the receiver.* ALFONSO *is aware that they can only speak for a few minutes.]*

ALFONSO: Hey girl. *[Pause.]* I'm getting you out, I promise.

CHUYIS: They were gonna beat me—

ALFONSO: I know.

CHUYIS: I didn't mean to kill Edgar. I didn't even mean to shoot him.

ALFONSO: I know.

CHUYIS: Is Juan okay?

ALFONSO: I heard he was out of the hospital. ¡Desgraciado!

CHUYIS: What's gonna happen to me?

ALFONSO: You just wait. I went to speak with Salvador, from the AIDS agency. We saw a lawyer. Don't worry. It'll all work out. Okay? *[Pause.]* All the girls are on your side. They're praying for you. That kid was a gangbanger.

CHUYIS: Please, Alma, I don't wanna be nobody's hero.

ALFONSO: No te mortifiques, amor. It'll take some time. Pero vas a ver que todo sale bien, okay? Remember our walks to the park late at night? Just think about that. How beautiful the skyline was, and we thought we each were a light shining all the way across the bay. We'll find our blue prince and have our double wedding, just like we always planned it.

CHUYIS: You still can find your prince.

ALFONSO: Look, just try not to be too pessimistic. You have to have faith. *[Pause.]* You look so thin. ¿Te están dando de comer?

A LOUD VOICE: Time's up!

CHUYIS: Me tengo que ir. *[She hangs up.]*

ALFONSO: Okay. I'll be back. Tomorrow. I love you!

[Lights out.]

Scene Six

*[*CELIA *and* LUZ PALOMA *are in their living room, immersed in their work.* CELIA *has scattered papers all over; she is entering grades in a grade book.* LUZ PALOMA, *in her bathrobe and slippers, browses through two huge law books and some files. The television is on.]*

LUZ PALOMA: *[unable to find what she is looking for, speaking rapidly]* There they go again. How many times do we have to watch this woman be discredited and maligned? *[Stands up, grabbing a cup from the coffee table, with the seeming intention to refill it but without moving, just staring at the TV.]* It ain't like he's not gonna get away with it. What are they gonna do? Deny him the post, as conservative as he is? He's perfect for it. Así se pueden llenar el hocico en decir que no son racistas. *[Pause.]* And that's just how it is. Now that they've got everything, they can proclaim to the hills how they want to be our representatives and friends. *[She walks away, dragging her feet, then stops and stares at the TV again. She walks back to watch more closely.]* Well, I suppose if a few sisters can figure his solidarity with the black race is as big as the size of his penis, that'll be something good out of this case. He can sit around and compare dick size with the other boys, white or colored for all I care, and they can all leave pubic hairs on their Coke cans to compare as well. *[CELIA stares at her, clearly annoyed; LUZ PALOMA does not notice.]* What the hell, we've got the word betrayal inscribed on our foreheads. But it was them who taught us that shit in the first place. How many generations hearing we were different and less than. So we internalized it really well, until we didn't care about our own any longer. *[Beat. Talking to the television.]* If we sisters weren't so isolated we wouldn't put up with this mockery of our issues. 'Cuz when have we been able to define things for ourselves, especially around sexuality? Zora was right. We've been nothing but the white men's mules.

CELIA: Are you gonna drink coffee at this hour?

LUZ PALOMA: I always do.

CELIA: And then you don't sleep enough and you end up feeling tired.

LUZ PALOMA: I'd sleep just as much if I didn't drink coffee. I'm not tired because of the coffee, the coffee helps me feel less tired. I'm tired because life is tiring. Every day is a fucking aggravation.

CELIA: Want a massage?

LUZ PALOMA: ¡Ay, sí, tengo la espalda hecha trizas! Parece como que me hubieran dado un cantazo.

[CELIA starts giving her a back rub.]

LUZ PALOMA: ¡Ay, qué alivio!

CELIA: You've been working really hard.

LUZ PALOMA: I'm trying to figure out what to do about the case of the transsexual.

CELIA: You think you'll take it?

LUZ PALOMA: I don't know. It's a bitch of a case. And I already know they don't have money.

CELIA: Maybe the firm will back you up.

LUZ PALOMA: Maybe. Let's not talk about that now. Oh, that feels nice. *[Pause.]* I'm really determined to start working less. I want to make more time for other things. I need to write more. I need to make more time for you and for our baby.

[CELIA stops rubbing her back.]

LUZ PALOMA: Well, so much for my back rub.

[She stands up and grabs her coffee mug.]

CELIA: Where are you going?

LUZ PALOMA: To the kitchen to get my coffee, where does it look like I'm going?

CELIA: I wasn't finished.

LUZ PALOMA: Yes, you were.

CELIA: Why are you mad?

LUZ PALOMA: Because. Why are we having this conversation again? I've told you I want a baby. I'm thirty-six years old, and I ain't gonna wait much longer.

CELIA: I just think you've worked too hard your whole life taking care of other people.

LUZ PALOMA: So what? I want to extend my family with a child of my own. And I want you to be a part of that family. I need you to support my choice to have a baby, Celia.

CELIA: We have a family. Isn't this a family?

LUZ PALOMA: What are you so afraid of? Why don't you just come out with it? I mean, you think our lives are always gonna stay the same?

CELIA: I don't want to be a parent.

LUZ PALOMA: Why not?

CELIA: Because I don't want to devote that kind of energy to raising a child.

LUZ PALOMA: I don't think you're being honest.

CELIA: I am too being honest. There are many things I still want to do.

LUZ PALOMA: So you're gonna sit here and tell me that if I were to get really sick with lung cancer or some shit tomorrow, you wouldn't stay close with me to at least help me take care of myself because you would still have many things you want to do?

CELIA: What does that have to do with you having a baby?

LUZ PALOMA: Well, aside from the fact that it would be something growing inside me, it's an example of a change in our lives that would require us to reaffirm our commitment to one another and deal with the situation. Together.

CELIA: So you're saying I don't want to commit to you.

LUZ PALOMA: I think you're afraid to.

CELIA: Haven't I committed to you? Don't I live with you? Don't I love you?

LUZ PALOMA: Yes.

CELIA: Then why are you saying that?

LUZ PALOMA: Well, if not that, ¡coño! What the hell are you afraid of?

CELIA: I told you already!

LUZ PALOMA: Fine. Forget the coffee. I'm going to bed.

[She gathers her books and files. CELIA stares away, paralyzed. LUZ PALOMA begins to walk away and almost exits.]

CELIA: All right, it wouldn't be my child!

[LUZ PALOMA stops dead in her tracks, then slowly turns around.]

CELIA: I'm sorry.

LUZ PALOMA: [walks up to her] What do you mean it wouldn't be your child? Of course it would be your child. It would be our child. Do you think I would wanna raise a child with any old person? If I did, I might as well raise it on my own.

CELIA: I just keep thinking, I'm afraid I couldn't love her enough. I'm afraid every time I looked at her I would know she didn't look like me. You know? Nothing of hers would have come from me.

[Silence.]

LUZ PALOMA: *[softly]* Well, that would be true, if by that you mean geneti-cally. But that doesn't mean you wouldn't be a good mother. I'd rather have a child with you, knowing that you love her, that you love us, instead of with someone who happened to share her genes but didn't love her. *[Pause.]* I mean, I think I would be a good mother. But there really are no guarantees that my own child would love me. She might relate better to you.

[Pause.]

CELIA: I'm afraid I might lose you and the child one day.

LUZ PALOMA: Well, that could also happen to me. But, I don't think it helps to think that. I mean, I don't think that should be the reason not to have a baby.

CELIA: I'm sorry.

LUZ PALOMA: Anyway, it's just…a dream. It may or may not be meant to happen for us.

[She looks at CELIA, who lowers her eyes. Affected, she walks away. Lights out.]

Scene Seven

[Crossfade to SALVADOR's apartment. He and ALFONSO sit next to each other on a sofa. They are looking at a picture album, sipping drinks. Music by Mercedez Sosa plays in the background.]

ALFONSO: ¿Y él? ¿También lo mataron?

SALVADOR: Yup.

ALFONSO: ¿Quién era?

SALVADOR: My brother's lover.

ALFONSO: No lo puedo creer. You can tell they really loved each other.

SALVADOR: They set an example for me of what true love is and should be. Love for each other, for their cause, for the people. Love of freedom.

ALFONSO: How did you cope with everything?

SALVADOR: At first, I didn't. I was traveling, studying at fancy American schools. I guess I might have been an elitist homosexual of sorts. But deep inside I was hurting. My parents always gave priority to their busi-nesses and their money, so my brother was the one who really took care of me and loved me as a child. When I found out that he had disappeared, I felt like something inside me had been ripped out, as if I'd lost a limb. *[Pause.]* My parents didn't want to have anything to do with him. They were ashamed of him. They couldn't see themselves having a queer son who was also fighting the dictatorship. They could have helped find him before it was too late. I'll never forgive them for that.

ALFONSO: I know how you feel. My parents were really mean to me. That's why I ran away. The last time my dad hit me, he almost killed me, left me all bloodied, chorreando en sangre. It was the day he found me putting make-up on. I don't know why it surprised him so much. I guess it shocked him to confirm what he had suspected all along, that I was a faggot.

SALVADOR: Don't say that about yourself.

ALFONSO: It's true, I've always been a sissy! That's why nobody in my family could tolerate me. They wanted me to be a "real" man. Well, except for my baby sister. She was the only one I got along with. But she was so helpless. I think my dad was messing with her. He was such a pig. Anyway, after that beating, I was like, yo me largo. Tenía quince años. I made it all the way from Mexico City to San Francisco selling my body. *[Pause.]* God knows I've seen some ugly things. *[He closes the picture album and comes up behind* SALVADOR.*]* Sírveme otra copa, ¿si?

SALVADOR: ¿Lo mismo?

ALFONSO: Sí, mi niño. Un ruso blanco. Es mi bebida favorita. Besides it ain't good to mix, luego termina una mareada o guacaleándose. This music is so sad.

SALVADOR: *[goes to prepare the drink]* Es música de protesta.

ALFONSO: You and your politics.

SALVADOR: You think I'm wasting my time fighting for a better world?

ALFONSO: No, I just think you're too serious. I don't trust people who are always serious. My father was always serious. He wanted to give the impression that he was a respectable man, but deep inside he was a mean motherfucker. *[Beat.]* Is that what motivates you too? Rage?

SALVADOR: *[gives* ALFONSO *the drink]* Anger is not always a bad thing.

ALFONSO: Personally I think a little glamour and laughter can't hurt. I think that changes more people in the long run.

SALVADOR: It can make people falsely conscious.

ALFONSO: Oh, puh-lease! It helps people deal with life. Hey, you got some salsa or something, algo más movidito?

SALVADOR: Sure.

[He goes to look for a CD and hands it to ALFONSO.*]*

ALFONSO: All right, Hector Lavoe! *[Goes to play the CD.]* Let's add some life to this party!

[Music starts. ALFONSO *begins to dance.* SALVADOR *watches him.]*

ALFONSO: There you go! That's a pretty smile.

[He approaches SALVADOR. SALVADOR *becomes instantly uptight. Oblivious to this,* ALFONSO *dances around him. The phone rings.* SALVADOR *goes to answer.* ALFONSO *lowers the volume on the CD player.]*

SALVADOR: Hello? How are you? It's good to hear your voice. *[To* ALFONSO.*]* Es Luz Paloma. *[To* LUZ PALOMA.*]* Hold on a sec, he's right here.

ALFONSO: ¿Bueno? Bien, ¿y tú? Yes? Oh my god, you're gonna do it!? *[To* SALVADOR.*]* She's gonna defend Chuyis! *[Responding to* LUZ PALOMA.*]* What? Okay…oh, my god, thank you so much. Yes, I'll be there. Thank you. *[He hangs up and starts jumping up and down.]* She's gonna defend Chuyis! I'm so excited!

SALVADOR: I told you she would.

ALFONSO: Thank you!

SALVADOR: You're welcome.

ALFONSO: *[hugs* SALVADOR *impulsively]* You were so sweet to take me to see her.

*[*SALVADOR *tenses up.* ALFONSO *steps back. They stand looking at each other silently.]*

ALFONSO: I'll never be grateful enough to you.

[*They remain immobile. Then, unexpectedly,* ALFONSO *steps forward and kisses him softly on the lips.* SALVADOR *seems startled.* ALFONSO *kisses him again, first softly, then more aggressively.* SALVADOR *is suddenly taken over by desire. As he responds, the kiss becomes passionate. The salsa rises as the lights gradually fade to black.*]

ACT II

Scene One

[*A single light rises, dimly illuminating one of the dressing rooms at Las Cariñosas.* ALMA *sits in front of an empty mirror frame, slowly taking off her make-up after a performance. She wears lingerie and high heels. Her look is somber. As she stares at herself,* EDGAR'S SPIRIT *runs in, holding an African fabric stretched from arm to arm, covering her body and face.* ALMA *freezes.* EDGAR'S SPIRIT *runs from one side of the stage to the other and back, then stops behind the mirror frame, facing* ALMA. *She sits down and slowly pulls down the fabric, revealing a bitter expression. She wraps her body in the fabric, her eyes fixed on* ALMA'*s. She hisses at her.*]

EDGAR'S SPIRIT: *I-could-not-care-less-about-your-fucking-friend!* She shot me! So what if my brother was an asshole. I had my whole life ahead of me. I had dreams. I was going to make it. I was going to be rich, and buy my mother a big house, and my father a new tombstone. I was going to get married and have children, and I was going to love them! Love them like I wanted to be loved. Play with them and talk to them and explain to them the difference between right and wrong, and hold them in my arms when they felt scared, and never, never hurt them! And I was never going to hit my wife. And I was never going to tell my children that I hated them and I wished they hadn't been born. Never burn their skin with matches, and cut their legs and buttocks with wires, and force them to drink hydrogen peroxide, and never, ever imagine they were horrible monsters because I was too drunk to tell the difference! She killed me. I was just defending my brother. I'm supposed to understand that it happened for a reason? How was I supposed to know any better? I only lived to be fourteen! You tell me now, you tell me why your friend pulled the trigger. You tell me.

[*She stands up, slowly walking away backwards, and exits.* ALMA *unfreezes.*]

ALMA: ¿Por qué lo hiciste, Chuyis?

Scene Two

[Crossfade to LUZ PALOMA *and* CELIA*'s living room.* LUZ PALOMA *enters, dressed in a suit and carrying a briefcase. She sets the briefcase on the coffee table, opens it and takes out a tape player. She looks at it, confronted by its realness. She takes out a cigarette and presses the play button on the recorder.* CHUYIS' *voice is heard.* LUZ PALOMA *listens.]*

CHUYIS' VOICE: *[breathing deeply]* Why should I trust you?

LUZ PALOMA'S VOICE: Do you not want to trust me?

CHUYIS' VOICE: It's not very pretty, what I have to say.

*[*CELIA *walks in and sits quietly next to* LUZ PALOMA.*]*

LUZ PALOMA'S VOICE: I'm not expecting you to cheer me up, or make my life colorful. I'm not here to profit at your expense. I have reason to believe you may have been wronged.

CHUYIS' VOICE: I killed a boy.

LUZ PALOMA'S VOICE: You seem like a good person. You could be my baby sister. Please tell me what happened. I will not use what you say against you.

CHUYIS' VOICE: He was…he had been hitting me a lot, putting me down a lot. Calling me a cunt, una puta, threatening to kill me. *[Pause.]* There were times when he said he loved me, but…I…I was scared. I bought a gun. I told him that if he laid a hand on me again, I would kill him, lo mataba. I had the gun in my purse that night. I was with Alma. We were dancing inside the club and then the show started. I watched for a little while. Luego de un rato, no sé, I felt I needed to go outside, get some air.

[Crossfade to the alleyway outside Las Cariñosas, the night of Edgar's death. CHUYIS *comes out the bar doors and walks downstage. She takes a deep breath and looks up, admiring the full moon shining brightly. She unzips her purse, takes out a pack of cigarettes, and puts one in her mouth, searching for a lighter.* JUAN GALLO *and* EDGAR *enter.* JUAN GALLO *has a mean look on his face, which* EDGAR *more or less imitates.* EDGAR *is carrying a baseball bat.* CHUYIS *spots them. Her body jerks as if suddenly possessed. The jerk makes her cigarette fall out of her lips.]*

CHUYIS: Mira, mira, mira, look who's here. El mismísimo Juan Gallo.

[EDGAR and JUAN GALLO *stop dead in their tracks.]*

CHUYIS: What's the matter, sugah? You've finally seen the error of your ways?

JUAN GALLO: How the fuck you know my name, fucking faggot!

CHUYIS: Oh, I see, you don't want your little brother to know we've been involved.

JUAN GALLO: I'ma beat the shit out of you, fucking punk-ass faggot. Fucking queer!

EDGAR: What's she talking 'bout, man?

JUAN GALLO: Shut up! *[To* CHUYIS.*]* I'ma send this faggot to fucking hell, where it belongs. Smart-ass motherfucking punk! *[He approaches* CHUYIS *menacingly.]* You like to take it up the ass? You weird-ass sissy! I'ma stick a fucking bat up your butthole and hump you so hard you'll bleed to death.

*[*CHUYIS *staggers back.* EDGAR *stands still.]*

CHUYIS: Stay away from me!

JUAN GALLO: Fucking cunt! Fucking puta! Who the fuck do you think you are talking to me that way?

CHUYIS: ¡Déjame en paz, Juan!

JUAN GALLO: Shut the fuck up!

CHUYIS: *[gripping her purse]* If you get any closer I'll kill you!

JUAN GALLO: You're the one who's gonna die, fucking freak!

*[*CHUYIS *pulls out a gun from her purse, trembling.]*

CHUYIS: Get back! I'm telling you to get back!

JUAN GALLO: You freak! Give me that goddamn gun!

[He charges after CHUYIS. *She falls backwards and shoots, screaming.* JUAN GALLO *jerks violently and wails in pain, wounded on the left shoulder. He covers the wound and falls to the ground, squirming. He is bleeding profusely.* EDGAR *looks at his brother. He shouts his name, then looks at* CHUYIS, *who stares at him, still holding the gun in her hand. Instantly,* EDGAR *jumps, swinging his bat, determined to kill* CHUYIS. CHUYIS *shoots a second time,*

hitting EDGAR *in the heart.* EDGAR *falls to the ground, dead.* CHUYIS *drops the gun. A shrieking voice is heard screaming, "¡Auxilio, auxilio! ¡Mataron a la Chuyis! ¡Mataron a la Chuyis!"]*

[Crossfade to LUZ PALOMA *and* CELIA. *They look at each other and embrace.]*

Scene Three

[At LUZ PALOMA'*s office,* SALVADOR *and* ALFONSO *browse through thick law books. There is an awkwardness between them.* LUZ PALOMA *enters. She walks around the desk, placing her briefcase down across from* ALFONSO, *staring at him.]*

ALFONSO: Why you looking at me like that?

LUZ PALOMA: Did you arrange the interview with the news network?

ALFONSO: What news network?

LUZ PALOMA: For the six o'clock news.

ALFONSO: Oh, that one. Yes.

LUZ PALOMA: What is the matter with you? You know how most people feel about drag queens and transsexuals. I don't care if we live in San Francisco. This is not a drag show.

ALFONSO: Why are you coming at me like that?

LUZ PALOMA: I'm trying to put together an almost impossible case where the odds are against us. I don't need you to be on the news dressed like it's a show at Las Cariñosas! That is not how you're gonna get support. As a matter of fact, you're not gonna get any support if you keep doing that.

ALFONSO: You want me to go back in the closet.

LUZ PALOMA: I am not asking you to go back in the closet. I'm telling you that if you really want to get some support for your friend you're gonna have to play the game based on the rules of the system. This case is getting a lot of attention nationwide, and in case you haven't noticed—perhaps because you have been too busy trying to look pretty in front of the cameras—neither your friend, nor you, nor anybody at Las Cariñosas is being portrayed in a good light.

ALFONSO: That's not my fault.

LUZ PALOMA: No one's saying it's your fault. But the networks are discrediting our case because of it.

ALFONSO: You're telling me I shouldn't be myself.

LUZ PALOMA: Right now you are dressed as a man, and you are still yourself. So if you can be yourself dressed as a man right now in my office, why can't you also be yourself dressed as a man in front of the cameras, if you feel so strongly that you have to be in front of the cameras?

ALFONSO: This is unbelievable.

LUZ PALOMA: Look, Alfonso. I'm gonna be real up front with you. If you wanna live in your fantasy world, you go ahead and do that. But I'm gonna have to ask you to please stand aside and not get involved with this case. Because this is about reality. It ain't glamorous. It ain't pretty. It ain't about movie stars and performances and applause and recognition. It is about serious work that I have to do in a legal system which tends not to give a shit about people like you. Now I don't think I have to stand here and remind you of how people who choose the kind of life that you've chosen can get treated, do I?

ALFONSO: No. Of course not. I know, 'cuz I've experienced it in the flesh, because people like you felt that it would be better to keep us invisible so you could pursue your careers and make a hundred fifty thousand dollars a year at our expense. Lucky for you that you don't feel uncomfortable as a woman acting and dressing the way *you* think women should act and dress.

LUZ PALOMA: I am a woman. And as a woman, I'm going to tell you something that perhaps you, who would like to be a woman, should learn, which is that as a woman—I don't care if you're straight or queer, butch, fem, whatever—sometimes you get more by staying quote-unquote in your place. And if you're smart, you know just when to do that, because when you don't, it may very well mean the end of your life or your children's lives. Disgusting? No doubt. But that's the way it is. Do you understand?

[ALFONSO *stares at her and storms out.* SALVADOR *follows him. Lights down on* LUZ PALOMA.]

SALVADOR: Hey, wait up.

[ALFONSO *stops and starts pacing.*]

ALFONSO: Fucking lawyer. Thinks she's so smart. Why would anybody wanna be reading those books all the time anyway? Nobody can under-stand half the words in them. *[He looks at* SALVADOR.*]* Y tú como siempre, ido. Tal parece que le está uno hablando a la pared. *[Beat.]* Hey, tell me something. Why is it that you only care about the shit you're doing? No, not even what you're doing, just what's inside your head, like the world revolves around your thoughts. You make it look like you pay attention to other people, but you really don't. I guess it must be that you grew up alone, away from your family. You didn't have to deal with people around you and their feelings. So sad.

SALVADOR: Hey, what's this all about?

ALFONSO: Exactly which part? Tell me so I know if you were listening to me or not.

SALVADOR: What the hell are you so mad at *me* for?

ALFONSO: 'Cuz I'm getting tired of me always trying to relate with you and you being lost in la la land.

SALVADOR: What do you mean? I talk with you all the time.

ALFONSO: No, you talk to your fucking self.

SALVADOR: That's not true.

ALFONSO: Oh yes it is, always talking those big-ass words and complicated sentences. The dictatorship of the proletariat, the social relations of production, the transhistorical dialectical wounds. You're just like that lawyer. You think you're so smart 'cuz you went to college.

SALVADOR: You're just as smart. You can understand everything we say.

ALFONSO: I understand everything you say is *trite*, that's what I understand.

SALVADOR: It is not trite. It's what I believe in.

ALFONSO: You're such a white boy.

SALVADOR: A white boy?!

ALFONSO: Always in your head—

SALVADOR: I am not a white boy!

ALFONSO: —controlling your emotions.

SALVADOR: That's not what you say when we're in bed.

ALFONSO: Oh, god, don't even go there! 'Cuz you know something? That's exactly the point. I'm the one who does all the work, talking sweetly to you, making up fantasies, seduciéndote. All you do is sit there till I've gotten you so hot and bothered you can't wait to stick it inside me, just like every other man I've been with.

SALVADOR: Please don't vulgarize our lovemaking.

ALFONSO: Lovemaking! Ha! See, this is just what I mean. I'm telling you that I don't feel like you listen to me. ¡No-me-escuchas!

SALVADOR: Okay Alfonso, if that's how you feel about me, then there's nothing I can do about it. So let's just drop this whole thing and forget about it.

ALFONSO: You're really scared to deal with your feelings, aren't you?

SALVADOR: No, I am not. I acknowledge my feelings. But I'm not gonna get caught in them and get all hysterical like you. Things need to get done. And if I wasn't in my head all the time, as you say I am, we wouldn't be trying to figure out how to help Chuyis get out of jail.

ALFONSO: And how is that? You're gonna organize a union at a factory and then convince the union of defending a Chicana transsexual, a member of the lumpen proletariat, like you call us?

SALVADOR: That's enough. I don't have to be the recipient of your attacks.

ALFONSO: You've been so caught up in your ideas about the working class, you've forgotten about real working people. But it's cool, it's alright. Since you're so good with your political strategies, I'll tell you what. You make one on your own, okay? 'Cuz I got my own way for dealing with this. And you know what it is? First, I'm gonna go home and I'm gonna pour myself a nice drink, 'cuz I get more from a drink than I get from you most of the time. And then I'm gonna go to the prison to see Chuyis and tell her how much I care for her. And I'm gonna do that every day, 'cuz I think that's what she really needs right now. So have a nice day, and good luck with your revolution.

[He starts to walk away.]

SALVADOR: You know, for someone who distrusts people who act out of anger you're pretty damn angry yourself.

ALFONSO: So what!

SALVADOR: So maybe you should lighten up a bit. What are you so angry about? Because it isn't about me, or Luz Paloma.

ALFONSO: Well, since you know everything, why don't you tell me.

SALVADOR: I think you're angry because of what the system's done to you.

ALFONSO: ¿Ah si, sabelotodo?

SALVADOR: You're only gonna be able to voice your anger in a productive way if you organize with other people and fight the system, Alfonso.

ALFONSO: Fight the system…what do you think I've been doing my whole life?

SALVADOR: No, you haven't, you've been fighting individuals. You pick fights on individuals. Your life is wrapped up in yourself as an individual.

ALFONSO: I am an individual!

SALVADOR: You compete against people, instead of organizing *with* them. Don't you see unless we work together to change society we're doomed?

ALFONSO: What the hell are you, a goddamn Christian savior?

SALVADOR: There you go again, directing your anger at me.

ALFONSO: Look, motherfucker, you know what? I'm getting really bored with this conversation. Go do some more mental masturbation by yourself.

[He exits.]

Scene Four

[LUZ PALOMA stands in a courtroom, addressing ALEXIS, a potential juror in CHUYIS' case. ALEXIS is a well-educated transsexual. She is self-contained and expresses herself with studied social graces. As the scene progresses, a light slowly illuminates CHUYIS in the background, tossing and turning in her jail cell cot.]

LUZ PALOMA: Ms. Alexis.

ALEXIS: *[in perfect standard English]* Yes.

LUZ PALOMA: Ms. Alexis, let's clear the waters right away. You've mentioned that you belong to a…an organization of transgendered people. Do you personally consider yourself to be a transsexual or transvestite?

ALEXIS: I see myself as a transgendered woman.

LUZ PALOMA: Could you please explain what you mean by that?

ALEXIS: It means I've undergone a sex-change operation. I used to be a biological male, and now I am a female. I see myself and live my life as a woman.

LUZ PALOMA: Ms. Alexis, the case for which you would be serving as a juror involves a transsexual—let me just say that I'm using that word not knowing the exact term my client would use to describe herself. In any case, my client, just like you, is someone who had a sex-change operation.

ALEXIS: Okay.

LUZ PALOMA: Are you at all familiar with this case, from watching the news, perhaps?

ALEXIS: I'm not sure.

LUZ PALOMA: My client is being accused of murdering a minor. It's been in the news.

ALEXIS: I am familiar with what I've seen on television.

LUZ PALOMA: Ms. Alexis, is your organization aware of this case?

ALEXIS: Some of us have heard about it. But I don't think everyone knows about it.

LUZ PALOMA: Has your organization taken an official or unofficial stand on this case?

ALEXIS: No, to be honest with you it's not something that we've discussed. We've been busy dealing with other issues.

LUZ PALOMA: Do you see it being discussed in the future?

ALEXIS: I have no idea.

LUZ PALOMA: Okay.

ALEXIS: I mean, we advocate for the right of all individuals to express their gender identity free of discrimination. So the murder cases that we have discussed in the past have been cases where the victim was a transgender person. This is a totally different situation. I doubt the organization would take a stand on this case without looking at the facts first.

LUZ PALOMA: So what you're saying, if I'm hearing you correctly, is that as an organization, you wouldn't automatically stand in defense of my client just because my client is a transsexual.

ALEXIS: Yes, that's right. If your client committed the murder, then she is guilty of murder. I mean, it doesn't matter what her gender identity is. See what I'm saying? Uh…Let me be very clear to you, if I may.

LUZ PALOMA: Go ahead.

ALEXIS: It might seem odd to some people, but I personally believe in the U.S. Constitution. And I believe in obeying the law. I personally would not defend a murderer no matter what.

LUZ PALOMA: From what you have heard about this case, do you believe that my client committed the murder of which she is being accused?

ALEXIS: From the limited information I have, I couldn't possibly conclude that. As I understand it, in our country a person is innocent until proven guilty. I would have to look at the evidence to assess if your client committed the murder.

LUZ PALOMA: Are you saying, then, that you think my client is innocent, based on what you have heard?

ALEXIS: No, I couldn't conclude that either. I am saying that, as I understand it, the law says that a person is innocent until proven guilty. If the evidence in this case showed that your client committed the murder, then I would conclude that she is guilty. But if the evidence showed she didn't commit the murder, then I would conclude that she is innocent and she should be free.

LUZ PALOMA: I see you are a firm believer of the law.

ALEXIS: Yes, I am.

LUZ PALOMA: Is it fair, then, to state that you have no position in this case and you would be open to hearing the evidence without bias?

ALEXIS: Yes, I am absolutely certain of that.

LUZ PALOMA: Ms. Alexis, do you feel a personal conviction to be a juror in this case because it involves a transgendered woman like yourself?

ALEXIS: No, not particularly. My only conviction with regard to this case is to serve my country. If I'm selected to be a member of the jury, that's what I intend to do, as I would with any other case. The fact that I am a transgendered woman and the case also involves someone like myself is a coincidence, but I don't see it as any more of a coincidence than, say, a male being considered to serve as a juror in a case where the defendant is also a male.

LUZ PALOMA: Ms. Alexis, honestly, has it always been your conviction to defend your country? Or has there ever been a time when you felt you'd rather not serve your country, perhaps because you might have felt let down by its treatment of homosexuals, of transgender people?

ALEXIS: Honestly, I see being a transgendered person as a right granted to me by the first amendment of the U.S. Constitution. If I didn't believe in the Constitution, I'd have to go against who I am.

LUZ PALOMA: So you've never felt hurt by how transgender people are treated in this country?

ALEXIS: Sure I have. But we are not treated with respect anywhere. In fact, we are treated worse in most other countries. I really feel that here in the U.S. we are mistreated because the Constitution is not being interpreted correctly. And I believe one day it will be.

LUZ PALOMA: Have you ever participated in any demonstration against the government or in any protest or action that criticizes its policies?

ALEXIS: No.

LUZ PALOMA: Are you sure?

ALEXIS: I really haven't. Really. I'm a peaceful kind of a person. I believe in working to achieve things, not in fighting. I write letters. I try to talk to people. I try to explain, to have a friendly dialogue, to persuade.

LUZ PALOMA: So you don't feel angry about how you're treated in society.

ALEXIS: Sometimes I do. But I don't really stay angry. I mean, I'm very lucky when it comes down to it. I have a lot of things to be thankful for. I have loving parents who support me, a loving family. It just happened that way. My parents are very kind, very nice and peaceful people. It was a little hard for them at first, but they accept me. They've given me everything I've ever asked them for.

LUZ PALOMA: What do your parents do for a living, Ms. Alexis, if you don't mind my asking?

ALEXIS: My father is a professor and my mother is a scientist.

LUZ PALOMA: So you would say your family is well to do?

ALEXIS: Yes, you could say that. I grew up in the Berkeley Hills. My family is well off.

LUZ PALOMA: Okay. I appreciate and thank you for your honesty, and I am happy that you have found so much support in your life to be who you want to be. Now, Ms. Alexis, would you stand for your decision in this case even if it went against the opinion of your peers?

ALEXIS: Sure. It wouldn't be the first time. I believe in speaking the truth. It's because I'm true to myself that I am who I am.

LUZ PALOMA: One last question, Ms. Alexis. Would you be able to remove yourself from participation in your organization while the case lasts?

ALEXIS: If I'm chosen as a juror and that's what I'm instructed to do, then that's what I'll do.

LUZ PALOMA: Thank you, Ms. Alexis. Mr. Gonzalez?

MR. GONZALEZ: We have no further questions. We are satisfied with this juror, Your Honor.

LUZ PALOMA: And I, too, am satisfied with this juror. Thank you again, Ms. Alexis.

[Crossfade. Lights up entirely on CHUYIS' *cell.* CHUYIS *continues to toss and turn, her breaths becoming heavier and increasing in speed. She mumbles words mixed with gurgled sounds, pushing against the mattress with her hands.]*

CHUYIS: No…dad…please…get off me…mom get him off me…get it out of me…get it out of me…it hurts…it hurts!

[Sudden crossfade to CELIA *and* LUZ PALOMA's *apartment. Home alone,* CELIA *kneels in front of an altar of seashells, pebbles, and palm seeds which she has placed on the floor over a fisher's net. As she prays, barely moving her lips, she lights a lantern and holds it up with both hands, making big circles with her arms.]*

[Sudden crossfade to JUAN GALLO *in a dream. Illuminated by a dim light, he walks slowly towards the center of the stage, his arms extended in front of him,*

clearing the space as if walking through tall, thick bushes in a battlefield. He scouts the stage from side to side.]

JUAN GALLO: Papá, papá. Where are you, man? Man, don't be playing games with me, man, where are you? *[Pause. He stands still at the center.]* I…I need your help with something. I got something to tell you. Uh…you might not like hearing this, but…I keep having these feelings, like, like sometimes…*[Pause.]* I think….I think I like men…and shit, you know what'm sayin'? *[Pause.]* I know I shouldn't be having these feelings, 'cuz it's fucked up. I mean, I don't want to…Look, man, I'm confused here. So, like, there's this chick…I dig her. She's a Chicana homegirl from Texas. Pretty down, real pretty and sweet and everything. We've been having a good time, you know what I mean? But…somethin' about her. I think she ain't really a chick, you know what'm sayin'? I mean, she is, but, I think…I think she was a man before. Man, I don't know what to do. *[Pause.]* You gotta help me, man. I mean, what should I do? Fuck man, where the hell are you? Where the fuck are you, motherfucker?! Where the fuck have you been? Why'd you leave me, man? Why'd you abandon me? Come back, man! Come back!

[Sudden crossfade to CELIA. *She is lost in her prayer, her body swaying back and forth, her head jerking a bit.]*

[Sudden crossfade to DOÑA IRENE'S *apartment. Dressed conservatively in black,* DOÑA IRENE *sits stoically in a chair, staring at a spot in the distance.* LUZ PALOMA *stands a few feet to her right.]*

LUZ PALOMA: Señora, le pido por favor que me escuche, tan solo unos minutos.

DOÑA IRENE: I am listening. Hable ya.

LUZ PALOMA: I'm very sorry about your son's death. I don't know what it's like to lose a child, but I can only imagine. *[Pause.]* When I was ten years old my parents were killed in an accident. They had worked very hard to follow their dreams and bring our family here from el Caribe. I had to raise my two younger sisters. They're twins. I would not be able to stand losing one of them.

DOÑA IRENE: Why are you here? To rub my son's death in my face?! To tell me how sorry you are that he was killed by that…ese pervertido, that freak that you are defending?

LUZ PALOMA: Doña Irene, please. My intention is not to hurt you.

DOÑA IRENE: You don't know about hurt! You don't know what it's like to bury the very being that came out of your insides, that you fed with your own breasts, that you took care of when he was sick and worked hard to feed and clothe, the child that you watched grow up, smiling to you, and that smile reminded you of yourself, like a mirror…there you were, hoping, dreaming. Una madre. Una madre que amaba a su hijo. *[Silence.]* That freak killed my baby.

LUZ PALOMA: Doña Irene, she was trying to defend herself.

DOÑA IRENE: ¡Mentira!

LUZ PALOMA: Doña Irene, míreme a los ojos. *[Pause.]* Years ago one of my sisters was assaulted. She was chased up what was left of the stairs of a burned, abandoned building in the South Bronx by a sick, disgusting man who put a knife to her neck. He assaulted her right there on the stairs, left her, a child, beaten, cut up, bleeding. *[Pause.]* Nobody on the block did or said anything to defend her. The women were afraid to speak up. The men admired him for it. He would get high on heroin and cocaine and beat his wife and his children and pick fights in the street because he wanted to believe that he was king and needed to prove it. He branded my sister a slut, and just about everyone chose to believe that lie. She was only a child, trying to live her life. *[Pause.]* Don't let your fears blind you any further to the truth. Ya ha sufrido suficiente engañándose a sí misma.

DOÑA IRENE: Váyase.

*[*LUZ PALOMA *grabs her briefcase and exits. Sudden crossfade to* CELIA. *She is kneeling in front of the altar, holding an ancient vase with a mix of milk, honey, and sunflower petals, some of which she pours on her hands.]*

[Sudden crossfade to the prison's visiting room, where ALFONSO *has gone to see* CHUYIS. CHUYIS' *expression is one of utter despair. She is very ill, short of breath.]*

ALFONSO: Tienes que ver a un médico.

CHUYIS: There's no one here.

ALFONSO: There has to be a doctor who can see you.

CHUYIS: They don't care. I don't want to be butchered anyway. Don't think about me. How are you?

ALFONSO: Cómo voy a estar. Preocupada. Triste. The apartment seems so empty without you. Todos los días pongo las canciones de Luis Miguel, para que no las extrañen tus cosas.

CHUYIS: I'm not getting out alive. *[Beat.]* I have AIDS.

ALFONSO: AIDS! What do you mean? Did they test you?

CHUYIS: No, I don't want them to test me. If they find out, they'll put me in a different unit and you won't be able to visit me. You're the only person I care about now.

ALFONSO: No me espantes Chuyis.

CHUYIS: It's okay. I'll be joining my mami and all our friends.

ALFONSO: Estás delirando.

CHUYIS: No. I never used protection with Juan. I don't know why. He's been the only one. I guess I was afraid. Or maybe I wanted to believe that he loved me as much as I loved him.

ALFONSO: But how do you know you have the virus?

CHUYIS: Nine months ago I went and got myself tested, 'cuz I felt I had gotten infected from him. I was really sick. The test came out positive. A couple of months later I took a second test.

ALFONSO: You never told me any of this.

CHUYIS: Because I couldn't admit it.

ALFONSO: But you were an AIDS educator, a community leader.

CHUYIS: Stop.

ALFONSO: It can't be. You're making this whole thing up.

CHUYIS: Why would I make this up?

ALFONSO: To get attention. Why else, I mean, isn't that why you shot Juan and his brother? You couldn't stand it, right? You couldn't stand the fact that I was more popular than you. It's not like I've been blind to it, you know.

CHUYIS: My god, you are so immature!

ALFONSO: No. Look at me in the eyes and tell me that deep inside what you wanted wasn't some attention. Why else would you do something so stupid like buy a gun and shoot a child?

CHUYIS: You would have done the same thing, Alma!

ALFONSO: No, I wouldn't have done the same thing. You could have avoided this whole mess. You knew you could have. I told you a long time ago to stay away from Juan. I told you *months* ago, right after you met him. I mean, did you even stop for a moment to think how it might affect me and the people who care about you?

CHUYIS: Stop trying to make me feel guilty. I hate it when you do that.

ALFONSO: I'm not trying to make you feel guilty.

CHUYIS: Yes you are. You do that all the time. Endlessly talking about how you crossed the border and lost your country and how no one's ever suffered as much as you and everyone's always hurting you somehow.

ALFONSO: What—

CHUYIS: And if anyone's forever trying to get attention it's you, Alma. Always centering the conversation on you, and *who* has the prettiest dresses, and *who's* the best performer, and *who's* gonna make it to college and be rich and famous one day.

ALFONSO: I see now, you hate me.

CHUYIS: No, I don't hate you, I'm just sick of your shit. No more secrets. That's all.

ALFONSO: You are such a bitch!

CHUYIS: Fine, I'm a bitch. I admit it. I envy your popularity. Is that what you wanted to hear? And I've felt very happy knowing I had my sex change operation and that I have breasts and you don't, and I was able to pay for my operation because my mother saved the money. She wanted me to do it because she knew it would make me happy. Because she loved me, 'cuz she was a nice woman, unlike your mother who despised you. So now you know how I feel. Satisfied?

ALFONSO: Oh my god, and all along I thought we were sisters. *[Stands up to leave.]*

CHUYIS: Alma, don't you dare leave me now.

ALFONSO: Good luck to you with your case.

CHUYIS: I'm not lying about my status!

[ALFONSO *stands still.*]

CHUYIS: I don't want us to fight. I need you.

[ALFONSO *remains standing.*]

CHUYIS: We only have a few seconds. You must hear this. *[Gathers all her courage.]* I don't know why I've been attracted to men who've hurt me. Now that I've been here so alone, I realize I wish you and I could have been closer. I just want you to know that. I wish we could have loved each other in a different way.

A LOUD VOICE: Time's up!

[ALFONSO *holds the telephone tightly for a few moments.* CHUYIS *hangs up. They place both of their hands on the glass separating them. Lights are dimmed slowly until all that can be seen is the flame from the lantern* CELIA *is holding. Softly, with her eyes closed, she blows out the lantern. Blackout.]*

ACT III

Scene One

[*Lights rise on the prison cell, illuminating* EDGAR'S SPIRIT. *She sits next to* CHUYIS, *who is in a deep sleep. She is in a traditional Pipil (Indigenous) dress, watching* CHUYIS *intently.]*

EDGAR'S SPIRIT: *[to* CHUYIS*]* In a past life, I was the daughter of a prominent landowner. My family lived in a beautiful small town adorned with luscious hills caressed by the warm, tropical breeze and the fall and winter rains. I was looked at with awe, envied by the women, secretly desired by the men, resented by the campesinos who could merely aspire to survive in the face of my family's opulence. Era la patrona. *[Pause.]* And for this very reason I was afraid and felt I could not speak. In my silence I was married off to a man much older than myself whom I never loved and gave birth to seventeen children. *[Pause.]* One day, the campesinos revolted. My husband, my father, and my older sons left to fight them. The little ones and the women stayed with me. I continued to live in fear, protecting my children as best I could, but the family's land was taken over by the peasants. *[Pause.]* The day the peasants stormed into my house, my children were literally pulled from my arms, lined up and forced to watch me be raped by countless men before they were massacred. I wanted very much to die, but I could not take my own life without knowing what had happened to the rest of my children. Every Sunday, before the church bells announced noontime, I walked to the town square, joining many other women searching through piles of bloodied corpses and limbs, heads, arms, legs, in hopes that none would be those of my children, or that they would be so my ordeal could end. "Quién viene?" the rebels asked. "Soy Villista," I responded, swallowing my pride and pain. *[Pause. She stands up and takes a few steps away from* CHUYIS.*]* To want to die is natural. There was a time when this desire signified our readiness to engage in the ultimate rite of passage, a necessary step requiring the bravery of birth itself, in order that we could experience full communion with the Universe, free of the constraints inherent to all matter, leaving the body behind, rightfully, to the Earth. Then came the invasions. Our cosmos was destroyed, and our hearts were filled with fear. Our ancient beliefs were forever distorted. Our readiness for fulfillment after life became a desperate need to find respite, a litany of regrets, a shaming of ourselves in an effort to escape punishment and enslavement. *[To* CHUYIS.*]* You wish to be at peace, to accept the temporariness of your humanity, to reach the crucial moment at which you will return to the Creator's womb. Your dignity, your fearlessness and love of self, your mother's greatest gifts to you, have kept you in touch with your purpose. Everyone you've called upon who is here has heard you. *[She remains still, then walks back to* CHUYIS, *leans over and kisses her on the forehead. Slowly, she begins to walk backwards, whispering what could be prayer.]*

[As EDGAR'S SPIRIT *walks into the surrounding darkness and off the stage,* CHUYIS *wakes up and begins to cry.]*

CHUYIS: Perdóname Dios mío. Forgive me, Edgar.

[Fadeout.]

Scene Two

[A desk and chair suggest a judge's chamber.]

LUZ PALOMA: Your Honor, my client has taken ill. She was tested for HIV and the result was positive. She's been placed in a separate unit without family visitation rights. She is not being treated humanely.

JUDGE: If your client has been placed in an HIV unit, then the correct thing has been done, Ms. Castillo.

LUZ PALOMA: Your Honor, the HIV unit is overcrowded. I found out that there is no appropriate medical care. There is a pediatrician who sees inmates once a month if they are lucky. The medical technical aides are not sufficiently qualified. My client has been suffering from severe chest pain, open sores on her legs, and has been coughing blood. She's been given Motrin, Tylenol, and Vaseline Intensive Care Lotion. There is no infectious disease specialist, not to mention gynecological care for her.

JUDGE: Ms. Castillo, now, what kind of gynecological care could your client possibly need? Your client is not a real woman.

LUZ PALOMA: Your Honor, my client underwent a sex-change operation. She needs gynecological care. She is now, for all intents and purposes, a biological woman. She is a woman with HIV. And it is likely that she would be diagnosed with AIDS given the symptoms she is presenting.

JUDGE: What is it that you want from me, Ms. Castillo?

LUZ PALOMA: I want you to release her.

JUDGE: Ms. Castillo—

LUZ PALOMA: Your Honor, please. I don't believe my client will live for six months. There are people who care about her, who want to take care of her. My client's culpability has not even been established. She is innocent, according to the law. If my client and her family were wealthy, bail would have been paid and she would be receiving the care she deserves, instead of the cruel and unusual punishment she is being subjected to.

JUDGE: Ms. Castillo—

LUZ PALOMA: Your Honor, there has got to be a way.

[*Crossfade to* SALVADOR'*s apartment. Both he and* ALFONSO *are stuffing envelopes, tired, looking ragged.*]

ALFONSO: [*simultaneously with* LUZ PALOMA] There has got to be a way.

SALVADOR: I'm looking into it. I don't know the legalities, but I'm speaking with a prisoners' rights coalition and a group of AIDS activists to see if she can be released through a compassionate release. I mean, it sounds reasonable, but I don't know.

ALFONSO: And if that works we could organize a salsa contest, make it a benefit so she can have some cash.

SALVADOR: We could. *[Silence. Stops working.]* Listen Alfonso…It's true I really haven't been present for you. I need to apologize to you.

ALFONSO: To tell you the truth I don't know what to think any more. This whole situation is making me question everything.

SALVADOR: I just want you to know that I really am here for you. I want Chuyis to be free as much as you do, like I wanted my brother to be free. *[Pause.]* And…also I'd be lying to you if I didn't tell you I'm doing this because I'm in love with you, and I want you to be happy. And I would give anything to spare you the pain you're feeling. *[Pause.]* You're right, it does scare me to feel this. But I also know how happy and peaceful I feel when I hold you in my arms after we've made love, and I can feel your heart beating. *[Pause.]* You're a brave and remarkable individual. I respect you.

ALFONSO: Wow. Maybe I should follow your example and start respecting myself more. *[Pause.]* I've been thinking I would like to try and find my little sister in México. She deserves to have a loving family, and a better world, like the one you're fighting for.

SALVADOR: *[attempts to get close to him]* I'll help you find her.

ALFONSO: *[uneasy]* Ya se me hizo tarde.

[Understanding, SALVADOR begins to escort ALFONSO off the stage. Just then a newspaper on the coffee table catches ALFONSO's attention. He picks it up and starts to read it.]

ALFONSO: "Transsexuals involved in Mission murder case set up anti-imperialist study group." *[To SALVADOR.]* What is this?

SALVADOR: It's just a newspaper…

ALFONSO: *[reading]* "Alma, a drag performer at Las Cariñosas, a Latino gay club in the Mission, has become a leader in the struggle to organize transgender sex workers. With the guidance and support of comrade R8361 she has set up an anti-imperialist study group to smash the capitalist machine and its effect on the peoples and immigrants from Latin America." *[To SALVADOR.]* This is a lie.

SALVADOR: Permíteme que te explique.

ALFONSO: No me expliques nada. No es necesario.

[ALFONSO puts the paper down and grabs his backpack, beginning to exit.]

SALVADOR: Wait…

[SALVADOR *tries to stop him, but* ALFONSO *pushes him away.*]

SALVADOR: Please don't walk out like that. Look, I'm sorry.

ALFONSO: Leave me alone, Salvador.

SALVADOR: Please don't make me grovel at your feet. Look. I know what I wrote isn't true. I'm sorry. I didn't mean to play with you. It's my own drama inside my head. I promise I won't do it again.

[ALFONSO *stares at him in silence.*]

SALVADOR: You don't have to use this or anything else to push me away. We can get along and love each other. I want to try.

ALFONSO: Try what?

SALVADOR: A relationship. Don't you want one?

[*Silence.*]

ALFONSO: It's not okay to be dishonest.

SALVADOR: I won't be.

ALFONSO: You can't play with my feelings.

SALVADOR: You got it.

ALFONSO: Si vamos a estar juntos como pareja necesito que seas sincero, que me quieras y me escuches y estés a mi lado.

[SALVADOR *takes a step closer to him.*]

SALVADOR: No more games.

[*He touches* ALFONSO's *face gently.* ALFONSO *struggles within himself for a moment, then gives in. They embrace.*]

[*Fadeout.*]

Scene Three

[*Crossfade to* LUZ PALOMA *and* CELIA's *apartment. They are sitting at opposite sides of the sofa with their legs intertwined under a blanket. They are looking at each other in a loving, contemplative manner, each holding a drink in her hands. Relaxed, attuned to one another, it is as if their love were meant to make the night less cold.*]

CELIA: You told the twins?

LUZ PALOMA: Yes.

CELIA: What'd they say?

LUZ PALOMA: Estaban felicísimas.

CELIA: I also told Fatima.

LUZ PALOMA: Oh yeah?

CELIA: She said it would have made my father very happy. She's right. It would have made for another wonderful story he could share with everyone.

LUZ PALOMA: Well, everyone will hear it from her now. She's also a great storyteller.

CELIA: Yeah. She said she was gonna tell María. You know, I was thinking, maybe by the time the baby's born María could come visit us. Don't you think it'd be good for her?

LUZ PALOMA: Sure. It'll make her wanna have an alternative family of her own.

CELIA: Oh, come on. She's only fifteen. Besides, she already has an alternative family.

LUZ PALOMA: Not a *lesbian* alternative family.

CELIA: That would be wonderful. She'd have all the space in the world, and all the love, support, and acceptance to come out. Proudly.

LUZ PALOMA: You know, we've done good for ourselves.

CELIA: Haven't we?

LUZ PALOMA: Not bad at all for four years.

CELIA: I still wanna go back and visit my parents' grave this summer. But after the baby's born, I'll stick around. I'm gonna work very hard and save lots of money, so we can send her or him to a good college.

LUZ PALOMA: That child's gonna have one fascinating life.

CELIA: Never a dull moment.

LUZ PALOMA: Can't break the tradition.

CELIA: The drama will have to be a little toned down.

LUZ PALOMA: Of course. Otherwise what would be the point of so much work on ourselves?

CELIA: Are you ready for tomorrow?

LUZ PALOMA: Ready for the big battle.

CELIA: I'm real proud of you, you know that?

LUZ PALOMA: Thank you. *[Pause.]* I'm sorry I made you feel ashamed because you didn't agree to having the baby right away like I wanted to.

CELIA: We don't have to talk about that any more.

LUZ PALOMA: I just want to acknowledge it wasn't about you. I'm working on it. *[Pause.]* After all I'm not one hundred percent sure I want to be a mother.

CELIA: Well, either way, I love you, and I'm here for you.

LUZ PALOMA: I love you, too.

Scene Four

[Church bells and African drums are heard out of synchrony. The sound creates a background of dissonance and confusion, presaging the clashing of opposing forces. EDGAR'S SPIRIT enters, carrying a bundle of red carnations. She wears the dark cloak worn originally by the PRIESTESS. She walks ceremoniously, looking straight ahead, plucking petals and letting them fall on the floor. As she reaches centerstage, she turns quickly to the audience. She brings her index finger to her lips, demanding silence. Suddenly she turns away and continues her procession, exiting. All stage lights are up on the courtroom. LUZ PALOMA is positioned stage left. Stage right, JUAN GALLO sits on the witness stand wearing a suit, his left arm no longer in a cast. The JUDGE sits behind a podium to his side. MR. GONZALEZ sits behind a desk near LUZ PALOMA.]

LUZ PALOMA: Mr. Roque, do you have a different name that you go by?

JUAN GALLO: What do you mean?

LUZ PALOMA: An endearing name perhaps, a nickname.

JUAN GALLO: Just Juan.

LUZ PALOMA: Your close friends call you Juan?

JUAN GALLO: They call me—they call me Juan Gallo.

LUZ PALOMA: They call you Juan Gallo?

JUAN GALLO: Yes.

LUZ PALOMA: Mr. Roque, would you be so kind to tell the jury what the word "gallo" means?

JUAN GALLO: In English it means…cock.

LUZ PALOMA: You mean "cock" as in a rooster.

JUAN GALLO: Yes.

LUZ PALOMA: Mr. Roque, if I may ask you, why is it that your nickname is "rooster"?

MR. GONZALEZ: Objection, Your Honor, I don't see the relevance of this question.

LUZ PALOMA: Your Honor, I'm trying to establish whether or not there was a relationship between Mr. Roque and my client prior to the death of Edgar Roque. I feel plaintiff's answer to my question will help inform that.

JUDGE: Overruled. *[To* JUAN GALLO.*]* Please answer counsel's question.

LUZ PALOMA: The question is, why is your nickname "rooster," as far as you know?

JUAN GALLO: Uh, out of respect.

LUZ PALOMA: Out of respect?

JUAN GALLO: Yes.

LUZ PALOMA: What is it that you're respected for, Mr. Roque?

MR. GONZALEZ: Objection. This clearly has no bearing on any possible relationship between the plaintiff and the defendant.

JUDGE: Counsel, what are you trying to get at?

LUZ PALOMA: I'll withdraw the question, Your Honor. *[To* JUAN GALLO.*]* Mr. Roque, prior to the night of your brother's death, did you know or were you related in any way to María de Jesús Garza?

JUAN GALLO: No.

LUZ PALOMA: María de Jesús Garza also goes by the nickname of Chuyis. Prior to the night of your brother's death, did you know or were you in any way related to a woman named Chuyis?

JUAN GALLO: No.

LUZ PALOMA: Mr. Roque, let me remind you that you have been sworn to tell the truth only. I'll ask the question again. Did you know or were you in any way related to a woman by the name of Chuyis?

JUAN GALLO: I don't know.

LUZ PALOMA: Mr. Roque, several people have testified in this court that prior to the night that your brother died, that you were acquainted with Ms. Garza, also known as Chuyis.

JUAN GALLO: I don't know, maybe.

LUZ PALOMA: You weren't acquainted with her, you don't know if you were, maybe you were. Which one is it, Mr. Roque?

JUAN GALLO: It could be. I mean, I might have seen her around a couple of times. I know a lot of people.

LUZ PALOMA: Isn't it true, Mr. Roque, that you actually were well acquainted with Ms. Garza prior to the night of the incident?

JUAN GALLO: No.

LUZ PALOMA: You were not.

JUAN GALLO: No.

LUZ PALOMA: Isn't it true that you had a fourteen-month-long intimate relationship—and by that I mean a sexually and emotionally intimate relationship—with María de Jesús Garza?

JUAN GALLO: No, it ain't true.

LUZ PALOMA: Let me try to refresh your memory a bit, Mr. Roque. I ask that Exhibit A be admitted by the court to be presented to plaintiff and the members of the jury.

[She brings an envelope up to the JUDGE; he opens it, pulls out a photograph, and looks at it, nodding. LUZ PALOMA then hands it JUAN GALLO.]

LUZ PALOMA: Take a close look at that photograph, Mr. Roque. Do you recognize yourself in that picture?

JUAN GALLO: It kind of looks like me.

LUZ PALOMA: You can't say for sure that it's you in the photograph?

JUAN GALLO: No.

LUZ PALOMA: Do you recognize the person who is being embraced by you—or the individual who, as you say, looks kind of like you in that photograph?

JUAN GALLO: No.

LUZ PALOMA: Mr. Roque, isn't it the case that you and Ms. Garza took that photograph together at a photo studio a few months ago and that you gave it to her in a frame with a birthday card attached to it as proof of your professed love for her?

JUAN GALLO: No, it ain't true. I never loved nobody that looked like that. That person right there in the picture looks like a freak to me. I wouldn't fall in love with no freak.

LUZ PALOMA: Mr. Roque, I don't understand what you're trying to accomplish by denying something so blatantly obvious.

JUAN GALLO: I'm telling you it ain't true!

LUZ PALOMA: Are you feeling angry, Mr. Roque?

JUAN GALLO: Yeah, 'cuz you're saying something that ain't true, and you're embarrassing me in front of my mother.

LUZ PALOMA: Mr. Roque, isn't it true that as a matter of fact you tend to get angry easily, especially when you drink, and that you indiscriminately pick fights in the streets, hence your nickname "rooster," as symbolic of a fighting rooster?

JUAN GALLO: Look lady, I don't know why you saying that stuff about me.

LUZ PALOMA: Mr. Roque, I'm asking you a question. Please answer my question.

JUAN GALLO: No, it's not true.

LUZ PALOMA: Mr. Roque, because I believe the person next to Ms. Garza in the photograph is in fact none other than you, I must ask the following question for clarification, and I am sure you will respond truthfully as you have up until now. Isn't it the case that you not only were involved in an intimate relationship with Ms. Garza—

JUAN GALLO: No!

JUDGE: Don't interrupt nor shout at counsel, Mr. Roque! *[To* LUZ PALOMA.*]* Proceed with your question.

LUZ PALOMA: Isn't it the case that you had a relationship with Ms. Garza in which you verbally demeaned her and also hit her on countless occasions, calling her names like, quote, bitch, ho, cunt, and puta, unquote, and leaving visible bruises on her body and face, even making her bleed on several occasions, and that you also threatened to kill her—

JUAN GALLO: *[whispering loudly]* Shut up already, you fucking dyke!

LUZ PALOMA: —and…Excuse me?

JUAN GALLO: What. I didn't say nuthin'.

LUZ PALOMA: What did you just say, Mr. Roque?

JUAN GALLO: I didn't say nuthin', Ms. Lawyer.

LUZ PALOMA: *[walks up slowly to him and stands inches away from his face, all the time staring him in the eyes defiantly]* Well, then answer my question, Mr. Roque. Did you or did you not physically and verbally abuse Ms. Garza on numerous occasions in the course of your fourteen-month relationship with her?

JUAN GALLO: I told you already, I never had no relationship with no disgusting freak! I hate freaks!

[Lights out simultaneously as church bells and drums are heard again, increasing in speed and synchronicity, until they become a disturbing, muddled sound which, almost imperceptibly, fuses into the beginning of the salsa "Dicen Que Soy" by La India.]

[All stage lights are turned on. It is no longer the courthouse but the dance floor at Las Cariñosas. Three couples—two women, a "butch" woman and a man in drag, and two men, all dressed up and carrying number cards—dance masterfully, performing beautiful, fancy steps and turns. Suddenly, SALVADOR *enters, pushing* CHUYIS *in a wheelchair. He and* CHUYIS *remain still, admiring the dancing, until one of the women dancing spots* CHUYIS *and freezes. Everyone else stops and turns to look. Nobody moves or says anything.* CHUYIS *stares at everybody. The woman who first spotted* CHUYIS *walks up to her and stands a few feet before her. For a moment no one does anything. Then* CHUYIS *begins to lip-synch the words to the salsa, at first with shyness, then with increasing enthusiasm. As the song progresses,* CHUYIS *cops an outrageous attitude. At the*

peak of her excitement, she begins to laugh hysterically. Everyone joins her, clapping and cheering, ecstatic that CHUYIS *is free. After a few moments,* EDGAR'S SPIRIT *enters, also clapping; the scene freezes and the music stops. She is wearing the dark cloak. She claps assertively, never ceasing to look at* CHUYIS *as she approaches her, getting closer to her than anyone. She stops clapping, kneels before her, and removes her cloak, folding it gently and placing it on* CHUYIS' *lap. She rests her head on it, closing her eyes.]*

[Fadeout.]

Scene Five

[Full darkness JUAN GALLO's *voice can be heard from different spots on the stage. A sofa and coffee table have been positioned stage center.]*

JUAN GALLO: You can't do this no more. It don't feel good. You gotta help me, Dad. You gotta stop hiding. Edgar, bro, you gotta make him come out of hiding. You gotta help him come out, bro. You gotta come out…Come out…

[Loud knocking.]

ALMA: *[offstage]* Open the door. Open the goddamn door, you scumbag.

[A spotlight suddenly illuminates JUAN GALLO, *asleep on the sofa. He wakes up, jolted. He looks around, trying to identify the source of the noise. He stands up quickly, realizing someone's at the door. Lights up.]*

JUAN GALLO: Who the fuck is that?

ALMA: Open the door! I got something to say to you.

JUAN GALLO: *[recognizing* ALMA's *voice]* Get the hell out of here.

ALMA: You'd better open the door 'cuz if you don't you're gonna be sorry.

JUAN GALLO: Go away.

ALMA: Ábreme o tiro la puerta y hago que te arrepientas por el resto de tus días.

JUAN GALLO: I said go away.

ALMA: Open it, you goddamn closeted queer!

JUAN GALLO: You stupid bitch! I'ma teach you how to treat people with respect. *[Opening the door.]* What the—

[ALMA walks on stage, dressed in an elegant nightgown and heels, fearlessly pointing a gun at JUAN GALLO. He staggers backwards.]

ALMA: I'm not afraid of you. I'm gonna kill you like Chuyis should have, you rotten son of a bitch. Arms up!

JUAN GALLO: *[obeying]* Hey, take it easy.

ALMA: You've never given a shit about anybody. Not even your brother, who was a little macho fuckhead like you.

JUAN GALLO: Just chill, baby.

ALMA: Don't try to sweet talk me motherfucker! Fucking dick. Ain't nothing you can say that'll make me change my mind now. Closeted bastard.

[She spits at him. JUAN GALLO jumps back, falling backwards on the sofa.]

ALMA: I pity you.

JUAN GALLO: *[extending his hands to protect himself]* Hey, man, take it easy!

ALMA: Shut up! You should have allowed yourself to get fucked up the ass a long time ago. It's what you secretly wanted anyway, somebody to do you real good, so you could know what it's like to be submitted and have your entrails stirred. You would have treated Chuyis much better.

JUAN GALLO: *[whimpering]* She killed my little brother.

ALMA: You killed your little brother! You dragged him into your scummy, no good, blood-sucking, sorry-ass lifestyle. You were gonna teach him to be Mr. Stud, is that it? Mr. Stick-your-dick-in-the-hole-and-slap-the-shit-out-of-them-bitches-and-dump-'em-afterwards? *[She kicks the coffee table.]* Well, I have a surprise for you. Chuyis is probably gonna die, even if her lawyer manages to get her out of jail. You wanna know why?

[JUAN GALLO is huddled against the end of the sofa.]

ALMA: 'Cuz she got AIDS. From you! 'Cuz you didn't give a shit about her!

JUAN GALLO: I ain't got AIDS.

ALMA: You will. 'Cuz you infected her.

JUAN GALLO: I did not! She fooled around with everybody.

ALMA: Bullshit! But it doesn't matter, I didn't come here to convince you. I just came to tell you before I blew your brains out.

[JUAN GALLO *looks in different directions, trying to figure how to free himself.* ALMA *cocks the gun.* JUAN GALLO *freezes.*]

ALMA: Pathetic.

JUAN GALLO: [*making a last effort to defend himself*] You're pathetic!

ALMA: Maybe. But at least I don't go around destroying people's lives for fun.

JUAN GALLO: All I've done is survive.

ALMA: As what? A macho wannabe? I've survived, too!

[*She straightens her arms, aiming assertively at* JUAN GALLO, *preparing to shoot.*]

ALMA: [*beyond herself*] When I found out that Chuyis had the AIDS virus and she had gotten it from you, I felt you were gonna be getting the punishment you deserved. But then I realized you didn't deserve to die from AIDS. That would be too dignifying. You deserve a violent death, as violent as you've been to everyone. So here's this gift, from me and Chuyis, and all the women fucked over by roaches like you.

[*She begins to breathe faster, her finger on the trigger moving ever so slightly, shaking a bit.* JUAN GALLO *shuts his eyes tight and covers his ears. She takes a step forward, grinning her teeth. Suddenly, she breaks down.*]

ALMA: I can't! I can't kill myself!

[*She falls on her knees, dropping the gun. Drums pound in the background.* JUAN GALLO *shivers, completely unable to move.*]

[*Fadeout.*]

Scene Six

[*A dimmed spotlight rises backstage, revealing* SALVADOR, CELIA, ALMA, *and other friends sitting around* CHUYIS *on her deathbed, frozen in their grief.* EDGAR'S SPIRIT *is also present. She stands behind the headboard in her Pipil dress, looking over the bed.* CHUYIS' BODY *is covered entirely with a white blanket.*]

[*Another spotlight rises stage center, where* LUZ PALOMA *stands in the court-house. She addresses the audience.*]

LUZ PALOMA: Ladies and gentlemen of the jury. We have come to the end of this trial, and it is time for you to determine among yourselves whether my client, María de Jesús Garza, lovingly known as Chuyis, is guilty of murdering fourteen-year-old Edgar Roque and attempting to murder Edgar's older brother, Juan. *[Pause.]* I have shown you that María de Jesús Garza is far from the monstrous, murderous freak that her accusers have painted her to be, and that on the night of Edgar Roque's death, she acted out of self-defense in a desperate attempt to save her own life, threatened by Edgar and his brother Juan, who in fact had the intention to kill her. *[Pause.]* As you know, my client was unable to be present at this trial because she was gravely ill. I regret to inform you that, in the early hours of the morning, Chuyis died from AIDS-related complications. Therefore, it won't be necessary for you to convene to make your judgment. *[Pause.]* I want to thank you for your patience and commitment to the task that you were assigned. I also want to take a moment to share with you, in closing, my deep condolences for Chuyis' death. She was a brave young lady whose crime was to allow herself to experience what it was like to be a woman, and be committed to that with all of her heart. A woman, not unlike many of us, who was loving, caring, yet a fighter, who had dreams, hopes, and who, despite how hard she tried to do what was expected of her, still ended up a victim of her circumstances, of her past, her identity, and the dishonoring and contempt towards her gender. I regret Chuyis' death as much as that of young Edgar, who, as a child, was also victimized. *[Pause.]* If by chance you should find yourselves feeling that Chuyis was guilty of the crimes of which she was accused, I ask that you consider a lesson I learned recently, which is that true forgiveness only occurs when we finally forgive ourselves for defending those who first wounded us. *[Pause.]* I know that those who love Chuyis understand this lesson, and for that reason, Chuyis didn't die alone, and neither her life nor her death have been in vain.

[Light on LUZ PALOMA *fades. She exits. As with* EDGAR's *death at the beginning of the play, seashells, rattles, and drums announce the moment of* CHUYIS' *spiritual transition. The sound of drums is accompanied by traditional Native American chants and prayers. Two* HEYOEHKAH SPIRITS *in festive, colorful Indigenous clothing, one wearing an African, the other an Asian mask, and holding candleholders with lit candles, platters of fruit, and baskets full of flowers, enter.* EDGAR's SPIRIT *looks at them respectfully as they walk backwards ceremoniously toward the center of the stage and, making an offering, hold up the candleholders and the other items and place them on the floor. Still backwards, they walk up to the bed where* CHUYIS' BODY *lies covered with the*

blanket and pick it up, carrying it stage center, followed by EDGAR'S SPIRIT. *At this point, lights on the bed scene fade out. The* SPIRITS *place the body on the floor by the candleholders and together with* EDGAR'S SPIRIT, *dance around it backwards, outlining an imaginary circle, exiting afterwards. The drums and the chants intensify as* EDGAR'S SPIRIT *enters a trance and blesses the body. She passes her hand over it, removing the blanket. The drums and chants stop.* EDGAR'S SPIRIT *exits quickly, using the blanket as wings, mimicking flight.* CHUYIS' SPIRIT *is in the form of a young Native American boy, in traditional, colorful and festive Native American religious dress.* CHUYIS' SPIRIT *opens his eyes, as from a deep sleep. Realizing he's alone, he becomes frightened and impulsively screams, "Ma! Ma! Ma!" beginning to cry as he curls into fetal position.* EDGAR'S SPIRIT *and the* HEYOEHKAH SPIRITS *enter again and sit around* CHUYIS' SPIRIT, *extending their hands out to him.]*

[Blackout.]

Epilogue

[Lights rise on the stage of Las Cariñosas, simultaneously with song "A Nadie" by Liliana Felipe. The candleholders and offerings from the previous scene remain on the floor stage center. ALMA, *wearing the same outfit she wore on the night* EDGAR *was killed, and once again made to perfection, begins her lip-synching performance.* CELIA *and* LUZ PALOMA *sit at a table holding hands, dressed up for the occasion. In mid-performance, during the instrumental section of the song,* SALVADOR *enters, dressed elegantly. He walks up to* ALMA *and gives her a red carnation. At the instant that both of their hands are touching the flower,* EDGAR'S SPIRIT *and* CHUYIS' SPIRIT *enter. The music stops and the scene freezes, capturing* ALMA's *and* SALVADOR's *looks. The two* SPIRITS *walk hand in hand.]*

EDGAR'S SPIRIT: Now you know everything.

CHUYIS' SPIRIT: Can I say hi to my future mom?

EDGAR'S SPIRIT: Sure.

[They walk to CELIA's *and* LUZ PALOMA's *table.]*

EDGAR'S SPIRIT: Give me your hands.

[She positions CHUYIS' SPIRIT's *hands gently on* LUZ PALOMA's *belly.* CHUYIS' SPIRIT *listens attentively.]*

EDGAR'S SPIRIT: Remember that now you have to look after her. Later in her life, she will meet the woman who used to be my father the last time I lived. They will love each other very much, but they'll need us to help show them how. When they've learned, she will birth you again. Come along…

[They take a last brief look at CELIA *and* LUZ PALOMA *and at* SALVADOR *and* ALMA. CHUYIS' SPIRIT *turns to the audience and winks. Both exit. The scene unfreezes and the music continues.* SALVADOR *kisses* ALMA *softly on the lips.* CELIA *and* LUZ PALOMA *smile for them.* SALVADOR *goes to sit with* CELIA *and* LUZ PALOMA. ALMA *proceeds to finish her song, which she has been performing in loving memory of* CHUYIS. *As the song nears the end, she approaches* LUZ PALOMA *and hands her the red carnation.* CELIA *and* LUZ PALOMA *kiss on the lips. Lights gradually fade. Song "Te Extraño" rises.]*

END

The Watermelon Factory

Alfonso Ramirez

Characters

MARIA CONCEPCIÓN FUENTES (CONNIE): Mid- to late forties, middle class, medium height, strong sense of humor, slightly accented English.

GABRIEL RIOS: Late twenties, thin, intelligent, intense, driven, formerly a lawyer.

Setting: The entire play takes place on a park bench in Golden Gate Park, San Francisco. There could be a small tree or a water fountain in the background, but otherwise the stage is bare.

Time: Mother's Day, from about 8:30 A.M. until noon.

Playwright's Note: During a recent production, rather than have the two actors read the first monologues out loud, I decided to tape-record the actors' voices and have the words play with the actors reacting as if they were inner monologues. Also, the director opted to include less Spanish and more English in the performances. There are various passages that could be translated, but they would be subject to the playwright's approval. Another aspect was added in a different prodution by having the two actors' body language, behavior and mannerisms mirror each other. The music cues that I have added at various times are just suggestions and don't necessarily have to be adhered to.

[Birds are heard chirping in the background and the light is diffused. As the play progresses, the light should become stronger until it reaches midday brightness. CONNIE enters, dressed in overcoat or light raincoat, giving the impression of confidence and control.]

CONNIE: *[voice-over]* Wouldn't you know it, I arrive first. Where can he be? *[Looks around.]* But how will I know what he looks like? I better shut up or someone will think I am crazy, Dios mío, talking to myself como

una loca. *[Sits and looks at her watch.]* Well, he said I might recognize
him. Of course, he could be the Zodiac Killer and here I am like a sitting dove. *[Stands.]* Oh, I knew this was a bad idea. ¡Qué locura! Ay,
maybe he won't even show up. Bien, y se acabó el cuento. Ay, I knew I
should have peed before I left the house. It's just nervios. Like when I
go to confession. The minute I get inside that little confessional box, I
always have to pee so bad. Then I get anxious and I rush my sins.
Momento. Maybe I'm in the wrong place. He said across from the
Aquarium, near the main entrance to the Japanese gardens, no? Or
maybe it was the rear entrance. *[Reaches into her pocket, removes a
folded letter and reads.]* "The priest said—" I wonder what priest he's
talking about. *[Continues reading.]* Oh here it is. "Golden Gate Park,
May tenth, nine A.M., near the Aquarium, third bench." *[Counts the
benches.]* Uno, dos, tres. Okay, here I am, but where is he? *[Sits.]* I'll
give him a few more minutes, then adios y a los pajaros. Maybe he
won't come. He's changed his mind. *[Stands, grimaces.]* Hmm…maybe
I better walk around and find a ladies' room. That way I won't look so
anxious being early. *[Exits briskly stage right.]*

*[*GABRIEL *enters from stage left and walks around slowly. He turns and counts
the benches.]*

GABRIEL: *[voice-over]* One, two, three. *[Sits.]* This is the one. *[Removes his
scarf and places it on the bench beside him.]* Oh, the bench is warm.
Maybe she came and left already. Or it could have been some homeless
person sleeping here. Maybe I should have given her more information
in that letter, or I could have mentioned Father Contreras, or maybe I
should have…Oh, this is crazy. Stop torturing yourself, Gabriel. Who
am I kidding? After so many years, why should she even care? She
probably just agreed to meet me out of curiosity. She has no intention
of coming. I am wasting my time. *[Shakes his head. Stands.]* I should
have asked for her phone number. Yeah, I should have called her
instead of writing her. *[Sits.]* Okay, calm down. Give her a chance to get
here before you lose your mind. Five more minutes, then…then what? I
guess I'll try calling information to get her phone number. Or I'll go
directly to her house. No, that would be wrong. What if it isn't even
her? I'll be disturbing the peace. She'll have me arrested. *[Pause.]* Well,
this sure seemed like a good idea at one time. Forget it. Just drop it. Go
home and give up this wild goose chase. Just give it up. *[Stands.]* Get
on with your life Gabriel. *[Sniffles.]* And this weather can't be good for
my allergies. *[Exits stage left, leaving scarf behind.]*

[CONNIE *enters, stage right. She sees the scarf, picks it up, and turns it around in her hands.*]

CONNIE: Oh, no. I missed him. ¡Ay, qué demonios! I knew I should have peed before I left the house. [*Smells the scarf.*] Mmm…Old Spice. Same as Father Contreras used to wear. Dios mío, that's a name I haven't heard in such a long time. A flashbulb from the past. [*She sits and clutches the scarf, becoming a little tearful.*] Angel. My Angel.

[GABRIEL *enters quietly stage left and watches* CONNIE *for a few seconds.*]

GABRIEL: Ahem. Mrs. Fuentes?

CONNIE: Yes. Gabriel Rios? Is this yours? [*Hands him the scarf.*] Old Spice?

GABRIEL: No, Obsession. Thank you. Thanks a lot for coming today. I'm sorry it was on such short notice. Oh, sorry—please sit down. [*Indicates the bench, then sits beside her.*]

CONNIE: Thank you. You are very kind. [*Uncomfortable pause.*] So, what's this all about? What is so urgent that you get me out of bed so early on a Sunday morning? It's the only day that I get to sleep late.

GABRIEL: I'm sorry.

CONNIE: That's okay. So, anyway, you're a friend of Father Romo. We were so lucky to get him as our parish priest. Is he your friend?

GABRIEL: No, actually, his name was given to me by Father Contreras—or I should say, Archbishop Contreras.

CONNIE: Archbishop? My, my, he certainly has come a long way all these years. How do you know him?

GABRIEL: He was the bishop in my neighborhood.

CONNIE: And where is that?

GABRIEL: You know, where I grew up.

CONNIE: I mean, where? What town?

GABRIEL: Oh, sorry. Sacramento.

CONNIE: [*Glances away.*] So, he's still there.

GABRIEL: Pardon?

CONNIE: Father Contreras; he's still living in Sacramento?

GABRIEL: Yes. So, you've been there?

CONNIE: Yes, a long time ago—when I was a teenager.

GABRIEL: That's not so long ago, I think.

CONNIE: [Smiles] You are very sweet. The last time I saw Father Contreras I was about sixteen years old. I had some cousins who lived in Sacramento, and we used to come up from Fresno on Christmas and Easter.

GABRIEL: Is that where you're from, Fresno?

CONNIE: No, I was born in Mexico, in a town called Aguascalientes.

GABRIEL: Hot waters?

CONNIE: Yes. Named after a hot springs close by. Somebody in my village caught polio from the water, so we moved to Fresno when I was about fifteen.

GABRIEL: How did you meet Father Contreras?

CONNIE: I guess you could say he was like a…spiritual advisor. He celebrated the mass at my quinceañera. He was so funny. He always had us laughing. [Laughs] And, he could do a mean Twist.

GABRIEL: Well, I doubt he does much dancing these days now that he's an archbishop.

CONNIE: Oh, I certainly hope not. [Laughs] What would the Pope say? [Crosses herself]

GABRIEL: I hope I'm not keeping you from attending Mass today.

CONNIE: No, I usually go to the last Mass. But today I just might miss it. I hope the Lord forgives me. [Crosses herself]

GABRIEL: I promise not to tell Father Contreras.

CONNIE: Thank you. It will be our little secret. Actually, I'm supposed to go out to dinner with my family. Once a year my husband and children are nice to me.

GABRIEL: [Interested] Tell me something about them. How many kids do you have? What are their names? How old are they? What about your husband? What does he do for—

CONNIE: Wait, wait. Un momento. Slow down. Are you always such a Columbo and in such a hurry like this? And why do you need to know so much? Do you work for the *National Enquirer*? Or are you a lawyer?

GABRIEL: I used to be a lawyer. Forgive me. Sometimes I get carried away. Let's backtrack a bit. You said you were going out to dinner. What time do you have to leave?

CONNIE: No later than noon. I've got to find the right dress, and I have a special appointment at the beauty shop at three for some French tips. I also promised my husband that I would iron his tuxedo shirt.

GABRIEL: So much commotion. Do you always go to through this much trouble for Sunday dinner?

CONNIE: What? You mean you don't know what today is?

GABRIEL: [*Shrugs his shoulders and looks at his watch.*] May tenth?

CONNIE: It's Mother's Day.

GABRIEL: Is it? Oh, that's right.

CONNIE: Were you a good son? Did you remember to send your mother an RTD?

GABRIEL: FTD.

CONNIE: RTD, FTD, FDS. ¿Qué importa? Did you?

GABRIEL: [*Sadly*] No.

CONNIE: Why not? [*Catches herself.*] Oh, I'm sorry. How inconsiderate of me. Is she dead?

GABRIEL: For all intents and purposes she is.

CONNIE: I don't understand.

GABRIEL: She's very much alive and kicking. [*Pause*] We're not speaking.

CONNIE: That's terrible. You must write to her or call her. My husband, his name's Enrique, but everyone calls him Hank, he says, "Communication, that's the most important. When there's no communication, there's no family."

GABRIEL: He sounds like a very smart man. But that's the problem right there, you see. We don't communicate. Or we seem to speak different languages. *[Stands and walks slightly away from the bench.]* Can we please change the subject?

CONNIE: Sure. Sorry. *[Pause]* You still haven't told me why we are here— what your letter was about. You sounded so desperate to meet me.

GABRIEL: It's kind of a long story, Mrs. Fuentes.

CONNIE: That's okay. I have until noon, and I like long stories. But, please call me Connie.

GABRIEL: I thought your name was Maria.

CONNIE: Maria Concepción, actually. We're all named Maria. They just add another name so they can tell us apart. Everyone calls me Connie.

GABRIEL: Okay, Connie. *[Sits, removes his coat, takes a deep breath.]* Where to begin? A couple of years ago I was very sick and spent a couple of months in the hospital.

CONNIE: And your mother never visited you, is that it?

GABRIEL: Please, just let me finish. This is very difficult for me. I had a bad case of PCP—

CONNIE: PCP? Isn't that a drug, or maybe an insect spray? No, that's DDT.

GABRIEL: No, it stands for pneumocystis carinii pneumonia. I almost died. My parents were there at the hospital every day, until my doctor informed them that I had AIDS.

CONNIE: *[Startled]* Ay, Dios mío. No! Is that true?

GABRIEL: Yes. You see the doctor that diagnosed me is a friend of theirs. They all belong to the same country club. He and my dad play golf together. *[Pause]* I was so pissed. I'd known this doctor all my life and he betrayed my wishes. The Hippocratic Oath clearly states—

CONNIE: Excuse me again for interrupting, but you'll have to use simple words. I'm having trouble following you.

GABRIEL: Never mind, that's not important. What is important is that after the doctor told them the truth about my condition, I didn't hear from them for a long time.

CONNIE: Are you a part of—what do they call themselves now—Queer Nation? I read about that in the *National Enquirer*.

GABRIEL: No, but I *am* gay. And they've known that since I was sixteen, when I first came out to them.

CONNIE: What did they say?

GABRIEL: They never seemed to care one way or the other. They were too busy with their work, their cocktail parties, their vacations, their country club activities.

CONNIE: What are they—Argentinos?

GABRIEL: *[Laughs]* No, they're Mexican, but very upwardly mobile. They may be brown on the outside, but they're pure white on the inside, like Oreo cookies. You know, I'm surprised they never changed their names from Rios to O'Rios, since they'd prefer being Irish to Mexican. They even bought tickets to *Riverdance*. Anyway, they hardly ever spoke Spanish to me. I knew they spoke it since they used it at work with their employees, with the cleaning ladies at home, anyone a shade darker than them.

CONNIE: ¡Sinverguenzas! ¡Qué cabrones!

GABRIEL: So, when I got out of the hospital, I had nobody to talk to. I'm an only child, so I couldn't call anyone to find out why my parents wouldn't return my phone calls. When I called them at home, they would just hang up.

CONNIE: Pobrecito. *[Rubs his arms.]*

GABRIEL: After I'd been home from the hospital for over a month, they showed up at my apartment. They said they had come to apologize.

CONNIE: Bueno, at least they apologized.

GABRIEL: It didn't mean anything. I yelled at them. I said, "How could you be so unfeeling? You're probably not even my real parents. Maybe someone switched me at the hospital when I was born."

CONNIE: What did they say?

GABRIEL: That was when I finally found out the truth.

CONNIE: What? What?

GABRIEL: They told me that I was adopted. Can you believe it? I was twenty-seven years old and they finally tell me they adopted me when I was a couple of days old. My mother was infertile…I'm sorry, that means she couldn't bear children.

CONNIE: Well, sometimes I can't stand them either. *[Pause]* I'm very sorry to hear all this, but what does it have to do with me? I didn't know your parents.

GABRIEL: I insisted that they tell me who my real parents were. They said they didn't know, that I should speak to Father Contreras. He had arranged for the adoption through some church agency.

CONNIE: *[Uneasy]* What did he tell you? Probably some lie. He was a sneaky one, that Father Contreras. Always playing practical jokes, chasing the girls, teasing them. He had quite an imagination, to put it politely.

GABRIEL: *[Looks at her for an extended moment.]* He gave me your address. Told me to look you up. *[Pauses, takes a deep breath.]* He said you were my mother. *[Pauses]* I am your son.

CONNIE: ¿Qué? No, wait a minute here. That can't be true. No way.

GABRIEL: Why not?

CONNIE: That was just a convenient lie for him. ¡Qué atrevido!

GABRIEL So, you're denying me too? You're saying you're not my mother?

CONNIE: I am sterile. I can't have children.

GABRIEL: How can that be true when you just finished telling me about your kids? You're going to have dinner with them, isn't that what you said?

CONNIE: Bueno, I should have explained before. Hank was almost a widower when I met him. He already had four kids, all of them very young. I used to clean house and cook for the old Mrs. Fuentes because she was sick with cancer. When she died, Hank asked me to take on more responsibilities. I took care of the children and after about a year they started calling me "Mami." One day Hank proposed to me. *[She turns away from him.]* It all happened so fast.

GABRIEL: Is that the truth?

CONNIE: Yes. Why?

GABRIEL: It sounds so far-fetched, and you just turned away from me at the end. As lawyers, we're taught to view body language and behavior as clues to untruths.

CONNIE: Palabra de honor. Oops, I'm sorry. You don't speak Spanish.

GABRIEL: I never said that.

CONNIE: You said that your parents...and you haven't really used any Spanish...and, well...do you speak Spanish?

GABRIEL: Sí. Estudié en la secundaria y en el colegio. Siempre quise aprender español.

CONNIE: *[Applauds]* I'm impressed.

GABRIEL: I wasn't sure if you spoke any English. Father Contreras said you hardly spoke a word when he knew you.

CONNIE: A lot he knows. What makes him think he knows so much? I haven't seen him in twenty-seven or twenty-eight years. Not since they sent me away... *[Stops]* Mira, que pretty cardinal.

GABRIEL: Where? Who sent you where?

CONNIE: Nada. Never mind. Just talking to myself. No importa.

GABRIEL: *[Stands]* Yes, it is important. He told me the same thing. Said you left your family when you were seventeen, but he neglected to explain why.

CONNIE: Why, who, what! You're beginning to sound like that Stacked Robert in *Unsolved Mysteries*. Is that all you lawyers know how to do— ask questions? *[Rubs forehead]* You're giving me a headache. Making me remember things, things buried so deep in my mind. I tried so hard to forget. *[Walks away]* So many years trying to forget...Do you have any Advil?

GABRIEL: Take your time. It's alright. Try to remember. It's important. *[Puts his arm on her shoulder.]*

CONNIE: *[Turns to him.]* I lied to you.

GABRIEL: So you are my mother?

CONNIE: No, I lied about not being able to have children. Ay, this is so hard for me. I never told nobody about this, not even Hank. *[Composes herself and takes a deep breath, exactly in the way that GABRIEL does.]*

When I was about sixteen, during one of our Christmas visits to Sacramento, I got pregnant. The family consulted with Father Contreras and he advised them what to do. He handled everything and sent me to the watermelon factory here in San Francisco.

GABRIEL: The watermelon factory? He sent you to work?

CONNIE: *[Laughs]* No, that's what we used to call the home for unwed mothers, the one that was maintained by the Archdiocese. All the women walked around like they swallowed a watermelon. It was quite a sight. You stayed there until the baby was born and put up for adoption.

GABRIEL: That must have been so hard for you, separated from your family.

CONNIE: I hated it. Six months of no contact with normal people. Oh, they had lots of activities to keep us busy, to keep us from going crazy. All I did was knit. I didn't speak much English then, so I sat in a corner for six months knitting clothes for the baby. Booties, sweaters, little blankets. One day blue, next day pink.

GABRIEL: What year was that?

CONNIE: Ay, who can remember?

GABRIEL: Please try. The date is very important to me.

CONNIE: I think it was…*[Looks skyward]* let me see…I'm thirty-eight. *[Pause]* Okay, I'm forty-five now, so that would make it—

GABRIEL: And you were seventeen then?

CONNIE: Yes.

GABRIEL: 1968?

CONNIE: Oh, you're fast. How did you figure that out so quick?

GABRIEL: Never mind. Continue, please.

CONNIE: *[Takes a breath]* So, I had the baby towards the end of summer. I even had a name picked out—Angel or Angela. I had convinced myself that the baby was an angel sent from Heaven. Towards the end of the pregnancy, I decided I was going to keep the baby. Of course, I didn't tell anyone.

GABRIEL: And they didn't let you keep it, did they?

CONNIE: She was stillborn.

GABRIEL: She?

CONNIE: Yes. Father Contreras told me that it was a little girl but that she was born dead. I was so sad. I cried for months. How could my baby be dead? I couldn't believe it. I couldn't even look at all the clothes I had knit and I started to burn everything, until one of the nuns took the rest of the clothes away from me.

GABRIEL: What happened then?

CONNIE: I couldn't stand the thought of going back to my family after that experience, so the Archdiocese here helped me to find work cleaning houses, and Angel found me a place to live.

GABRIEL: Who?

CONNIE: What did I say?

GABRIEL: You said Angel.

CONNIE: I meant Father Contreras. I used to call him by his first name because…um…he became such a good friend.

GABRIEL: You planned to name the baby after him?

CONNIE: *[Nods, looks at him.]* What now? What's that look mean?

GABRIEL: Nothing.

CONNIE: More lawyer psychology? You don't believe me, do you?

GABRIEL: Well…not really. Consider this: You tell me an insipid story about—

CONNIE: Momento. Stop using these lawyer words. ¿Qué quiere decir "insipid"?

GABRIEL: It means…innocuous…silly.

CONNIE: Okay, now I know. *[To herself]* Insipid, innocuous. I like the sound of those words. Let me get my pad and pencil.

GABRIEL: You're changing the subject. You don't think that Father Contreras could have lied to you about the baby?

CONNIE: Why would he do that? He's a…priest.

GABRIEL: Come on, don't you read the newspapers? Where did you get this idea that they're so holy? They always lie, to protect themselves, other priests, even the church. *[Pause]* Let's take a hard look at the facts here. I was born on September twenty-seventh, 1968, supposedly right here in San Francisco.

CONNIE: ¿Y qué? You think you were the only person born here on that day?

GABRIEL: No, but that's exactly nine months after Christmas.

CONNIE: But, they said it was a girl.

GABRIEL: Another lie. Where's she buried? Have you seen the grave?

CONNIE: They cremated her.

GABRIEL: Another lie.

CONNIE: *[Covers her ears.]* Stop it! You just don't give up.

GABRIEL: *[Desperate]* I have spent the last two years, two whole years of my very short life, looking for my real mother. It's the only thing keeping me alive. And, before I die, I'd like to know who she is. I want to talk to her. I want to know what kind of food she likes, what kind of music she listens to. All I want is the truth.

CONNIE: Truth? That's a lot to ask for. I guess you'll just have to keep on looking. I'm sure it's not me.

GABRIEL: Why are you so sure?

CONNIE: *[Exasperated]* Otra pregunta. Because…we don't even look alike. You're tall, I'm short; you're dark-haired, I'm not; you're—

GABRIEL: *[Touches her hair.]* I see roots.

CONNIE: *[Slaps his hand.]* Don't touch my hair! What makes you think you have a right to touch me? ¡Esto no lo soporto!

GABRIEL: Forget it. I'm sorry.

CONNIE: You think you can just show up one day after so many years and annunciate to some stranger that she's your mother? No, Gabriel. No.

GABRIEL: I said I was sorry. I guess I'm just wasting your time. *[Stands]* You know what, I think I'll just go. *[Tries another tactic and pretends to leave.]*

CONNIE: No, wait! I'm sorry. Forgive me. I...I overreacted. I shouldn't be so sensitive. Please don't go. Just stay and talk a while longer.

GABRIEL: I can't. *[Pacing around]* I need to go back to Father Contreras. I'm running out of time. And money. You don't understand the situation I'm in. You don't understand the desperation—I'm dying.

CONNIE: I'm trying to understand. But, I'm sorry mijo, I can't pretend to be your mother just to make you happy. It wouldn't be fair to you, or to your real mother.

GABRIEL: I'm just having a hard time accepting things, that's all. It's like there's a...bomb ticking inside of me, and only one person can defuse it. These last two years have been so hard for me.

CONNIE: How many other women have you visited?

GABRIEL: What do you mean?

CONNIE: How many names did Father Contreras give you?

GABRIEL: Just yours.

CONNIE: Ya ves, you've only started to look. Go back to him and try again.

GABRIEL: No. It looks like I struck out on the first try.

CONNIE: *[Desperate]* Don't say that. There's still time. You're still young and energetic. Keep looking. Make it your mission!

GABRIEL: Mission. Ha! The gay, HIV-positive, adopted Junipero Serra in search of the Mother Church. Well, the Catholic Church can eat my afterbirth! That is, if I could ever find it. Do you see how every conversation, every thought in my brain leads to the same thing? Maybe I should go back to that...watermelon factory and talk to them. Maybe they can help me. *[Turns to her. She is looking at her watch.]* Sorry to waste your time.

CONNIE: You're not wasting my time.

GABRIEL: You can leave now. Go ahead.

CONNIE: What?

GABRIEL: Go back to your perfect little life in the suburbs. Back to perfect Hank, the great communicator, and your perfect little children who call you "Mami." No worries. Nobody disturbing the peace and making waves.

CONNIE: What are you talking about? Are you getting those deliriums? I saw something about that on Cristina's show, with all these AIDS people bitching and moaning, just like you right now.

GABRIEL: You know what I mean. Go home. You have a family waiting for you. I don't want to talk to you anymore.

CONNIE: You want me to feel sorry for you and your situation? Is that what you want?

GABRIEL: What do you know about my situation? You don't know anything about pain and suffering. You don't have the foggiest notion what it's like to be gay AND have AIDS.

CONNIE: Is that right? I paid a big price for what I did. I suffered too. You have no idea what it was like being pregnant in Fresno in 1968. It was no picnic. I was a condemned woman.

GABRIEL: Please, don't use that word.

CONNIE: Which one?

GABRIEL: Condemned. I hate it. Catholicism.

CONNIE: What I meant was that no one would want to marry me. I was a marked woman. Lucky for me I had Father Contreras to look after me. He paid for everything, God bless him.

GABRIEL: Why did he pay for everything?

CONNIE: ¡Ay, tú con tus "whys"! I don't know! Don't ask me questions like that. *[Angry]* Ask Father Contreras. You seem to be so friendly with him. Go ask him!

GABRIEL: Why are you getting angry?

CONNIE: Otra vez con esos "whys." Is that all you know—questions?

GABRIEL: That's exactly what I've been doing for two years—torturing myself with questions. And you're not answering any of them.

CONNIE: Perdón, pero esto es el colmo. You've asked me the last question. *[Stands to leave.]* I don't have to take this abuse. *[Walks away, then returns.]* You're just trying to find someone to blame. You'd love it if I took all the responsibility for whoever abandoned you. Maybe you'd even like to blame me for your AIDS. That was your doing. You had a choice in that matter. You should have been more careful.

GABRIEL: You don't know anything. How ignorant can you get living in that Mary Kay fantasy world of yours? *[Moves closer]* You have no idea how I got AIDS!

CONNIE: So, tell me. *[Takes a deep breath.]* Tell me how.

GABRIEL: Why should I? You'll just say what everybody else says.

CONNIE: No. I want to understand. I want to know more.

GABRIEL: You don't want to know.

CONNIE: I do. I care.

GABRIEL: Why?

CONNIE: *[Rolls her eyes]* Just tell me and spare me the Inquisition.

GABRIEL: Fine. I had sex with a priest. Someone I trusted. Someone I never imagined could get AIDS. He told me I was his first, the only one. That's what he told me. Now are you happy? *[Pause]* So…what do you think? Come on, say something!

CONNIE: *[Incredulous]* A priest? Are you sure?

GABRIEL: He wore black pants, a black shirt, little white collar, carried a Bible and a rosary. I'm pretty sure he was a priest.

CONNIE: I mean, are you sure he's the one that gave it to you?

GABRIEL: Are you calling me a liar? Yes, he gave it to me. Nice and gift-wrapped like a Christmas present. I hadn't slept with anybody else in five years.

CONNIE: Where's he now?

GABRIEL: He's dead. He died while I was in the hospital. I tried to look him up, but the church always told me lies. Finally, a friend of his, another priest, told me the truth. Did you know that there's a special rectory where all the priests with AIDS are sent to die? Even today they treat them like lepers.

CONNIE: *[Shakes her head.]* A man of the cloth. Hard to believe.

GABRIEL: I'm wasting my time here. I gotta go.

CONNIE: WAIT! You can't leave.

GABRIEL: Why not?

CONNIE: Because…because…I was already leaving. I was first.

GABRIEL: Fine. Go ahead. *[Sits]* Run away. Like you always have. Run away from your problems.

CONNIE: *[Taking baby steps]* I'm not running. I'm walking. See?

GABRIEL: Go on. Go back to your safe cocoon. Go back to your Volvo station wagon and your precious little children and your PTA meetings.

CONNIE: *[Turns]* Ha! Look who's talking. Mr. Country Club himself. How dare you criticize me and talk about suffering like it's something you can buy at K-mart! You have no right. I went through a lot of pain too. Who was there for me, huh? Who?

GABRIEL: That's not my fault. You had a choice.

CONNIE: *[Yells]* CHOICE? What choice? Do you think he would have let me have an abortion? He was so charming, such a smooth talker. His words were like milk and honey to me, like a choir of angels. I didn't stand a chance. He promised me so many things. He promised to take care of me. *[Crying]* So many promises.

GABRIEL: Who?

CONNIE: We were on a field trip to San Francisco to see the Pope. I was still a virgin. He said it wouldn't hurt. It hurt so much. It still hurts sometimes.

GABRIEL: *[Pressing her]* Who? Who was it that hurt you?

CONNIE: *[Closes her eyes and remembers for the first time]* He said it was God's will that we should be together. I was so stupid. *[Sits]* Why did I believe him? *[Opens her eyes]* ¡Condenado! I never should have done it. NEVER!

GABRIEL: *[Softer]* I'm right here. *[Rubs her back]* Let it all out. Let it go. Come on.

CONNIE: I feel so much pain, so much sadness. So many years of holding it all in. ¡Sinverguenza! He always lied to me. *[Slams her fist on the bench a few times.]* I was so young, so green. I didn't know any better. He was so convincing. *[Sobbing]* All these years and I could not forget. Deep inside me it was like there was a piece missing. No matter what I did, no matter where I went, it was always there, a red hole in my stomach.

You have no idea what it is like to have something, I mean, someone taken away from you.

GABRIEL: Yes I do. *[Hands her a red hankie from breast pocket.]*

CONNIE: I was a good girl. I didn't smoke or drink. I didn't take drugs. One mistake, one little mistake…Why should I be punished for the rest of my life? *[Cries]* Ay, Dios, ¿por qué, por qué?…

GABRIEL: It wasn't your fault. Don't beat up on yourself. There comes a time when you have to have closure. You have to let it go or it could kill you.

CONNIE: I'm sorry. *[Pauses, wipes her eyes, and takes a deep breath. She hands him the hankie.]* Thank you. I think I feel a little better now. Oh, what an old fool I am. I'm so sorry…*[He hands her the hankie again and she blows her nose.]* That's better. Please forgive me.

GABRIEL: Nothing to forgive. Now, aren't you glad you came here today and got that off your chest?

CONNIE: *[Smiles]* Yes. But, what about you?

GABRIEL: Believe me, I've had my share of crying.

CONNIE: No, I meant we still haven't found your mother.

GABRIEL: *[Pauses, shakes his head.]* It doesn't seem so important right now. Maybe I don't need to. Maybe it would be too painful for me, for both of us. But it's been eating away at me for so long. I'm probably better off not knowing for sure.

CONNIE: That's not true. You will find her. And when you do find her, I'm sure she'll take you in her arms and give you all the love you deserve. *[Pause]* You are such a kind person. You came to me with your problems and all I do is burden you with mine.

GABRIEL: My perception is different now. I think all problems, like all pains, are universal. People should help each other more. This whole planet is crying out in pain. Sometimes, when I meditate and it's very quiet, I can almost hear the moans and the sighs of those who have gone before me.

CONNIE: Ay, Dios mío, that's too much for me to worry about. It's hard enough deciding what to wear in the morning, keeping my family's clothes clean, and choosing between Tuna Helper or Hamburger Helper for dinner.

GABRIEL: *[Laughs]* You're so funny. At least you made me laugh a while and forget about my own headaches. Gracias.

CONNIE: I'll bet you really liked it when I lost control and took it out on this bench. I'm sorry I let my emotions run away. Oh, before I forget. *[Takes an envelope out of her purse.]* Write your address here please. Maybe we can start communicating.

GABRIEL: It's okay if I write you?

CONNIE: ¿Y por qué no?

GABRIEL: How will you explain me to Hank?

CONNIE: He won't even notice. He practically lives in his garage—farting around, breaking things then fixing them. He's like a toolbox zombie. If he asks, I'll just tell him that I have a new boyfriend. A handsome one too. *[Arches her eyebrows.]*

GABRIEL: Oh God. Then he'll come looking for me with his power drill or his chain saw. *[Writes his address on the paper.]*

CONNIE: Don't worry. He still hasn't figured out how to plug in the extension cord. *[Takes his address from him.]*

[In the distance, church bells chime noon.]

GABRIEL: *[Glances at his watch.]* Hey, you hear that? You'd better get going or you'll be late.

CONNIE: Okay. *[She slowly begins to gather her belongings.]* Will…you…be alright?

GABRIEL: Yeah, sure. I'm a big boy. I might go over to the Aquarium.

CONNIE: I meant about…the…AIDS.

GABRIEL: Mas o menos. I'm on a new medication.

CONNIE: Have you been taking your medicine?

GABRIEL: *[Sheepishly]* Sometimes I forget.

CONNIE: When are you supposed to take it?

GABRIEL: *[Embarrassed]* Two hours ago.

CONNIE: *[Shakes her head]* Ay, Dios mío. Do you have it with you?

GABRIEL: *[Reaches into his pocket and pulls out a small plastic container.]* Here.

CONNIE: *[Pulls out a small bottle of water from her purse and hands it to him.]* Take it. Andale, take one out and swallow it now.

GABRIEL: Sí, Señora. *[Takes the water and several pills.]* Thanks.

CONNIE: Bien. You know, you are going to have to start taking better care of yourself. *[She pulls out a Kleenex and wipes the side of his mouth.]*

GABRIEL: I know.

CONNIE: I hope this crazy mission to find your mother isn't hurting your health.

GABRIEL: Al contrario, it's the only thing that keeps me alive.

CONNIE: Bueno, then you keep on looking. Just remember to take your pills. And if I was you, I would try to make peace with your parents, the Oreos. They may be crummy people, but they did the best they could, and they still care about you.

GABRIEL: Yeah, whatever...*[Pause]* You better go now.

CONNIE: I wish I could stay longer, but the kids are expecting me.

GABRIEL: It's okay. I understand. Oh, I meant to ask you—

CONNIE: *[Reaches into her purse and quickly retrieves a photograph.]* Mira, aquí están.

GABRIEL: That purse is like Felix the Cat's magic bag. What else have you got in there? *[Looks in.]* Is there a salsa bar in there?

CONNIE: No. *[Laughs]* That's Hank Junior on the left, he's the oldest. He's at Stanford Medical School. Esta es Gloria. She's married and lives in Santa Cruz.

GABRIEL: So, you're a grandmother?

CONNIE: No, not yet. They want to wait a while. *[Back to photographs.]* After Gloria, it's Maria del Carmen—

GABRIEL: What do they call her?

CONNIE: Just Carmen. That's my husband Hank next to me, and this is the baby Joselito.

GABRIEL: He's not exactly a baby. He must be about six feet tall and weighs about…two hundred pounds.

CONNIE: He's the tallest of all of them. He's the quarterback of the high school football team.

GABRIEL: ¡Qué guapo! He's very handsome.

CONNIE: *[Slaps his knee.]* Hands off! He likes girls.

GABRIEL: You never can be too sure. I'm sure he's familiar with conversion plays.

CONNIE: *[Pauses]* Do you still…I mean, can you still…?

GABRIEL: I can, but I've got more important things to worry about now, like staying alive.

CONNIE: Well, be careful, please. *[Puts the photographs away.]* That's all of them.

GABRIEL: Good-looking family—all of them. You're very lucky.

CONNIE: Yes. *[Pause]* Listen, do you want to have dinner with us? I'm sure it will be okay, so long as you keep your hands off Joselito.

GABRIEL: No, no, really. Thank you for asking anyway. It's almost time for my nap. I always make intricate plans to do so much every day, then I get tired. *[Yawns]* Quisiera dormir por cien años.

CONNIE: *[Smacks him gently]* Don't joke like that. *[Pause]* Hablas español muy bien. You have a good accent.

GABRIEL: Gracias. I guess it's all in the genes. *[Smiles a little.]*

CONNIE: Just out of curiosity, what are your parents' names?

GABRIEL: Clem and Rosie. They used to be Clemente and Rosario, until they got delusions of grandeur.

CONNIE: Delusions? Are they sick too? I saw that show on *Lifetime,* "Families in Delusion."

GABRIEL: No, they're just crazy.

CONNIE: Well, they did a good job of raising you. So polite, and smart.

GABRIEL: They can take credit for polite, but the smart part, that's all in the genes.

CONNIE: Sorry, I really should get going. *[Stands.]* Well, mijo. God bless you and keep you.

GABRIEL: *[Jokes]* I hope so 'cause nobody else seems to want to.

CONNIE: Let me know if you need anything. *[Awkward pause]* I feel bad abandoning you here. *[Quickly]* I mean, I wish I could do more.

GABRIEL: You've done a lot already, believe me. I guess I just needed somebody to listen to me, a shoulder to lean on. Thanks again. *[Pauses, looks skyward]* I better go. Looks like it might rain and I didn't bring an umbrella. The last thing I need is a cold. *[Stands]*

[As they hug, he pulls out a little box and envelope from his coat, which he secretly places on the bench next to her purse.]

GABRIEL: Oh, I keep meaning to ask you this—what was your maiden name?

CONNIE: Nieves. Like snows.

GABRIEL: Maria Concepción Nieves. That's cool. *[Pause. Starts backing away.]*

CONNIE: *[Waving]* You keep in touch now. No olvides. ¡Y cuídate! *[They hug.]*

GABRIEL: Adios. Gracias. *[Exits]*

CONNIE: *[Stands watching him for a few seconds. She turns to grab her purse and sees the box and envelope. She sits, opens the envelope, and pulls out a pair of knitted blue baby booties, which she brings to her face and smells. She begins to cry.]* Angel. Angelito. My little Angel.

[Lights go down slowly, as Chavela Vargas' "Con Las Manos Vacías" comes up.]

END

Dolly: Old Lady, Love, and Life

Q. V. Atkins

This monologue is excerpted from the playscript Russian Roulette/Poison Places: Teens Living in the Age of AIDS.

[DOLLY *is downstage. She might have a cart and should also have a cigarette butt in her mouth. As she crosses the stage, she mutters to herself. She is the proverbial "bag lady," a member of the invisible society. She has tried to numb herself with drugs to forget her pain and anger, but it hasn't always been like that.* DOLLY *lets herself remember.*]

[*After a few moments of inaudible muttering,* DOLLY *shouts*]

It wasn't always this way! [*She repeats this a few times*] IT—WASN'T—ALWAYS—THIS—WAY. Hell, I was smart. I WAS. And I was cute, YES I WAS, and, and, I could siiiiiiinnng! Oooh Bobby use to love to hear me sing. [*She takes a beat*] Bobby, my best friend, my love. We had been best friends since preschool. We did everything together, including having sex— "making love" we liked to call it. Everyone said, "You're too young to be in love, you're only seventeen." But when Bobby died, everything changed. For the longest time, I didn't even know what AIDS was and Bobby didn't know too much either. He said he must have "caught" it when he was younger…I don't know, whatever. I didn't know what to believe anymore. Hell, it was too late by that time anyway cause I had started to get sick and we went to the hospital, and sure nuff they told me I was HIV-positive. HIV-positive, AIDS, it all meant the same thing to us. We both felt so lonely, so we stayed with each other and kept having sex. I mean what else could go wrong. . .it couldn't get much worse than that. HA! [*Laughs sarcastically*] We got reinfected. Reinfected! What the hell is that? How the hell can you do that? Oh, we found out all about it, after the fact. The virus hit Bobby twice as hard. Within months, Bobby was dead. He passed away without seeing his child. And I missed him. He had been my best friend my whole life. But I was happy about one thing—I'd always wanted a baby, something of my own to love me and never leave me. *[Her pain returns with the next thought]* It never occurred to me that my baby might be born positive…I wouldn't hurt my baby…I wouldn't hurt my baby on purpose…I wouldn't. *[She starts to break down. She escapes this painful thought and starts to mutter again]* I don't wanna talk about that. *[Shaking her head.]* I don't want to talk about that…But it wasn't always this way. I don't even know why God is keeping me here. Why are you keeping me here? *[Stops, listens, and then answers]* I know, but ain't nobody listening to me. I try telling them about love and this taker of life, but these hard head kids ain't trying to hear me. *[She stops, listens again and then she smiles]* Do what? Sing! *[She takes a beat, shakes her head, closes her eyes and begins to sing her song to God. She is glowing. It's as if in this moment she is in no pain—she is beautiful and transformed. As the song ends, she continues her walk across the stage, humming and then pausing. She looks to her right and sees a* GIRL *at a gravesite, but the* GIRL *does not see her. It can be intimated that she is talking to* DOLLY *as her Mom, and that* DOLLY *has "gone home."]*

Like Mama Like Daughter

Kulwa Apara

This monologue is excerpted from the playscript Russian Roulette/Poison Places: Teens Living in the Age of AIDS.

[A young GIRL *kneels down at a gravesite to speak to her mother. She has with her a bouquet of flowers. She affectionately places them upon the grave. In this scene, she expresses her grief and longing for her mother and her innermost thoughts, which also reveal how much she is like her mother.]*

Mama, it's been ten years since you've said you love me. Ten years since I felt your warm kisses against my cold cheek. Ten years since I've heard the sweet lullaby of your voice. I told you he wasn't good for you. Damn, why couldn't you listen? He gave you HIV, and now I'm left here to ponder in my pain, alone. My diary is kept on my skin. Each wound, bruise, and scar revealing my sadness. But my boo is there for me Mama, he's there so much. Even though he does treat me bad at times, but he just can't help it, you know, he's hurting too. I told him if you was here you would tell him, "you ain't good enough for my baby, naw, you just a good for nothin' nigga!" Yeah, yeah, that's what you would tell 'em. But you ain't here. So what now Mama? Mama, I got something to tell you…I'm positive, but my boo he still love me and he say he'll be wit me always, even though he gave it to me. I told Aunt Sharon 'bout it and she said I'm a damn fool for getting the same shit my Mama died from. Ooh mama, I hope this don't count as suicide, 'cause Lord knows I wanna go to heaven. Shit! It seems like I been in hell ever since you left. Mama I'm sorry, I know you don't like me cussing on a Sunday. Well, I'll talk to you later. Bye…Mama, I love you.

SECTION 3
DANGER/DEATH

Numb

Zelma Brown

How did I get here—into this designer chair with its own purifier? My
beginning was in an alleyway, dark with distrust, shadows bending,
drawing venom and pushing sleep into my veins. My story starts here.

Slow, pulling thorns from
my arms.
This place where I sleep is covered with
nasty dreams.
My chest pulls the stench that's caught up in the air.
I breathe.
My mind pounds with the thoughts of
what ifs.
I try to look to tomorrows yet I only end up
with today.
The thorns have infected my body with a tinge
of disgust,
that smells like candy left in the sun.
It's poison,
and it's killing me.

*I would swear that H, I and V are phantoms that haunt me, hunting me down
like an animal in strange lands. My paranoia is surrounding my very thought.*

What do they have planned for me?
I know they plot my destruction.
They work hand in hand
towards my demise.
They hope to torture my body
and steal my mind.
I see them ducking in and out of crowds
with smiles as big as rainbows.
There is no pleasure here.

What do they have planned for me?
Will it be a painful end?
Slow?
Some of them have already penetrated my blood
and they pull even more
at my soul.

What do they have planned for me,
these fucked up new friends called
H, I and V?

I'm hopeless. Gradually I lose control of my body and my mind. I'm tired of
hiding the truth about me. Worried about being ostracized, not being
touched, no longer the freedom of love from strangers. Was it really love?
Someone didn't love me too much, now did they? The thought of loneliness
will surely kill me. The pain of it, I can't bear. I can't stand it.

Help me! Help me! Help me! This must end. It must end now!

I SIT
My feet dangle over this golden gateway,
the waters seduce me with every wave and curl.
I INHALE
And taste the salt of the ocean
mixing with my fears.
I FLY
And it's almost like I float on air.
I HIT
And the rush of the cold sea embraces me.
A LIGHT
As I rise towards it I feel relief. It's almost over.
I AWAKE
And I breathe the air from a machine's purity.
I FEEL
Nothing from my neck down.
I DIE.

Daily there is no smile.
I WAIT. I CRY. I'VE FAILED.
And now I suffer.
I regret.

My loneliness, my hopelessness is mine, and it is ok to have. With these lessons of failure I've learned that life is still life. It didn't have to be this way. I
mean, I've always made bad choices, but not any more.

I've learned to accept my new life-time companions, and I'm positive.
With the aid of my new friends, H, I and V, I am learning the true
importance of life.

Black Power Barbie

Shay Youngblood

Characters

TABITHA: African American female, late twenties; also YOUNG TABITHA

JACKSON: African American male, mid-twenties; also YOUNG JACKSON

THERAPIST: White female, 30-60 years old

PAOLO: Hispanic male, 25-30 years old; also HANNIBAL, the father

MADONNA: Hispanic female, 25-30 years old; also LENA, the mother

Author's Note:

TABITHA and her younger brother, JACKSON, the children of murdered revolutionaries, battle over Black Power Barbie as they relive vivid and frightening memories in therapy sessions. As adults, TABITHA remains psychologically wounded, living in the past, while JACKSON faces the reality of living with AIDS. They both discover romantic love and struggle to hold on to it.

Costume Notes:

TABITHA (also YOUNG TABITHA) wears a white T-shirt underneath a black flared jersey dress and dark flats or sneakers.

JACKSON (also YOUNG JACKSON) wears a white T-shirt, black jeans and sneakers. He changes into a bra, pink petticoat and red baby-jane shoes; then an afro wig, red dress and red high heels.

THERAPIST wears a conservative suit with white blouse and pumps.

PAOLO (also HANNIBAL) wears a white shirt, loose pants and bare feet or sandals.

MADONNA (also LENA) wears her hair short or pulled back, dark lipstick, a black leather jacket, white T-shirt, a short dress or skirt and black work boots. A pink ribbon is pinned to her jacket.

Prologue: Therapist's office

[TABITHA *lies motionless on the floor clutching* BLACK POWER BARBIE *as the* THERAPIST *speaks.*]

THERAPIST: When I was a little girl I used to like climbing trees. I wasn't content to sit on the low branches and watch the world go by. I would climb higher and higher into the heart of a tree as easy as a monkey. I would keep climbing higher and higher until I reached the very top. I would look down on the rest of the world as if I were a god. I would make cars disappear, whole families would vanish from my kingdom with the wave of my hand. One day I fell out of the tree and I broke my arm and sprained my ankle. I tried to forget the pain, to wave it away, but it didn't work. Yet, when I cried out someone was there to comfort me and wipe away my tears. I'll always remember the pain but I'll never stop climbing to the very tops of trees or waving my hand to make bad things disappear. Sometimes it works. Sometimes I remember how to take the pain away.

[JACKSON *enters and helps* TABITHA *to sit upright on the sofa.*]

TABITHA: My name is Nzingah Sojourner Afri'can.

JACKSON: My name is Noble Adesanya Afri'can. We changed our names to protect our innocence.

TABITHA: *Bewitched* was my favorite TV show. I wanted to be a little witch with magic powers just like Tabitha.

JACKSON: I named myself after one of the Black Panthers.

TABITHA: You are so black.

JACKSON: What do you mean by that?

TABITHA: You could've been John Doe or Jack Smith, but you had to be the center of attention. You could've gotten us killed trying to be so black.

THERAPIST: What do you mean Tabitha?

TABITHA: He forgot about the tool kit.

JACKSON: What tool kit?

TABITHA: Daddy put me in charge of the Black Person's Tool Kit for Survival After a Major Action Against Your Community. Number one:

Change your appearance. Number two: Change your address. Number three: Change your name. Number four: Defend yourself in ways the enemy wouldn't think of. But you must never, my little warrior, change your attitude.

Scene One: Tabitha and Jackson's living room, 1973

[A silent mini TV glows in the darkness. Spotlight on YOUNG TABITHA, *a melodramatic eight-year-old child lost in her play world. She sings as she plays with* BLACK POWER BARBIE. YOUNG JACKSON, *her brother, is five years old and very shy.]*

YOUNG TABITHA: *[sings]* My grandma and your grandma was sitting by the fire. My grandma called your grandma a gray-headed two-faced liar. Talking bout hey now, hey now, waffle waffle one day… *[hums a little as she dances* BLACK POWER BARBIE *around]* One day, when I'm grown, we gonna live in a big house. It's gonna have lots of windows so we can see outside, so we can look at birds flying south for the winter. Our house gonna be big, its gonna be bigger than Florida, bigger than the whole United States. We gonna have parties in our house with lots of food. Lemon cake and champagne and oranges. I'm gonna invite all our friends. And if he want to, Jesse Jackson can come. Aaaaand Mohammed Ali, aaaaand Angela Davis. She so pretty ain't she? I wouldn't cry if she combed my hair, cause then, when I'm grown, I'm gonna look like Tina Turner and my hair gonna be so long, Mama's gonna have to take a bus all the way to California to brush it at the end. Then we'll be in Hollywood and we'll be in the movies and we'll be famous.

*[*YOUNG JACKSON *enters]*

YOUNG JACKSON: That's so stupid.

YOUNG TABITHA: Get back Jack or I'll have to attack. *[Points her fingers at him like pistols]*

YOUNG JACKSON: Your hair can't be that long.

YOUNG TABITHA: But I can be a movie star like Dorothy Dandridge was in *Carmen.* I can be pretty and sing and dance and wear zebra bikini panties and a pink dress just like in that movie.

YOUNG JACKSON: I wanna be somebody.

YOUNG TABITHA: Silver.

YOUNG JACKSON: Silver?!

YOUNG TABITHA: Yes. You can be Silver, the rich and famous horse who rides with the Lone Ranger. Silver is the star of that show. If you be Silver I'll let you play with Black Power Barbie.

YOUNG JACKSON: OK.

YOUNG TABITHA: First I gotta brand you.

YOUNG JACKSON: What for?

YOUNG TABITHA: Cause that's what they do to horses on TV. C'mon, let's go out to the kitchen.

YOUNG TABITHA and YOUNG JACKSON: *[Singing as they go to the kitchen]* Home, home on the range, where the deer and the spiders wear lace. Where seldom is heard a dis-turbing turd and the skies are not cloudy all day.

YOUNG TABITHA: Close your eyes and count to a hundred.

YOUNG JACKSON: What for?

YOUNG TABITHA: Be-caaaaause.

[YOUNG JACKSON closes his eyes. YOUNG TABITHA turns on the stove and heats a potato masher. She hums as she dances BLACK POWER BARBIE around.]

YOUNG TABITHA: Don't look. *[She brands him on the forehead.]*

[YOUNG JACKSON screams. YOUNG TABITHA laughs wickedly.]

Scene Two: Therapist's office

[TABITHA plays with BLACK POWER BARBIE during her therapy session.]

THERAPIST: Tabitha, what was your motivation for branding your brother?

TABITHA: Motivation? I didn't want his nasty little hands on my Barbie.

THERAPIST: So you wanted to be in control?

[Flashback to an earlier time. LENA and HANNIBAL enter.]

LENA: I wish this trial was over. I've got a bad feeling. What if something happens to us?

HANNIBAL: I'm teaching Nzingah how to take care of the guns since she's the oldest.

LENA: You haven't been listening to me. They're too young for that, Han.

HANNIBAL: By the time I was seven years old I had seen two grown men hanging from a tree in my backyard. One of them was my uncle.

LENA: It doesn't have to be that way here. We're a long way from Alabama.

HANNIBAL: Not far enough. When does the trial start?

LENA: Next week. I'm trying to get them to drop the conspiracy charges, but they won't let up on first-degree murder.

HANNIBAL: They don't have one ounce of hard evidence.

LENA: They don't have to. They've got the legal power to keep all five of those men and women in jail for a long time.

HANNIBAL: Now, I believe they wanted to overthrow the government. But I don't believe they killed nobody.

LENA: They were trying to kill the devil, but all they did was wake him up.

HANNIBAL: I'm gonna teach my little girl, my little warrior, how to put him to sleep.

LENA: She's only five years old.

HANNIBAL: She's old enough.

[LENA *and* HANNIBAL *exit. Action returns to present therapy session.*]

THERAPIST: So you wanted to be in control?

TABITHA: I didn't mean to hurt him.

THERAPIST: You have to take responsibility for your actions, Tabitha.

TABITHA: It wasn't my fault.

THERAPIST: How old were you both then?

TABITHA: I was eight and he was about four or five.

THERAPIST: How did you feel about your brother?

TABITHA: I didn't feel anything special. I put up with him. He was a pain in the ass when he wasn't getting on my nerves. He was really cute back then, especially when I dressed him up. I guess [pause] I...

THERAPIST: Loved him?

TABITHA: I didn't say that.

THERAPIST: Do you love him?

TABITHA: That's not a fair question, he's not dead yet.

Scene Three: Tabitha's bedroom

[YOUNG JACKSON *sneaks into his sister's room and puts on her red baby-jane shoes, pink petticoat and training bra as she watches unseen. He looks at himself in the full length mirror, pretends to put on makeup. Satisfied, he closes his eyes, clicks his heels together three times, and wishes with all his might. When he opens his eyes,* YOUNG TABITHA *is standing behind him laughing. Silently he takes off each piece of clothing and replaces it.* YOUNG TABITHA *continues laughing uncontrollably as he leaves the room dejected.*]

Scene Four: Therapist's office

THERAPIST: How did you feel when you kidnapped your sister's Barbie doll?

JACKSON: She wasn't a doll. Black Power Barbie was very much alive for me then. We were going to have twin daughters and live in a dream house. We were going to live in a tree house on the edge of a canyon. We would watch the sunsets. I would swim in the ocean every day.

THERAPIST: Jackson, how do you feel about your sister?

JACKSON: She's my hero. I love my sister, but I wanted to live with Barbie.

[*Flashback to* YOUNG JACKSON *and* YOUNG TABITHA*'s living room.* YOUNG JACKSON *and* YOUNG TABITHA, *ages nine and twelve, are in a children's play world.*]

YOUNG JACKSON: Why do I have to wear the dress?

YOUNG TABITHA: Be-caaaause I'm in charge.

[YOUNG JACKSON *puts on the dress*]

YOUNG JACKSON: Now can I play with Barbie?

YOUNG TABITHA: Black Power Barbie! Not until you put on Mama's afro wig.

YOUNG JACKSON: You crazy!

YOUNG TABITHA: You want to play with her don't you?

YOUNG JACKSON: Yeah, but...

YOUNG TABITHA: Here, put it on. *[Hands him the wig]*

*[*YOUNG JACKSON *puts on wig.* YOUNG TABITHA *hands him a mirror.* YOUNG JACKSON *looks in the mirror and begins to primp.]*

TABITHA: Here, you can play with her for four-and-three-quarter minutes.

*[*YOUNG TABITHA *hesitantly hands* BLACK POWER BARBIE *to* YOUNG JACKSON, *who is very excited.]*

YOUNG JACKSON: *[Sings as he plays with* BLACK POWER BARBIE*]* Miss Mary Mack, Mack, Mack, all dressed in black, black, black, with silver buttons, buttons, buttons, all down her back, back, back. And I love coffee, coffee, coffee, and I love tea, tea, tea, and I love the boys, boys, boys, and the boys love me, me, me.

YOUNG TABITHA: That's pretty good. Time's up.

YOUNG JACKSON: No fair.

YOUNG TABITHA: OK, one more minute.

YOUNG JACKSON: Turn around, I want private.

YOUNG TABITHA: Privacy.

YOUNG JACKSON: That's what I want.

YOUNG TABITHA: OK.

*[*YOUNG TABITHA *turns around.* YOUNG JACKSON *goes outside and climbs into the tree house. He pulls up the ladder and laughs.* YOUNG TABITHA *turns around and sees that he is gone.]*

YOUNG TABITHA: Get down out of that tree house this minute with Barbie.

YOUNG JACKSON: No!

YOUNG TABITHA: This is a federal crime. Kidnapping is serious, Jackson.

YOUNG JACKSON: When I grow up and be grown, I'm gonna live in a tree house with Barbie.

[Return to therapy session.]

THERAPIST: Are you afraid of Tabitha?

JACKSON: I'm afraid for her. What's gonna happen to her when I'm dead?

THERAPIST: I've suggested a comfortable facility.

JACKSON: She'd die in an institution. I wish I could take her with me.

THERAPIST: My baby sister had a little red piano once. It was a gift from our grandparents. They gave it to her because she was sick with measles and had to stay home from school for weeks. Well, I had to keep going to school, promise to be nice to her, and I had to listen to her incessant banging on the red piano every day and sometimes into the night. I became obsessed. I wanted that little red piano more than I wanted anything in the whole world. More than curly hair, more than dance lessons, more than a year of summers. I wanted it so badly that I wished my baby sister would disappear so that I could have it all to myself. I imagined all the songs I would sing, all the tunes I would play. I could even see my own ten little fingers touching each smooth black and white key. That summer my baby sister and I went swimming in an abandoned water tower. She drowned only a few feet away from me. After her funeral, to ease my pain, my parents gave me the little red piano. Be careful what you wish for Jackson.

Scene Five: Jackson's car

[TABITHA *plays with* BLACK POWER BARBIE *as* JACKSON *drives the car.*]

TABITHA: Close your eyes.

JACKSON: I'm driving the car, Tabitha.

TABITHA: If you close your eyes I'll let you play with Black Power Barbie.

JACKSON: That doesn't work anymore.

TABITHA: You don't love us anymore?

JACKSON: I love you too much.

TABITHA: What about Black Power Barbie?

JACKSON: I grew up and she didn't. What do you want for dinner tonight?

TABITHA: Black Power Barbie and I will be dining out tonight. She'll be wearing her gold lamé evening gown with a mink collar and her glass slippers, in case the Prince is there. We shall drink champagne and eat oranges. Black Power Barbie and I will be dining out tonight.

JACKSON: Paolo is coming over tonight.

TABITHA: I don't care.

JACKSON: What does that mean?

TABITHA: It means that I don't care if you fuck that cute young boy in Mama's bed.

JACKSON: You have a filthy mouth.

TABITHA: Just make sure you use a condom.

JACKSON: Tabitha!

[Pause]

TABITHA: Do you fuck him or does he fuck you?

JACKSON: We do a lot more than fuck.

TABITHA: Like what else, play Scrabble?

JACKSON: We talk, watch TV. *[Pause for effect]* Kiss…bite…wrestle…OK, sometimes we fuck, but I always use a condom.

TABITHA: Are you a top or a bottom?

JACKSON: Where do you get this…

TABITHA: Are you?

JACKSON: It depends.

TABITHA: On what?

JACKSON: Who's in charge?

TABITHA: Black Power Barbie is always in charge. *[Pause]* I learned some curse words in Portuguese, you want to hear?

JACKSON: Do you like Paolo?

TABITHA: I like him alright. Black Power Barbie likes him a lot. He taught us how to say "you fucking asshole" in Portuguese. *[Competitively]* He's been to Brazil you know.

JACKSON: I didn't know he spoke Portuguese too. Did he tell you about the rainforest? Did he tell you how it smells at night—like the breath of Angels?

TABITHA: No, but he told me he had a Barbie once. He didn't steal other people's.

JACKSON: Do you talk about Barbie in session?

TABITHA: That's my business.

JACKSON: Do you talk about me?

TABITHA: Isn't that why we have to go to see that nutty doctor every week? Will you put on the dress?

JACKSON: No.

TABITHA: Please Jackson.

JACKSON: No Tabitha, I don't want to be the mommy anymore.

Scene Six: Therapist's office

[JACKSON *is depressed and withdrawn.*]

JACKSON: After our parents were murdered, Tabitha was afraid to sleep by herself.

THERAPIST: When did you start touching her?

JACKSON: When she asked me to.

THERAPIST: Did she force you?

JACKSON: No, I liked touching her feet. It was private, between us. She has the most beautiful feet I've ever seen. Perfectly shaped toes. Elegantly curved ankles. I would put special oil between her toes and massage the soles of her feet with the heel of my hand. She never had to force me. Touching her feet was just part of loving her. I kissed them once, but she pushed me away. She said I couldn't love her like that. Sometimes when I couldn't sleep, she would press the soles of her feet against my forehead. She said she was taking the pain away by walking on it. My sister is very complex. She's smart too. I always thought she'd be the first Black Woman Superhero.

THERAPIST: What did you think you were going to be, Jackson?

[*Flashback to* LENA *and* HANNIBAL.]

LENA: Let's have an old-fashioned Christmas this year.

HANNIBAL: Lena, you know how I feel about all that shit.

LENA: Just this last time, I promise. *[Pause]* She wants a doll.

HANNIBAL: A doll! You can't be serious? She told me she wanted a pearl-handled pistol just like mine.

LENA: You know I don't want her messing with guns yet.

HANNIBAL: She's got to learn sometime.

LENA: Noble wants one too.

HANNIBAL: A gun?

LENA: No, a doll.

HANNIBAL: You want him to be a girl?

LENA: I want him to be happy. They want...Barbie dolls.

HANNIBAL: Barbie!

LENA: Shhh! You're gonna wake them up. They want Black Barbie.

HANNIBAL: Good old-fashioned capitalism.

LENA: They're still children.

HANNIBAL: How about a Black Power Barbie for our little revolutionary Nzingah?

LENA: What about Noble?

HANNIBAL: A tool box with a hammer and a box of new nails. My boy is gonna build a nation.

[Return to therapy session.]

THERAPIST: Jackson, what did you think you were going to be when you grew up?

JACKSON: A scientist. *[Pauses to think, upbeat]* Or a finger snapping, hip swinging, wig wearing sissy.

Scene Seven: Therapist's office

TABITHA: *[Chants as she circles the room]* Sinful, disgusting heathens! Sinful, disgusting, heathens! Sinful, disgusting heathens! You will burn in hell!

JACKSON: That's what Aunt Laurel screamed at us when she found us playing house. I became a man's man. Our uncle took me camping. I started hammering things. Aunt Laurel's good china…my head against the wall…nails into the palms of my hand.

TABITHA: You didn't want to be a sissy anymore?

THERAPIST: I'm the therapist, shouldn't I be asking the questions?

JACKSON: I was not a sissy.

TABITHA: Was too.

JACKSON: Was not.

TABITHA: Was.

JACKSON: Not.

TABITHA: When the bad men broke the windows, you made us hide.

JACKSON: The bad men wanted to kill all of us. The FBI. The CIA…

TABITHA: Shut up Jackson.

JACKSON: They thought we were dangerous Marxists. We were just a family.

TABITHA: Tell him to shut up. We can't talk about that.

THERAPIST: Why, Tabitha?

TABITHA: I never want to be that scared again. Sissies are scared of everything.

THERAPIST: Jackson saved your lives.

TABITHA: Now me and Black Power Barbie have got to save his.

THERAPIST: How, Tabitha? She's only a molded piece of plastic. She can't think, let alone discover a cure for your brother's disease.

TABITHA: Shut up. She's my hero. She can fix things. She made the bad men go away. She made them think we were dead like Mommy and Daddy. Bang, bang, you're dead. [TABITHA *points* BLACK POWER BARBIE *at the* THERAPIST]

Scene Eight: Jackson and Tabitha's living room

[TABITHA *and* PAOLO *are making brightly colored paper flowers.*]

TABITHA: Now tell me how to say "Fight the Power" in French.

PAOLO: I don't speak French.

TABITHA: I thought you said you used to live in France.

PAOLO: When I was a baby. I was born there. My parents moved around a lot. We lived like gypsies.

TABITHA: In tents? Did you ride camels in the desert?

PAOLO: No, we lived in very fancy apartments and I rode to school in a chauffer-driven Mercedes Benz.

TABITHA: You sound sad about it. Didn't you like being rich?

PAOLO: No. It wasn't much fun.

TABITHA: Didn't you have a lot of friends?

PAOLO: I didn't like making friends, because I was always saying good-bye.

TABITHA: Oh. *[Pause]* Why do you sleep with my brother when you know he's gonna die?

PAOLO: Because I love him.

TABITHA: You're not afraid to touch him?

PAOLO: There is danger when you don't touch. The first year after I left the University my brother and I took a trip to Spain with some boys we knew. We traveled together every spring. The first spring Marcel was missing. Then Isaac and Hector died. Then my brother Adrian. The two of us left were too sad to live but too scared to kill ourselves. It was very difficult to continue living, but we found ways.

TABITHA: How?

PAOLO: I keep loving. I'm not afraid to say good-bye anymore.

TABITHA: Do you love me too?

PAOLO: Yes.

TABITHA: *[Coy]* Do you want to touch me?

PAOLO: I have a different kind of love for you.

[PAOLO takes TABITHA in his arms and begins to tango around the room with her. JACKSON watches them.]

TABITHA: Paolo?

PAOLO: Yes, Tabitha?

TABITHA: When you leave, don't say good-bye.

Scene Nine: Jackson and Tabitha's living room

[TABITHA *and* JACKSON *are on the sofa. She is watching TV intently, her back to him.*]

JACKSON: I'm gonna miss you.

TABITHA: Then don't go.

JACKSON: I can't not die. I've got AIDS, Tabitha. You can't kiss it and make it go away.

TABITHA: You could try harder. I read about creative visualization.

[*A timer sounds*]

Time for your treat.

[*She gives him a pill and a glass of water.*]

Close your eyes and take a deep breath. [*Pause*] Breathe in. [*She breathes in and speaks. Slowly.*] Your breath is healing, massaging your internal organs. [*Pause*] Breathe out. [*Pause*] Breathe in. [*Pause*] Breathe out. [*Pause*] Now you must imagine the most beautiful place in the world.

JACKSON: All I see is black.

TABITHA: Look deeper.

JACKSON: Can I open my eyes?

TABITHA: It only works if you close your eyes.

JACKSON: Alright, my eyes are closed and I'm breathing.

TABITHA: Now imagine someplace beautiful, someplace calm, a perfect place. [*Pause*] Now you're in heaven with Mommy and Daddy. [*Pause*] Soon I'll be there with Black Power Barbie. [*Pause*] Do you think tofu tastes the same when you're dead?

[*Doorbell rings*]

TABITHA: That must be your two-legged treat.

Scene Ten: Jackson's bedroom

[Lying on a big bed, PAOLO *sings a few lines of an aria from an Italian opera in the dark. Lights up on* JACKSON *as he approaches the bed and joins* PAOLO *under the white sheets. They are playful and passionate.]*

PAOLO: What's this? *[Holds up a dreamcatcher hung from the bedpost]*

JACKSON: A dreamcatcher.

PAOLO: What does it do with the dreams you don't want?

JACKSON: A great winged spider swoops down and eats them alive.

PAOLO: I want all my dreams, even the bad ones. They give me strength. They guide me. They help me to understand where I'm going. I dreamed about your sister last night.

JACKSON: What did you dream?

PAOLO: *[Animated]* The three of us, me, you, your sister, were walking around in a zoo. On one of the paths we came face to face with a gathering of large exotic birds. They started flying around our heads, circling closer and closer until we could touch their feathers. They folded us beneath their wings and flew us to a garden filled with calla lilies and birds of paradise. There was a loud noise like thunder and when I looked around you were gone, the birds were gone. Your sister and I were alone but we could hear you, we could hear you singing an opera.

JACKSON: So you were safe and I was singing.

PAOLO: In Italian.

JACKSON: You're a great tutor, but my Italian still sucks.

PAOLO: Don't you think the dream means something?

JACKSON: I think it means you shouldn't eat pork so late at night. I dream the most ordinary dreams in this bed. Sometimes I don't dream at all.

PAOLO: I have the most vivid dreams when I sleep with you. This is an amazing bed.

JACKSON: It's my mother's bed.

PAOLO: Fucking in your mother's bed takes courage.

JACKSON: She's dead, so it doesn't matter.

[Pause]

PAOLO: When we go to Mexico…

JACKSON: I'm gonna swim in the ocean every day.

PAOLO: We'll eat fresh fish and run in the sand.

JACKSON: Tabitha doesn't like fish.

PAOLO: Then we'll eat steak.

JACKSON: She's a vegetarian.

PAOLO: Then we'll rent a villa with a garden near the ocean.

JACKSON: You make me want to live a long time.

PAOLO: You make me want to die so that I can be with you forever.

JACKSON: Who'd take care of Tabitha?

PAOLO: She's really strong. Have you seen her muscles lately? *[Pause]* Your sister is really into this Black Power Barbie thing, isn't she?

JACKSON: Yeah, she's very serious.

PAOLO: She's kind of like a superhero?

JACKSON: Barbie or my sister?

PAOLO: Both.

JACKSON: Yeah, I guess they're both superheroes.

PAOLO: Sometimes I wanted to be Barbie.

JACKSON: I wanted to possess her.

[JACKSON kisses PAOLO on the lips. Instrumental jazz plays as JACKSON and PAOLO make love.]

Scene Eleven: Therapist's office

THERAPIST: Tabitha, why are you so angry?

TABITHA: You've never been Black have you?

THERAPIST: Well, I…I…

TABITHA: The last time I went shopping in a big department store downtown, I had to remember to make sure I didn't open my bag for anything or make any sudden moves while I was being followed by store security in case they thought I was stealing. I have to try to remember to not look like a thief. When you go into a store you don't have to think about that do you? That's one reason I'm so damn mad.

THERAPIST: I'm not Black but my friend Alice is, and nobody thinks she's a thief.

TABITHA: Just because you know somebody Black doesn't mean you know me.

THERAPIST: I didn't mean…

TABITHA: We're not coming here anymore.

THERAPIST: You don't have a choice. These are court-ordered sessions.

TABITHA: So! Let the court find us in Mexico.

THERAPIST: You're running away then?

TABITHA: Not just me. All of us.

THERAPIST: We need to talk about why you're here. You set a fire and someone was hurt.

TABITHA: It wasn't my fault. Me and Black Power Barbie were searching for the cure. I saw it in the flames.

THERAPIST: The firefighters found you naked in a tree. You told them you wanted to die.

TABITHA: I wanted to be with mommy and daddy. I want to stay with Jackson. Paolo is teaching us Spanish so we can go to Mexico. We'll find a cure, we'll save him.

Scene Twelve: Jackson's bedroom

[JACKSON and PAOLO are wrestling on the bed. JACKSON begins to cough uncontrollably.]

PAOLO: I'm sorry. Did I hurt you?

JACKSON: No, I'm fine. Maybe we should start the lesson.

PAOLO: ¿De donde es usted?

JACKSON: ¿De donde es usted?

PAOLO: No, emphasis on each syllable. Otra vez. ¿De donde es usted?

JACKSON: ¿De donde es usted?

PAOLO: Bien, muy bien. Un besito.

[JACKSON and PAOLO pucker and kiss gently before continuing the Spanish lesson with occasional coughs from JACKSON. TABITHA looks on sadly then walks into the THERAPIST's office as JACKSON and PAOLO continue the lesson in the background.]

TABITHA: I wanted to hurt them. I wanted to make love to them both. I wanted to hurt myself. I wanted to fly and find a way to make everything beautiful again.

[As if photographs are being taken, stage lights flash. Lights up on TABITHA lying on the couch clutching BLACK POWER BARBIE, watching a blank TV screen. In the bedroom, JACKSON lies in bed coughing. PAOLO takes JACKSON's pulse, then kneels by the bed holding on to his hand. PAOLO kisses his hand and holds it to his cheek. Lights out.

Lights up on TABITHA, who is sitting on the couch alert, as if listening. PAOLO is in bed next to JACKSON, clutching his knees to his chest. JACKSON lies still and silent. Solemn jazz from the love scene up. PAOLO kisses JACKSON on the lips and covers him with the sheet. PAOLO lights candles at the head of the bed or around it and decorates the body with white roses. At the same time, TABITHA speaks to BLACK POWER BARBIE.]

TABITHA: Let's close our eyes and think of someplace beautiful. Morocco at midnight…Taos pueblo at dawn…Inside the mouth of a wet kiss…A Brazilian rainforest where the trees speak Portuguese…Hotel de Dream on Mardi Gras morning. I want lips on mine, hands testing my softness, the safety of arms wrapped around my back. Jackson? *[Calls out]* Jackson? Can you hear me in the rapture?

PAOLO: We miss you. I miss you. Like good…clean…rain.

[PAOLO approaches TABITHA and embraces her. TABITHA lets BLACK POWER BARBIE droop in her grip. She sobs in his arms as the lights fade to black. Lights up on THERAPIST alone on stage.]

THERAPIST: I know what if feels like to lose someone you love. My father accidentally flushed my pet turtle P-Quick down the toilet. He said he was sorry, but he wouldn't let me cry. My mother, to her credit, tried to comfort me with a plate of chocolate chip cookies, but my father didn't know how to deal with his feelings of guilt so he forced me into the car and drove me to the pet store at the mall. My father told me to choose a new pet on the spot. Now I was crying and could hardly see through my tears and my grief over losing my pet turtle, but my father wanted to hurry up and get this off his conscience. I just needed time to grieve. He kept pushing so hard that I turned around and picked the first thing I saw, a little black spider monkey I immediately named P-Quick. It was a disaster. P-Quick peed on the furniture, he ate my homework and finally ran away after two weeks in my house. I've lost things, I've cried over them, but that won't bring them back. You've just got to cry over each memory and grieve your guts raw before you move on. Sometimes it helps to go out and buy yourself a new pair of shoes.

Scene Thirteen: The shoe store

[BLACK POWER BARBIE *watches* TABITHA *try on shoes to the sound of shoe store music from tap to tango and rap to rumba.* MADONNA *enters, and watches* TABITHA. TABITHA *whispers into* BLACK POWER BARBIE*'s ear, then listens and agrees with her.* TABITHA *and* MADONNA *perform a choreographed mating dance. They sit in chairs back to back. They watch each other in the full-length mirror try out shoes in different situations (i.e., dancing, tiptoeing, fencing, tai chi, running, squashing bugs, stomping on an offensive instep). They dance/flirt together in the mirror.* MADONNA *pulls a shoe out of her leather jacket pocket and places it on* TABITHA*'s foot.* TABITHA *pulls a mate from her pocket and puts it on. They dance together offstage with* BLACK POWER BARBIE. *Lights fade to black.*]

Scene Fourteen

[*Lights fade up slowly to dark amber. The echoing sound of high heels clicking on a hard wood floor, walking into the distance. The sound of a door slamming shut.*]

[TABITHA *sits in the dark, watching visual images projected onto the wall behind the bed.*]

[*Painting of a vase of flowers.*]

TABITHA: Window.

[*Photograph of a large tree.*]

TABITHA: Wind.

[*Sculpture of a woman.*]

TABITHA: Wet kiss.

[Drawing of an open door.]

TABITHA: The color red.

[Photograph of PAOLO *dancing with the* THERAPIST.*]*

TABITHA: The number seven.

[Photograph of JACKSON *lying in a casket.]*

TABITHA: A beautiful poem.

[Lights begin to fade out slowly.]

[Dark silhouette of two women kissing.]

TABITHA: Strange blood on my pillow.

[Lights black.]

Scene Fifteen: Therapist's office

[A lamp clicks on.]

THERAPIST: Who is Madonna?

TABITHA: You would say Madonna is a dream I had about my mother.

THERAPIST: What would you say?

TABITHA: I would say that she is this femmy-butch girl I met in a shoe store.

THERAPIST: Femmy-butch girl?

TABITHA: At first I thought she was a boy, but I knew she was a lesbian by the way she looked at my shoes.

THERAPIST: How did she look at your shoes that was different, say, than a boy would look at your shoes?

TABITHA: Before she even touched me, she stroked my shoes with her eyelashes. Like this. *[*TABITHA *demonstrates looking at the* THERAPIST'*s shoes.]* Boys look at my breasts first. Like this. *[*TABITHA *demonstrates]*

THERAPIST: Do you like Madonna?

TABITHA: Black Power Barbie is fascinated.

THERAPIST: What about you? Do you like the way she looks at you?

TABITHA: I like the way she touches me.*[*TABITHA *demonstrates, perhaps kissing the tips of her fingers.]* It makes me nervous, but I like it. My skin tingles and I stop breathing when she touches me. Is that normal?

THERAPIST: It's quite natural to feel an attraction to someone of the same sex. It's quite another matter to do something about it. You've had a great loss in your life—perhaps you're trying to fill it up too quickly.

TABITHA: I think Jackson is jealous.

THERAPIST: Why do you think that?

TABITHA: Last night he showed me a beautiful poem. I wanted to show it to Paolo, but Black Power Barbie said he's not coming back from Brazil.

THERAPIST: Jackson's been dead for two months now and Paolo is very sick. Neither of them is coming back.

TABITHA: You know I don't want to go there.

THERAPIST: I wouldn't be doing my job as your therapist if we didn't go as deep as it's possible to dive. *[Beat]* My grandfather was one of the most successful cake designers in New York City in the twenties. For weddings he would create the most elaborate concoctions of sugar, spinning delicate webs that looked as if an army of possessed spiders had created them. His crystallized doves and bouquets of spring flowers dripping with teardrops of honey flavored dew were so lifelike. One summer my grandfather was asked to bake a twenty-seven tier cake for one of the most powerful Mafia-connected politicians in the country. He baked the cake on the hottest day of the year, and for the first time in his life my grandfather baked a cake that melted and fell twenty-seven layers flat. He was desperate to make an impression on his powerful new client, to keep his reputation—and his head attached to his shoulders—so he expertly iced twenty-seven flat round tins shaped like a wedding cake, with beautiful pink and white frosting. Now my grandfather didn't know that the night before the wedding, the bride had run off with the best man so when my grandfather got to the banquet hall he had no idea the danger he was in. The only reason my grandfather tried to cover up his mistake was to save his reputation, the perception people had of him. You can cover up the truth with pretty pink icing, but sooner or later you have to face the facts, look at what's being covered up underneath.

TABITHA: What happened to your grandfather?

THERAPIST: He told the politician what happened to the cake. The mafioso and his nervous guests laughed so hard they cried. Then my grandfather was made to eat all twenty-seven layers including the tin pans, accompanied by a ten-piece orchestra.

TABITHA: That must've hurt.

THERAPIST: There are consequences to the truth. Now, tell me about the shoe.

[JACKSON *is walking around in the background with the high heels on, admiring them, posing in them, dancing in them.*]

TABITHA: Madonna gave me a shoe from my mother's closet, like the ones my brother used to wear. It's a tall, red leather shoe with a pointed toe. I never saw my mother wear them. She kept them in a box underneath her bed. My mother wore shoes for running, running from the bad men. My father wore combat boots, he was always ready for war. When the bad men came to kill us, me and my brother were underneath the bed playing with my mother's shoes. We pretended to be dead. When we came back to life all we had left were Black Power Barbie and my mother's shoes.

THERAPIST: Why did the bad men want to kill you?

TABITHA: We were dangerous.

THERAPIST: In what way?

TABITHA: We were educated and armed. Mama wanted to kill all the pigs and Daddy wanted to put them on trial.

THERAPIST: Your parents were revolutionaries?

TABITHA: They were lawyers. They gave me Black Power Barbie when I was six years old. "The time has come for you to know things, little girl." Daddy's voice was thunder. "The time has come for you to do things, little girl." Mommy's voice was rain. Black Power Barbie said, "Be quiet as a mouse. Close your eyes against the blood. Fold your ears against the screams, close your mind to the memory. Sleep," she said, very quietly. "Pretend that you are dreaming." Don't make me remember this part.

[*Flashback to* LENA *and* HANNIBAL *dancing close around the room. There is a loud knock at the door.* HANNIBAL *answers the door.*]

HANNIBAL: Who sent you here?

LENA: What's the problem officer?

HANNIBAL: You better get out of my house with this bullshit.

LENA: Get your goddamn hands off me!

[Sound of gunshots. LENA *screams.* HANNIBAL *falls dead. More gunshots.* LENA *falls dead. Return to present.]*

TABITHA: And that is everything. That is all I know.

THERAPIST: You've had a very hard life.

TABITHA: Nothing is ever what it seems. This is nothing. This is not my life. One day when I'm old and gray I'll mix the ashes of everybody I ever loved with a teaspoon full of honey and I'll spread them on a piece of toast and I'll eat them for breakfast. I'll wash them down with ginger tea and lemon. Then I'll lay down and dream and we'll be together again.

THERAPIST: Are you sad? Do you want to cry?

TABITHA: Everybody's gone and nobody said good-bye.

Scene Sixteen: Tabitha's bedroom

[TABITHA lies in bed with her eyes closed. JACKSON appears and begins to interrogate her as he walks in circles around the room.]

JACKSON: Is Madonna your girlfriend?

TABITHA: Why are you asking me that?

JACKSON: I saw you whisper in her ear.

TABITHA: I whisper in your ear, but you're not my girlfriend.

JACKSON: I saw the way you kissed her. You didn't tell the therapist that.

TABITHA: So I kissed her. So I don't tell that witch everything.

JACKSON: So is she your girlfriend?

TABITHA: We've only had one date.

JACKSON: How did you meet her?

TABITHA: The way you meet people.

JACKSON: At the bookstore?

TABITHA: No.

JACKSON: Store 24?

TABITHA: No.

JACKSON: The hospital?

TABITHA: No.

JACKSON: Is it gonna be like this all night? Twenty questions? You didn't used to be like this.

TABITHA: You didn't used to be dead.

JACKSON: You used to hardly leave the house unless Paolo was with you. Now you're hanging out everyday with some Spanish chick.

TABITHA: She's not Spanish, she's Latina.

JACKSON: Same difference.

TABITHA: Bee brain, it's not the same.

JACKSON: OK, so she's Latina. Where did you meet her?

TABITHA: At a shoe store.

JACKSON: A shoe store?

TABITHA: I bought these. *[She holds up a pair of shoes]*

JACKSON: Where you gonna wear those?

TABITHA: On my next date with Madonna. There are some things I want to remember.

Scene Seventeen: Tabitha's living room

[Surrounded by shoes and shoe boxes, MADONNA and TABITHA play a storytelling game.]

MADONNA: You roll first.

[TABITHA rolls the dice.]

MADONNA: Now pick your man or your woman. Buddha, Mother Teresa, Yemaya, Tina Turner, Che or Shango?

TABITHA: Tina Turner.

*[*TABITHA *chooses a piece of green beach glass and holds it up to the light.]*

MADONNA: Yemaya.

*[*MADONNA *holds up a shiny blue disk.* TABITHA *rolls the dice, moves her playing piece, and picks a card which she reads aloud.]*

TABITHA: "Tell a story about something you do to relax." That's easy. I like to lie down in the closet on top of a couple of blankets with the door open just a crack. It feels safe when I'm inside. It smells like all the people who've ever lived in the house. It smells like moth balls and dust, old things and lavender. Sometimes I think I could stay inside of closets forever. But it's dark and it's lonely in there. Your turn.

MADONNA: I would die in a closet. I couldn't breathe or salsa very well. My leather jacket would get moldy...

TABITHA: You could leave it open just a little.

MADONNA: Either you're in the closet or you're out. *[Rolls the dice, moves her playing piece, and picks a card.]* "Tell a story about an aroma you remember from your childhood." That's hard. Let me think a minute. *[Closes her eyes and sniffs about, then makes a face.]* The smell of my brother's underwear. He used to wake me up in the mornings by throwing a pair of his dirty underwear on my face. The smelliest things you can imagine. Like rotten eggs and spoiled milk and sweat and piss. When I was about fifteen and he was twenty I got up my nerve and I paid him back by dumping an entire laundry basket full of dirty clothes on his head when he was sleeping. He beat me so bad I had bruises for weeks. My father put him out of the house and I haven't seen him to this day. I can't say I miss him or his funky underwear.

TABITHA: I used to be really mean to my brother, then he died. I'm sorry now.

MADONNA: I'm not. I mean, I'm not sorry my brother is gone. I have another perfectly good one. Manuelito...he's so sweet you could pour him on a pancake. He's still inside his closet waiting for someone to join him in the dark. He's married to a very nice girl and they have two sweet little boys. He puts on a suit every morning and puts in time at a downtown law firm. But he spends his evenings in the park by the river waiting for a little bit of pleasure and a bowl full of pain. Go on, it's your turn.

[TABITHA *rolls dice, moves, and picks a card.*]

TABITHA: "Describe something that made your father happy." My father used to love it when I would give him a manicure. I would soak his hands in green dish soap, squeezing each finger until he screamed, then I would brush underneath his nails and clean under each one with a long metal file. Then I would rinse his hands in warm water, dry them and push back the cuticles. He would let me paint them with clear nail polish when I was done. When they were dry I would kiss each finger and put his hands to my face like this. [*Demonstrates on* MADONNA's *face.*] His hands were big and rough and I felt so safe then. Sometimes he let me clean his guns. I'd forgotten about that. He was happy when I learned how to shoot his gun, to protect myself and my brother. [*Pause*] Your turn.

MADONNA: I don't like guns.

TABITHA: You don't have to like them to know how to use them. You never know when you might have to protect yourself.

MADONNA: I have other ways of protecting myself [*Does martial arts style kicks.*]

TABITHA: I'm impressed.

MADONNA: And Shango can kick some ass when he has to.

TABITHA: You believe in voodoo?

MADONNA: I believe in what works. Santeria has a rich history of results. My Egun guided me to you *and* a new pair of shoes.

TABITHA: I'd say you have an unfair advantage.

MADONNA: You're the one with the gun.

TABITHA: I don't use guns anymore. We don't have to. Your turn. [*Gives her the dice.*]

MADONNA: "What was one of the first ways you earned money?" [*Pause*] I'd rather not answer that one.

TABITHA: That's not fair. We promised to tell each other everything. How else are we gonna get to know each other?

MADONNA: OK. [*hesitantly*] Sitting on my uncle's lap.

TABITHA: What?

MADONNA: *[Louder]* Sitting on Uncle Nicky's lap. That's one of the first ways I earned money. He would sit me on his lap facing the TV and he would say, "Pretend you're riding a circus pony," and we would gallop through episodes of *Lassie* and *I Love Lucy* until his pants were wet.

TABITHA: I'm sorry.

MADONNA: It's OK. It was a long time ago. Can I pick another one?

TABITHA: Sure.

MADONNA: "With your eyes closed, draw a picture of a house."

[MADONNA closes her eyes and uses her hands to draw a house around TABITHA.]

MADONNA: I see you in my house. I see you every night in my dreams.

TABITHA: I see my brother in my house. Hotel de Dream, where nothing there is what it seems.

MADONNA: Is he living or dead in your dreams?

TABITHA: I'm not sure he really died when they said he did. He comes to me every night. He knows about you.

MADONNA: What does he know about me?

TABITHA: That you like me. He's jealous.

MADONNA: Why?

TABITHA: He thinks you'll take me away from him, keep me from dreaming.

MADONNA: He shouldn't be jealous.

TABITHA: Take another card.

MADONNA: OK. "Tell another player about something that makes you feel good."

[MADONNA leans toward TABITHA's ear and whispers. The sound of their loud, sensual whispers overlap in English and Spanish as MADONNA and TABITHA speak simultaneously.]

MADONNA: Besa mi sonrisa por la mañana, antes de que el día vuele por la ventana.

En la tarde, unta tu perfume a lo largo de mis piernas. Abre tus cristales empañados en la noche silenciosa y oscura.

Alumbra mi sendero con una llama que nunca muere.

Nunca muere. Muere nunca.

TABITHA: When you kiss my smile in the morning before day flies through the window.

When you spread your perfume upon my thighs in the twilight hours, opening all your shuttered windows in the dark and silent night.

When you crawl beneath my skin with jeweled fingers. Light my way with a flame that never dies.

Never dies. Never dies.

[MADONNA *and* TABITHA *begin to make love.*]

Scene Eighteen: Therapist's office

[*Lights click on.*]

TABITHA: I kissed her on the lips.

THERAPIST: Do you think that you're a lesbian now?

TABITHA: I don't know.

THERAPIST: You've only kissed her once.

TABITHA: I've slept with Black Power Barbie since I was six.

THERAPIST: Does that make you a doll?

TABITHA: No, Black Power Barbie is definitely a lesbian.

THERAPIST: What is your definition of a lesbian?

TABITHA: A girl who kisses other girls…on the lips.

THERAPIST: Then what does what does it mean that you've slept with Paolo?

TABITHA: That was my expression of love for him on that particular day.

THERAPIST: You also wanted to sleep with Jackson's nurse in the hospital.

TABITHA: Just because I want to sleep with a man in a dress doesn't mean I'm not me anymore. Some days I wake up and I feel like a boy and I want to wear boy clothes and do boy things like wrestle, climb trees, pee standing up. Some days I wake up and I feel like a girl and I want to wear girl clothes and do girl things, put on lipstick, lace underwear and pee sitting down. Some days I'm somewhere in the middle of boy-girl and it's all me.

THERAPIST: Why do you really want to be a lesbian, because it's cool or hip?

TABITHA: Let me put it to you like this, of all the things that I could be today, I'd rather be a lesbian. I like kissing girls.

Scene Nineteen: Tabitha's bedroom

[TABITHA *lies in bed with her eyes closed.* JACKSON *is standing on a stepladder, fishing with a gun in an old-fashioned bathtub.*]

TABITHA: What's it like being dead? Does it hurt?

JACKSON: My body doesn't feel anything, but my heart misses you.

TABITHA: Jackson I'm hungry. There's a hole where my heart used to be.

JACKSON: Fish. Would you like some fresh fish?

TABITHA: You know I hate fish. I don't like to eat anything with eyes that can look back at me.

JACKSON: I'll poke the eyes out. You have to eat something.

TABITHA: I have a hole in my heart.

JACKSON: Let's fill it up with this, Bugs Bunny.

[JACKSON *produces a head of cabbage, which he gives to* TABITHA, *who eats it, making lip-smacking sounds as if it is delicious.*]

TABITHA: I am not a rabbit. I am not a rabbit. I am *not* a rabbit.

Scene Twenty: Tabitha's bedroom

TABITHA: I think I'm pregnant.

MADONNA: What would make you think that?

TABITHA: I ate a head of cabbage in my dream last night.

MADONNA: I don't think that's enough to make you pregnant.

TABITHA: After Jackson died, I slept with his boyfriend.

MADONNA: More than once?

TABITHA: Twice. Once for Jackson and once for me. I didn't feel anything for a while. Sex was like a warm blanket. But each time I opened my eyes, I would remember that Jackson wasn't here anymore. I've still got a hole in my heart.

MADONNA: Let's hold on to each other for a really long time and maybe we can make it go away. *[They embrace]* I love you.

TABITHA: Just for one night I'd like to sleep without dreams.

MADONNA: I said I love you.

TABITHA: That's nice.

MADONNA: Don't you remember?

TABITHA: Remember what?

MADONNA: How to say it.

TABITHA: Say what?

MADONNA: The word for love in Portuguese.

TABITHA: I forgot.

MADONNA: How could you forget something like that?

TABITHA: I can say something else. Te quiero mucho. I want you.

MADONNA: That's not enough.

Scene Twenty-One: Therapist's office

*[*TABITHA *and* MADONNA *are talking to the* THERAPIST. JACKSON *and* PAOLO *are in the room listening.]*

THERAPIST: Why are you here?

TABITHA: Everything was fine.

THERAPIST: Until she read your diary?

TABITHA: Everything was perfect.

THERAPIST: Why did you read her diary?

MADONNA: She said she wanted to know everything—so do I. I wanted to be sure she loved me.

TABITHA: You could've asked me. If you ever read my diary again I'll poke your eyes out.

MADONNA: Don't be so dramatic.

TABITHA: I'm serious. I'll poke your eyes with my fingers, like this. [*Demonstrates.*] Maybe after I pluck them out I'll squash them between the pages of my diary so you can read all you want, but you can't ask me questions. Eyes don't have lips when they separate from the body.

MADONNA: I said I was sorry. In my house nothing was private. I never had anything that I didn't have to share with four brothers. I swear, reading your diary was an accident. It was lying on the kitchen table. I thought it was just a notebook with blank pages. I wanted to leave you a note. Something sweet, so you would smile. When I opened it and saw all those words I started reading and I couldn't stop.

THERAPIST: You could've, but you didn't.

MADONNA: OK I didn't. I wanted to know everything because I wanted to be everything for you that was missing.

TABITHA: You could never do that.

MADONNA: I could try.

TABITHA: I've lost too much. I've lost almost everything. My mother, my father, my brother…my brother Jackson was my air, my water, my blood and each one of my tears. Watching him leave this world was the hardest thing I've ever had to do next to remembering. I used to wonder how he could still have sex with Paolo without thinking about dying. I couldn't stop thinking about it. How could he leave me all by myself? And then the house was still and the whole world was quiet when his heart stopped beating. The taste went out of everything. The world turned gray. And I couldn't stop dreaming. Everyone seems to disappear.

THERAPIST: You're still dreaming about Jackson aren't you?

TABITHA: He sits at the foot of my bed every night, waking me up by pulling on my big toe. He doesn't come around when Madonna is there.

THERAPIST: Sometimes you have to let something go so you can make room for something else.

MADONNA: Why did you sleep with me?

TABITHA: Because I don't like sleeping alone.

THERAPIST: Is that all?

MADONNA: Why, Nzingah?

TABITHA: Because you made me feel something and I was afraid it would go away if I noticed it straight up, if I said it…I was afraid it would mean too much and then you'd go away…but I do. I do. *[Pause. Closes her eyes.]* Te amo.

MADONNA: What did you say?

TABITHA: I said, "Te amo." I love you.

MADONNA: Nzingah, open your eyes.

*[*TABITHA *opens her eyes]*

MADONNA: I'm still here.

TABITHA: But what if…

MADONNA: Let's start with today.

*[*MADONNA *and* TABITHA *kiss.* TABITHA *drops* BLACK POWER BARBIE *to the floor.* MADONNA *picks it up and gives it to her.* TABITHA *throws it across the room and embraces* MADONNA. *The* THERAPIST *closes her book and smiles.* JACKSON *and* PAOLO *embrace and exit as the lights fade.]*

THERAPIST: *[To audience]* Of all the possibilities, how do you choose to love?

END

Elegy

Joanne Bealy

Those sirens wailing in the background remind me of you, Carlos, how I went to visit you in the hospital for what turned out to be the last time I would see you, how you were so mountain water sweet, how you were so fucking thin I thought somebody else must have taken over your body, traded your beautiful one for this pokey-ass sack of bones.

I didn't say that to you of course. It's just something about the way the body disintegrates, not like you had anything to do with it or had any control over it. It's just the way disease eats its way through, bit by bit, and when it hits the brain, it doesn't discriminate, it keeps on eating. Pac-Man like. That's how I used to picture it. Or that stupid Duracell rabbit. It helped me keep my sense of humor.

But this time it seemed to have gone too far. You could no longer speak, for god's sake, how fair was that? Couldn't the fucking thing have let you keep your brain? After all, it seemed to be getting everything else. I think maybe you agreed with that particular point of view, though you never said as much, because you left for good shortly after that.

But here's the thing. Even though you could no longer talk, you never lost your voice. It came through your eyes and the tips of your fingers. It was there in the strength of your mouth and your smile. Do you remember, Carlos, how I always wanted to touch your mouth because that smile was such a knockout, how I used to beg you to give up all those boys so we could go make babies together? It was that blessed smile that caused that tomfoolery. Not that I would have really done it, but I was so crazy about you.

I did want you to take me home with you, though. That was true and that I would have done. I wanted to go to Venezuela, experience firsthand a country that could spit out the likes of you. I wanted your mother to teach me to dance and then I wanted to dance with you. I wanted to soak up the family love that oozed out of you these thousands of miles away from its center. I wanted to hold you, Carlos. I never expected you to die.

So that last day I went to the hospital to see you *(I remember John being there and someone else I didn't know, a woman, and they sat at the far side of the room so I could visit with you)*, I gave you my Hopi familiar. Despite the fact that you had teased me relentlessly for years about this three-inch tall figure that went everywhere with me, I knew it held no grudges. I knew it would help usher you gracefully to the other side. It was also the only way I could think to express the significance of your friendship in my life without relegating it to platitudes. That you looked away tore my heart open. That your tears so easily pulled out mine rankled me. I needed to be strong. I needed to be mad at someone—for you being sick *(hell, not even so much sick at that point as almost dead)*, for none of us knowing how to be with the very sick *(they don't teach that in school, do they?)*, for god taking you, the sweetest angel, instead of some flaming asshole nobody would even miss. I was mad at all of that and I was so very sad.

But because it was you, because I was so hopelessly enamoured with you, because I knew our time left was short, I tried to articulate what I'd been attempting to say with the gift. It had something to do with red sports cars and turkey noodle soup, with trust and passion and learning what it is that makes people move through the world in the way that they do, with loving someone for no particular reason other than for who they are.

It was about you throwing me the keys to your sports car when I jokingly asked you for them one day after work, never in a million years expecting that you would entrust me with your most precious possession. I remember catching the keys with my left hand, taking one long look at you, then running out of there before you could change your mind. Last thing I heard was you yelling after me to be back by five o'clock.

Years later when you came to visit me in the country *(you were already sick and I was feeding you homemade turkey noodle soup, remember, Carlos?)*, you told me you didn't think I would really take the car that day but it was too late to back down by the time you realized I would, how you learned to trust what you already knew to be true—that I would never do you wrong.

And here's something you didn't know, Carlos. When I kissed you good-bye and left your room that day, I didn't leave the hospital. I ran up six flights of stairs, like I was training for some athletic event. I ran really hard, without stopping, so I was wet with sweat and the only thing I could think about was how I was going to catch my next breath. I had no idea why I was running up instead of down, which is where the main entrance from the street is, but I found myself at the door leading to the roof, a door that, if you believed the signs, was always locked shut. Well, this time it was wide open. Understanding that everything happens for a reason, I decided to walk into the light that was shining through and step up onto the roof. It had one of those pebbly surfaces that crunched underfoot and, for some unknown to me reason, I stepped out into the middle and fell onto my back, sort of like I was making angels in the snow. I just lay there feeling the heat of the day, staring at the blue blankness of the sky. And every once in a short while some bird would fly through my vision range and I would follow her until either I didn't want to anymore or she left.

And suddenly I knew why I had been drawn up to the roof instead of down to the street. It was so I could hold that bird with my eyes, not hampering her freedom but appreciating her, against the vastness of the sky and her own possibilities. What you had been trying to tell me all along, Carlos, became, in that single moment, infinitely clear. You were not bereft over leaving, I was. You were not mad at anyone over your illness, I was. You were quite content with who you were, how you had lived your life, the love you were so effortlessly able to give and receive. You looked forward to discovering what was next, you told me that. I had chosen to forget. It was me who hadn't adjusted and I could do that on my own time.

I closed my eyes and let the calm—from my breath, from the sky, from the solitude—engulf me. I breathed you, Carlos. And I know you breathed me too.

Ashes to Ashes
Marijo

Characters (in playing order)

NARRATOR/STORYTELLER

MOTHER MATTIE MAE DUMPLER

LUCKY

REVEREND BILLY BOB BUMPUS

MISSIONARY CIRCLE LADY

USHER BOARD LADY

WEST INDIAN LADDER

CHURCH LADY #1

CHURCH HANDYMAN

MOTHER EARLITHA MO

LADY WITH SIX HAIRWEAVES

CHURCH MEMBERS AT THE LADDER

Production Note: Performed by Marijo and directed by Brian Freeman, 1995.

[The stage/performance area is bare, except for a 12-14 foot ladder and a 6-8 foot ladder; they are spiked at downstage right and downstage left. There is yellow plastic police tape with the words "Keep Out" and "Police Dept." on it wound around the legs of one ladder and through the steps of the other. The ends are left loose. At the top of the taller ladder sits a basket, filled with finely shredded paper. On the top of the other ladder is a flowered hat with bright pink feathers. Hanging from various points of the ladder are four or five pairs of pink gloves and church fans.]

[NARRATOR/STORYTELLER *enters performing space, crosses downstage by the taller ladder, and begins climbing up. Sings the first verse of a spiritual plainly, without much emotion, with the second verse sung in a full-out gospel belt.*]

NARRATOR/STORYTELLER: [*singing*]
We are climbing Jacob's ladder,
We are climbing Jacob's ladder,
We are climbing Jacob's ladder,
Soldiers of the Cross.

Ev'ry round gets higher and higher,
Ev'ry round gets higher, higher, higher and HIGHER

[*Interrupts song to speak to the audience*]

NARRATOR/STORYTELLER: Now, just what would make an eighty-eight-year-old woman climb a forty-foot ladder? Well, I don't gossip and I sho don't lie—but I'll tell you. Mother Mattie Mae Dumpler, beautiful, smooth, dark skin almost the color of eggplant, snow white hair with hot-pressed curls all done up in the same style from 1949 'til today! Mother Mattie Mae Dumpler, pink feathered church hat, pink lace gloves, and matchin pink plastic church pumps. She climbed that ladder one step at a time, and every time she took a step she'd stop, look up, and moan.

MOTHER MATTIE MAE DUMPLER: Oh Lawd! Give me strength!

NARRATOR/STORYTELLER: The sweat covered her face like a veil and she was pantin an puffin but she kept on goin until she reached the top. Now, Mother Mattie Mae Dumpler's son had been the director of a big theatre company downtown, and had worked so hard to keep it goin that he would joke with his mother.

LUCKY: [*Casually leaning over top of ladder as if audience was his mama*]
Mama, if I die before you, I want you to cremate my behind and put my ashes in that old closed-up heating pipe that hangs over the stage. Cause see that way I'll be able to keep my eyes on everything going on. Plus, I'll always have the best seat in the house every time the curtain goes up!

[NARRATOR/STORYTELLER *climbs down ladder, crosses to downstage center and speaks*]

NARRATOR/STORYTELLER: Well! Like I said before, I don't gossip and I sho
don't lie—but it just so happened that the boy came down wit a myste-
rious disease. Oops, I mean illness. Now his mother tried her best to get
her son to come to church so folks could pray for him. But the boy
didn't wanna go—and it's just as well, cause the folks in the church
didn't want him comin there no way. Aw, they got to whisperin an
carryin on about what was wrong wit the boy? And what was he sick
wit? But she wasn't tellin nobody nothin. Well, anyhow—it just so happened that after he was sick for a little time, the boy upped and died!

[NARRATOR/STORYTELLER crosses to one corner downstage while speaking]

Now, uh, I don't gossip and I sho don't lie—and you didn't hear it from
me, but Mother Mattie Mae Dumpler asked to have her son's service up
in her church. And she's a Saint up in the church, okay? Now, here's
where the story gets messy see, cause for some reason her pastor,
Reverend Billy Bob Bumpus, told her:

REVEREND BILLY BOB BUMPUS: Naw, you caint have your son's service in
this church. This here is a Christian church, an yo son was a sinnuh!

NARRATOR/STORYTELLER: Now, they say the preacher said it was because
her son was out in the world wit alla that thee-ayter mess! But the truth
be known—and this aint no hearsay, it wasn't bout no thee-ayter mess.
I told you bout them folks snickerin and a-whisperin about her son
when the boy first got sick—anh-hanh, you know they was tryin ta find
out what was wrong wit him, and so forth and so on. I know cause I
went to a music program at the church and just happened to hear some
of em talkin bout him right in the back of Mother Mattie Mae
Dumpler's pew! Lord have mercy—the poor old woman played like she
never even heard em, but her back sorta slumped and she started
moanin. Aww, it was pitiful!

Mother Dumpler felt angry and hurt about not havin her son's funeral
in her church, but she talked to the folks down at the thee-ayter about
havin the service there, and his ashes left in the pipes at the thee-ayter,
like her son used to joke about. And the thee-ayter folks honored her
son's wishes. *[NARRATOR/STORYTELLER pauses in mock-somber respect
for the dead, then rushes to continue.]* So anyways, they had a wonderful
service down at the thee-ayter. Everybody was there. Black folks and
white folks, brown folks and red folks, yellow folks—and even some
polka-dotted folks! They opened up with African drummers and

dancers dancin up and down the aisles. And they had praise singers, speechifyin and poems.

[Relishes telling the following information]

Ohhh, and even some of his friends from New York City and Hollywood were there, sho was. One of the girls from that singin group—uh…oh neva mind, but she sang a solo and the chile chirped like a bird! And lessee—who else, oh yes—what's-his-name who's seven feet tall? You know, he was in that movie called, uh, don't tell me, it's on the tip of my tongue. Well, any way, Freddy Lightfoot Ferguson even did a tap dance! Aww, it was somethin else. And they had Mother Dumpler sittin up there on the stage in all her best pink church clothes. On one side of her was a big poster of her fine son Lucky—that's what everybody called him—with them big dimples and smilin that beautiful gap-toothed smile of his, lawd! And on the other side of her was a tall tree of pink flowers. She looked like an African queen! To top it all off, they had a mass choir with Lucky's friends and some folks from the city council, singin and marchin.

[Demonstrates a funky choir march, with one hand on lower back, and sings]

We are/Soldiers/in the/Ar-r-meee
We have to fight/although/we have/to pray
boo-boo-boo-boomp,
We have to/hold up/the blood-stained banner
We have to/hold-it-up until-we-die
boo-boo-boo-boomp! Ohhh we are—

Lawd, you shoulda seen them white folks tryna keep up! And naturally, after the service they had all kinds of food. It was truly a wonderful home goin. They coulda sold tickets, cause it was standin room only. Folks kept talkin about that funeral for a long time!

Everythin was fine. Just fine—until the earthquake. You know that b-i-ig earthquake? Shook that theatre so bad it liked to fell apart, and the city had to close it down. Had them yellow plastic police somebody-been-shot-here-do-not-enter ribbons all over the place! They were gonna tear it down. Lawd, Mother Mattie Mae Dumpler had a fit. Got ta screamin and hollerin and carryin on in that gravelly voice of hers, her head shakin—you know she had that Parkinson's.

MOTHER MATTIE MAE DUMPLER: Whut gone happen to ma baby ashes?

Whut gone happen to ma baby ashes? WHO GONE HEP ME GIT MA BABY ASHES FUM OUTTA THAT PIPE?

NARRATOR/STORYTELLER: It was on a Sunday at church when she found out about it, when one of the ladies of the Missionary Circle was nice enough to tell her about it.

MISSIONARY CIRCLE LADY: Well, Mother Dumpler, I guess you gone hafta git yore boy's ashes outta that there pipe. I mean, now that the city's gonna close the place down. Oh yass, I read all about it in the mawnin papuh, amen.

NARRATOR/STORYTELLER: Mother Dumpler was wailin real loud as she asked the church members to help her get Lucky's ashes, but they all seemed to be too busy. One lady from the ursher-board whined in a sweet, high-pitched voice, wavin her fingers to and fro.

USHER BOARD LADY: Ohhh! Mother Mattie Dumpler. I broke three of my fingernails last night, an you know the little Ko-ree-yun lady whut do em? Well she promised ta fit me in taday right aftuh church service, so I caint go up there with ya, I'm awfully sorry, ay-man.

NARRATOR/STORYTELLER: Then she asked the church's handyman to help her. But he started coughin and sputterin and scratchin his head while he was tryin to find some kinda excuse. He was hunchin up his shoulders, and poppin his suspenders so hard over his big belly til it seemed like he would pop wide open.

CHURCH HANDYMAN: Aww...Sistuh Dumpluh. Uh, uh, well...er-ra... Help ya git yore son's ashes fum outten that pipe? You know I'ma hafta call Brotha Hyrus to come over an hep ya, since he do have his own carpentry bidness...an er-a, he know mo bout whut ta do wit a hammuh den me! Uh heh-heh-heh.

NARRATOR/STORYTELLER: Now, Mother Dumpler just knew her best friend and prayer warrior, Mother Earlitha Mo, would be the one person she could lean on. After all, she was one of the church Saints. They did missionary work out in the streets together. But Mother Mo bellowed out in a voice like a rusty tuba, as she struck herself on her big bosoms:

MOTHER EARLITHA MO: Mothuh Mattie Mae Dumpluh...mah HEART *[On the word "heart," she grabs her chest as if to rip her heart out]* goes OUT to ya, praise Gawd! *[On the word "out," she flings her invisible heart out to audience]* But taday is the fifth Sunday, the day I does mah prison ministry, so I caint come. And even though I caint be there witcha in the flersh *[punctuates by snapping a huge hanky towards audience]* I'm gonna be right there witcha—in tha spirit, Praise Gawd! I'll send a tamale pie ova latuh on!

NARRATOR/STORYTELLER: Well, the last person Mother Dumpler asked to help was her pastor, Reverend Billy Bob Bumpus, who never missed no occasion to deliver a sermon on any subject in that sing-song style of the old-time country preacher. Now I don't gossip, and I sho don't lie, but that man preaches everyday conversation.

REVEREND BILLY BOB BUMPUS: *[Delivered as an old-time preacher's sermon.]* Saint Mothuh Mattie Mae-Dumpluhh / Uhhhhh, ya know / the little wife just had serious surgery / bout a month ago / Well / on her bunions, yasss / an it look like her / wh-o-o-o-l-e leg done / swoll right on up / Unh-hunh / Couldn't even come ta church this mornin / Well / Imma hafta take her to the hospital / but when we get through / with ow-wa bidness / as yore Pastor / Imma drop by ta read some a my / favrit scriptures for ya, amen.

NARRATOR/STORYTELLER: Ooo! Mother Mattie Mae Dumpler snapped out: "Ain't nobody wanta hep me? All right then, I'll do it myself!" And she did. She tore outta that church in a huff. She was hotter than the fourth of July, and smokin like a firecracker! She slammed the church doors so hard that the stained glass windows in em fell out singin: "He-l-l-p me somebody—Hey, Hey, Heyyy!" *[The last lines sung in a gospel riff.]*

With her pink hat leadin the way, followed by those pink gloves an pink plastic church pumps, she stomped out to the parkin lot, jumped—I mean as well as she could jump—into a big shiny gray 1945 Cadillac; gunned the engine and took off! Aw, she tore past the stop signs and through the red lights, all the way downtown. Pink lace gloves justa grippin the steerin wheel. Oooo! she zoomed, hunchin over the steerin wheel and peekin through her pink bifocals, her nose almost through the windshield. She was madder than a crazy dog! She drove that car straight up on the sidewalk, underneath the marquee of her son's theeayter, and tore right through the yellow plastic police somebody's-been-shot-here ribbons! She slammed the brakes so hard that smoke was comin from the tires! Now, some folks from outside came runnin into the lobby to see if the old lady was hurt, but they see Mother Dumpler jump—well like I said before, as well as she could—out the car, stomp over to a corner, pull a long ladder into the stage area, and start climbin up.

Mother Dumpler's church members and Reverend Billy Bob Bumpus musta felt bad about not wantin to help the poor woman, so they all followed her down to the thee-ayter.

Well, by the time they got to the thee-ayter she was near the top of the ladder. They were circled all around the bottom of the ladder with their necks stretched up, and their mouths wide open, lookin just like a bunch of black birds! One woman was wearin six hairweaves and twelve pairs of those artificial dragon-lady fingernails. She was clawin up in the air with one hand and flippin through her hair with the other.

LADY WITH SIX HAIRWEAVES: Mothuh Dumpler come on down, we was just foolin. Reverend Billy Bob Bumpus, he's gone come up and do it for ya, aintchu, Rev'run?

NARRATOR/STORYTELLER: But the righteous Reverend Billy Bob Bumpus was flippin frantically through his Bible searchin for just the right passage to read. But Mother Dumpler called back down to him:

MOTHER MATTIE MAE DUMPLER: Naw! That's allright, yall Christians stay right there. I don't need your hep—I got JEE-zus ta gimme all tha hep I need!

NARRATOR/STORYTELLER: And she kept on climbin and moanin: "Oh Lord, give me strength!" Over and over, "Oh Lord, give me strength!" Finally, she's at the top of the ladder. She unhooks a hammer from her pink plastic belt and starts swingin at the plaster sealing the pipe, and wails: "Oh Lord, give me strength!" She swings—blam!—and keeps wailin, "Oh Lord, give me strength!" Blam! "Oh Lord, give me strength!" Then Reverend Billy Bob Bumpus shouts up in his best sing-song preachin voice:

REVEREND BILLY BOB BUMPUS: Saint Mother Mattie Mae Dump—luhh / These is the very last and evil days of the world / yes they they are / The Bible speaks all about folks dyin by the sword / Well / An mens lovin mens / yessusuh / and wimmens lovin wimmens / Well / So they deserves / to die-for-they wic-ked ways / Unh-hunhh / Iiiiiii / know all about your son / Yes I do / Your son was an abomination / to-the-Glory-of-God / Well.

NARRATOR/STORYTELLER: And I told you, I don't gossip and I sho don't lie, but the pages of his Bible were burnin up with flames of fire with all that preacher's hateful condemnations! Well now, it's funny that in all this time, the ladder had not moved. But that ladder checked out the situation and said:

[Actor mimics the rigidity of a ladder, speaking with a West Indian accent]

WEST INDIAN LADDER: Deh poh ol laydeh / ent hahb enybodeh ter hehlp heh / cept daht unseen Lawd sheh keep callin on / so AH go be deh strent daht sheh be needin.

NARRATOR/STORYTELLER: And the ladder was still. Everything was still. With one final blow—BA-LAM!—the last lump of plaster fell out the front of the pipe. The tears and sweat were all blended together now, makin the old woman's face look like some kind of ritual mask. Down below, the church members were shakin their heads and murmurin various comments or singin softly.

CHURCH MEMBERS AT THE LADDER: *[Overlapping]*
Gerrll, ain't this some'um?
And chile, chile, I would'nt na missed this for nuthin—
And ohhh Lord have mer-er-cy—
Ohh, Lord, have mer-er-cee—
My word, my word—
Gerrll, gimmee sum-a-that gum!

NARRATOR/STORYTELLER: With the plaster out of the pipe, Mother Dumpler reached her pink lace gloved hand into the pipe, her moans comin in waves.

MOTHER MATTIE MAE DUMPLER: Lord, Lord, Lord. Please Suh, hammercy on me.

NARRATOR/STORYTELLER The bag of ashes was huge—Lucky was a big man, so Mother Mattie Mae Dumpler had to use her hands like a wedge, wigglin her fingers around the bag inside the pipe bit by bit. At last with a loud suckin sound—FFOOWWKK!—the bag popped out. The old lady held the bag high over her head makin the ladder rock back and forth. She looked just like she was doin some kind of cere-mony. After a moment, she brought the bag to her bosom and hugged it like a baby and moaned.

MOTHER MATTIE MAE DUMPLER: Oh my baby! My baby! My las chile, yo mama have ya now!

NARRATOR/STORYTELLER: The church folks at the bottom of the ladder were chantin and wailin old spirituals: Some-tiiimes / I feeeel / like a mo-ther-less chi-ild; and I want Jee-zus / to wa-allk / with meee.

NARRATOR/STORYTELLER: Reverend Billy Bob Bumpus was still flippin the pages of his Bible, and when he'd find somethin important, he'd smack his lips, and say in his sing-song way: "Yessuh, yessuh, yessuh, my, my, my!" The woman with all the hairweaves was wavin those twelve pairs of dragon-lady fingernails in the air and pleadin.

LADY WITH SIX HAIRWEAVES: Aw Mothuh Dumpluh! Come on down. This ain't good for ya, witcha high blood an all!

NARRATOR/STORYTELLER: Mother Dumpler yelled down in between her sobbin:

MOTHER MATTIE MAE DUMPLER: Naw, that's allright, yall ain't wanted to hep me, so don't worry bout it. I GOT my baby's ashes now, high blood an all! Yall ought ta be ashamed before Gawd, callin yaselves Christians. Yall ain't got no Gawd IN ya—hipacrits. All of ya!

NARRATOR/STORYTELLER: The preacher started bellowin up to the top of the ladder:

REVEREND BILLY BOB BUMPUS: Now look-a-here, Mother Mattie Mae Dumpler, tha Lord don't—

[MOTHER DUMPLER *hugs the bag of ashes and calls down angrily*]

MOTHER MATTIE MAE DUMPLER: Ohh hush up, Pastor—I ain't through talkin yet! Pastor you don't know nothin bout no Gawd, or else you wouldn't preach so much hate against folks. Like Gawd didn't know nuthin bout no sinners. Didn't he say outta his own mouth, "Judge not, unless ye BE judged?" Well? An didn't he say that "What-sa-neva ye do for the least of my peoples, ye do also unto me?" Whilst my chile was sick, you didn't want him to come to yo church. And then you wouldn't even let me hold his fewnul service in yo church. [*Begins to cry, but continues*] I shoulda brought him ta church and dared yall ta put me out, cause it ain't yo church. It's Gawd's church. But I didn't do nuthin. Pastor, I bet theys some other families in tha church who chirren lead lives they don't understan, but that don't mean we got ta stop lovin em—or rejec em. And I don't rejec my chile. So you jus keep on preachin. But you hush up about my son!

NARRATOR/STORYTELLER: One church member said: "Well she sure told him, now didn't she?" Now, you know that big artificial-fake-rhine-stone-diamond brooch that Mother Dumpler wears to church every Sunday? You know, the one that was reeel big, shaped like a sunflower, with spikes all over it? Well, she was wearin it the day she climbed the ladder, unh-hunh. She musta leaned on the bag, or hugged it too tight, because right in the middle of her fussin at Reverend Billy Bob Bumpus there was a loud P-O-U-F-FFFF! Ooowee! Ashes were sprayin up in the air, flyin everywhere like a gray snowstorm! Pandemonium broke out below! *[Takes hat from top of ladder and toss the shredded paper up in air]* Mother Dumpler was cryin, "Oh Lawd, my baby's ashes! Yall help me get ma baby's ashes!"

She was hysterical now, reachin up, out, and all around her in the air, snatchin handfuls of the ashes that used to be the fruit of her womb. The church folk were screamin and runnin, bumpin into each other tryin to get away from the ashes.

CHURCH MEMBERS AT THE LADDER: *[Overlapping]*
Oh Jeezus, she done popped the damn bag—runnn!
Duck yall, duck!
Move outta my wayyy!
told ya we should'na come to this heathen house!
Oh Lord have mercy!

NARRATOR/STORYTELLER: Reverend Billy Bob Bumpus was tryin to shake and blow off ashes that sifted down between his Bible pages, but he ended up slammin that Bible down and hollerin like he was preachin a revival sermon:

REVEREND BILLY BOB BUMPUS: Mothuh Mattie Mae Dumpluhh / These is the very last / and evil days of the world / Unh-hunh / This is the Devil's work / I told ya the wrath of God is mighty, yesss it is / Well / Yore son was a sinnuh / And this here is the evidence / of the Lord's wrath / Unh-hunh / Well-a, well-a, well / Whatchoo gone say now / Motha Mattie Mae Dumpluh / Whatchoo gonna say nowww?

NARRATOR/STORYTELLER: The old lady grabbed handfuls of ashes, and stuffed them back into the hole in the bag, only makin the bag spew out more ashes into the air and down onto the folks who were coughin and gaggin as they ran out the exit door. Suddenly, Mother Dumpler started laughin as she cried.

MOTHER MATTIE MAE DUMPLER: What I'm gonna say, Reverend? Ahma say that I prayed and prayed fuh vengence, but ya got to be careful of whatcha pray fuh. I didn't expect the Lord to answer ma prayers—not this-away. And ya know what? Yall was so busy tryin ta figger out what ma Lucky had whilst he was alive, an so-o-o scairt of catchin sumthin from him. Well. *[She begins to laugh almost uncontrollably, gasping for her breath, crying and speaking at the same time.]* Well, yall sho done caught it now, aintcha? And you know what else, Reverend? I forgive ya. An ahma sing yall a song.

NARRATOR/STORYTELLER: Now I'm gonna say this one last time—can you guess what it is? That's right, I don't gossip and I sho don't lie, BUT— Mother Mattie Mae Dumpler actually sang one of her favorite church songs right through her tears. And she slowly climbed back down that ladder, tenderly cradlin the last remnants of her son's ashes.

[The gravelly voice of MOTHER DUMPLER *is heard singing "They Will Know We Are Christians By Our Love." The* NARRATOR/STORYTELLER *climbs down to the floor, crosses to downstage center and beckons to audience members in an invitation to join in the singing.* NARRATOR/STORYTELLER *exits as lights are going down to a slow fade, or while audience is still singing the second verse. Words to the song are on the back of the programs.]*

They Will Know We Are Christians By Our Love

> We are one in the spirit,
> we are one in the Lord.
> We are one in the spirit,
> we are one in the Lord.
> And we pray that our unity
> will one day be restored.
> And they'll know we are Christians
> by our love, by our love.
> Yes, they'll know
> we are Christians by our love.

We will join hands together,
we will walk hand in hand.
We will join hands together,
we will walk hand in hand.
And together we can show the world
that love is in the land.
And they'll know we are Christians
by our love, by our love.
Yes, they'll know
we are Christians by our love.

[No bows or curtain call.]

*[*NARRATOR/STORYTELLER *reenters with HIV/AIDS health educator for
Q & A.]*

Nothing Forever

Chiori Miyagawa
Lyrics by Mark Campbell

Characters:

WOMAN

WOMAN 2

MAN

Roles also played by WOMAN 2:

MAN ON THE STREET

WOMAN AT THE COUNTER

BOY
NICE WHITE WOMAN

TEACHER

WAITRESS

HOMELESS WOMAN

MOTHER

MAN AT THE DELI

Roles also played by MAN:
PIANO PLAYER

PAUL

[Darkness. Lights up on the PIANO PLAYER. *He sings "the bridge."]*

> In a leaden river
> I am spun away
> Whirling in its water and decay

And the hanging branches
I so vainly clutch
Brittle, snap off at my fingers' touch

Should I scream or cry out
Not a soul would come
So I float in silence, growing numb

Closer comes the ocean
Fierce and black as night
As the shoreline disappears from sight

I am taken under
Lost in the debris
Then above beyond my reach I see
A bridge
A bridge

[Lights up on WOMAN. *She is leaning on the piano reading from an application form.* PIANO PLAYER *listens.]*

WOMAN: "Have you ever: been a habitual drunkard? advocated or practiced polygamy? been a prostitute? been an illicit trafficker in narcotic drugs or marijuana? received income from illegal gambling? Have you ever been declared legally incompetent or confined as a patient in a mental institution? Are you now or have you ever been a member of, or in any way connected or associated with, the Communist Party, or ever knowingly aided or supported the Nazi Party directly, or indirectly through another organization, group or person, or ever advocated, taught, believed in, or knowingly supported or furthered the interests of atheism?"
[Pause]
Should I?

MAN: I don't know.

WOMAN: I think I'm pregnant.

MAN ON THE STREET: *[From a distance]* Hey, China Doll, come sit on my face.

WOMAN: I don't work at a Korean grocery. I don't wash shirts at a Chinese laundry. I'm not a waitress at a Vietnamese restaurant. I'm not a Filipina domestic. I don't know how to play the violin or write computer programs. I don't even know how to make sushi. I have no paper lanterns or shoji screens at home.

MAN ON THE STREET: China Doll, China Doll, China Doll, China Doll.

WOMAN: I can dress white, eat white, joke white, think white. I can marry white. I'm from the proud country of honorary white. A savage with silk and perfume. *[Pause]* Should I tell him?

MAN: I don't know.

[WOMAN moves away from the piano. Lights change. MAN ON THE STREET moves into the space and becomes WOMAN 2.]

WOMAN: I wish I could see the rainforest from my window. Instead I see construction on Hudson Street. Gray layered with dark gray, light gray and gray-black. I heard somewhere if a person doesn't see green for three days, she will go blind. At night I test my eyes with a postcard from Mexico. I'm afraid of going blind from not seeing the rainforest.

WOMAN 2: But you've never seen it.

WOMAN: I want to. Before it's too late for me.

[Lights change. Music.]

WOMAN: When I was growing up, the only window in the living room was frosted. So the outside didn't exist. I was always inside. At home, my mother wore the same shirt and skirt every day. But she dressed up to go to the department store in town. She looked very nice then.

WOMAN 2: Inside. Outside.

WOMAN: I wore the same shirt and skirt every day at home, too. We had to save the good clothes for school.
Shame. Beauty.

WOMAN 2: Inside. Outside.

WOMAN: The windows in my room were frosted also. I nearly went blind because I couldn't attach images to my childhood sounds. Cars, people, dogs.

WOMAN 2: Closed in a box, wrapped with gift paper.

WOMAN: Slowly my inside took over my outside. I became always unimportant. Always shabby. *[Pause]*

If a life grows inside me, wouldn't it turn rotten?

WOMAN 2: Why?

WOMAN: You know, I'm an orphan.

WOMAN 2: Liar.

[Lights change.]

WOMAN 2: But it doesn't mean anything.

WOMAN: There will be twice as many people in Ecuador in the next century.

WOMAN 2: She will be the most beautiful American…Japanese…Japanese American…whatever.

WOMAN: She?

WOMAN 2: She.

WOMAN: Ten million species sacrificed for one selfish desire.

WOMAN 2: But it doesn't mean anything.

WOMAN: Rain will stop falling on forests by the end of the century.

WOMAN 2: What will you name her?

WOMAN: *[Pause]* I'll name her September.

MAN: *[sings "After…"]*

> He turns and instantly
> Is swept into the sea
> Of his own breathing
>
> I seek a hiding place
> And crawl into the space
> Between his shoulders
>
> No solace, even there,
> I stumble to the chair,
> Beside the window.

It's raining hard and fast—
And then the rain has passed—
The street is soundless.

I watch the clock's dull glow.
The night will soon let go…
He does not know…
He will not know.

[Pause.]
[Lights change.]

WOMAN: October 1992. My last trip to Japan before becoming a U.S. citizen. The good-bye trip. At Narita International Airport, there are two huge signs.

WOMAN 2: "Welcome to Japan" in English.

WOMAN: "Welcome home" in Japanese. Okaeri nasai.

WOMAN: I can read both, but I am neither visiting nor going home. Thirty-two years. I have lived exactly half of my life in Japan, the other half in the U.S.

Tokyo train station. A metropolis. Full of men in dark business suits and beautifully dressed women. Here, you can buy anything—boxed lunches with rice balls and pickles, or spaghetti and salad. All kinds of bread. You can buy slippers, cream puffs, or Armani shirts.

WOMAN 2: Can you buy…what is it called? You know—the thing you put on the kitchen faucet to make the water spray?

WOMAN: I know what you mean…what is it called?

[They all think for a moment.]

MAN: I don't know.

WOMAN 2: Well, can you buy it?

WOMAN: Yes, you can. There are many stores in the station. Also, there are women in aprons selling flowers or marinated squid… *[unsure]* I think. I'll buy a newspaper.

*[*WOMAN *approaches the counter. Pause.]*

I don't know which one to buy.

[Pause.]

I'm in the way of men throwing change on the counter and dashing off with their usual paper. *[Pause. Nervous.]* I'll just get the one most people are buying. Men are bumping into me. People are waiting. Quickly I say "ham and cheese."

WOMAN AT THE COUNTER: What?

WOMAN: I mean, how much is it?

[Pause.]

WOMAN AT THE COUNTER: What do you mean?

WOMAN: The price is not printed on the paper.

WOMAN AT THE COUNTER: *[puzzled]* Don't you know it?

WOMAN: I can't read half the characters in the paper. I don't know the Japanese words for "consequence" or "wrench." I will never speak English like Connie Chung.

[WOMAN 2 takes WOMAN's hand and kisses it tenderly. WOMAN 2's movement changes into a throwing motion. Sound of shattering glass. Lights change.]

BOY: *[Yells]* Do you remember Pearl Harbor?

WOMAN: I don't have the words to throw back to these boys on the school bus, throwing ice at me. 1979. My first anniversary of Pearl Harbor in the United States of America.

NICE WHITE WOMAN: *[speaking very slowly]* You are so small. That's a cute red dress. And you eat like a bird.

WOMAN: I'm always hungry living up to my image of eating like a bird.

NICE WHITE WOMAN: *[very proud]* Today, we will do a good thing. We'll have carrot sticks and yogurt for lunch.

WOMAN: I don't understand this concept. *[She takes a bite of a carrot stick.]* I'll do anything to be "American." I wear high heels and tight jeans, blow-dry my hair just like the white girls. At lunch, I don't hesitate one moment in the cafeteria. There are people behind me. I can't let them know I don't really speak English. Quickly I say "ham and cheese" because that's all I know how to say. I eat ham and cheese sandwiches for months.

[Lights change.]

[A classroom.]

TEACHER: *[shouting]* THE CAPITAL OF NEW YORK STATE IS ALBANY.

WOMAN: I'm not deaf.

TEACHER: *[shouting]* DO YOU UNDERSTAND ME? WHO WAS THE FIRST PRESIDENT? WHO WAS ABRAHAM LINCOLN? HAVE YOU READ *THE CATCHER IN THE RYE?* WHO IS EVIL IN THE WORLD? NORTH KOREANS? CHINESE? WHERE IS THE THIRD WORLD? THESE ARE THE IMPORTANT THINGS IN LIFE.

WOMAN: I'm not deaf. I just don't know what's important.

[Lights change.]

WOMAN 2: How is your friend Paul?

WOMAN: He isn't feeling well. For the past six months he has been eating nothing but cereal. His creamy white skin now sags on his fragile bones. I make myself blind so I don't see his decay. All I see are his blue blue eyes, wet.

[Lights change. WOMAN *reads from the application.]*

WOMAN: Have you ever been a habitual drunkard?

WOMAN 2: No.

WOMAN: Advocated or practiced polygamy?

WOMAN 2: No.

WOMAN: A prostitute?

WOMAN 2: No.

WOMAN: Narcotic drugs?

WOMAN 2: No.

WOMAN: Illegal?

WOMAN 2: No.

WOMAN: Mental?

WOMAN 2: No.

WOMAN: If the law requires it, are you willing to bear arms on behalf of the U.S.?

WOMAN 2: No.

[Pause.]

WOMAN: I think the answer is supposed to be yes. Are you now or have ever been in any way connected or associated with the destruction of—

WOMAN 2: rainforests, or ever knowingly aided or supported the destruction of—

WOMAN: rainforests directly, or indirectly through another organization, group or person, or ever advocated—

WOMAN 2: taught, believed in, or knowingly supported or furthered the destruction of—

MAN: rainforests?

[Lights change. WOMAN *and* WOMAN 2 *begin eating toast.* WOMAN 2 *offers* MAN *some toast. He takes a piece and eats.]*

WOMAN 2: It didn't taste the same. It looked the same, but it didn't taste the same. I was disappointed and disgusted. Butter used to be really good. On a silver spoon, right out of the jar. I had done it many times before. But it didn't taste the same. I felt like throwing up. At nine years old, I stopped eating butter. I'm sure it was my mother. She didn't think I should eat butter by itself. It wasn't right.

WOMAN: *[puzzled]* Right?

WOMAN 2: Butter should be on toast. If I couldn't eat butter like a normal child, I shouldn't eat it.

WOMAN: Right, left.

WOMAN 2: So she stopped it. I don't know how. But I'm sure it was my mother.

WOMAN: Why is my right always your left?

WOMAN 2: The kitchen was dark, crowded with a cabinet, table, chairs, dish towels. Her pots and pans didn't match. This made her unhappy. I was married for six years to a man whose mother's pots and pans didn't match. He wanted matching pots and pans. It took me years to taste butter again. I felt queasy. I was twenty-two. Ten years later. I'm allowed to have mismatched pots and pans. But I still can't eat butter by itself, off a silver spoon.

WOMAN: *[Touches her stomach]* I have to eat Japanese food *now*.

[Lights change.]

WOMAN: A restaurant in midtown. I'm at the L-shaped counter, surrounded by Japanese businessmen in dark suits and glasses. Eating, eating, never looking up. Never once. Staring at their sushi, tempura, udon. Cutting me out of their world.

WAITRESS: What would you like?

WOMAN: The same thing those men are having. A bowlful of nostalgia.

WAITRESS: Would you like something else?

WOMAN: No.

[The WAITRESS goes away.]

WOMAN: Won't you look up? Unless you look at me, I won't exist. You'll never know what I look like. You'll remember nothing about me.

[Lights change.]

WOMAN 2: You are a racist.

WOMAN: *[Surprised]* Because I once married a white man? Because September isn't all Japanese?

WOMAN 2: Have you ever been in love with an Asian man?

WOMAN: No. *[Pause. Her speech gets faster and faster.]* Look. This is how a woman falls in love in Japan. She is asked out on a date to dinner. She is supposed to pour beer for the man. She should not touch her food first. Her shoulders should curve slightly inward, her eyes lowered, and her voice childlike. Innocent. She should constantly agree with the man throughout the conversation dominated by him. It's not a good idea to have a college degree. It's not a good idea to be too smart. Later, she gets to cook, clean, wash, have kids, and stay home alone every night with the kids. She looks forward to taking care of her aging in-laws. She eventually gets to clean their false teeth. *[Pause.]*

WOMAN 2: Are you sure?

[Lights change.]

WOMAN 2: What if September is a boy?

WOMAN: I don't know.

WOMAN 2: It's OK.

WOMAN: If September is a girl, the worst she will do is eat hamburgers, hot dogs, and TV dinners.

WOMAN 2: If he is a boy?

WOMAN: He can hold a chain saw.

[Pause. Lights change.]

WOMAN 2: You think you are Medea, don't you? What's your revenge?

WOMAN: Revenge?

[Lights change.]

WOMAN 2: Will you tell him?

WOMAN: I don't know.

MAN: *[sings "A Lie…"]*

> I lean across his table
> To let him know…
> But find that I'm unable
> And let it go
>
> And suddenly I've kissed him
> And with a sigh
> I whisper that I've missed him—
> He gropes my thigh.
>
> Removing all my clothing,
> He presses on.
> A second of self-loathing
> And then it's gone.
>
> A flicker of desire
> And we are caught
> I am a better liar
> Than I once thought.

[Lights change. WOMAN *leans on the piano and reads from the citizenship application.]*

WOMAN: "If your application is approved, you will be required to take the following oath of allegiance: I hereby declare, on oath, that I absolutely and entirely renounce and abjure all allegiance and fidelity to any foreign prince, potentate, state or sovereignty, of whom or which I have heretofore been a subject or citizen…"

WOMAN: What does that mean?

MAN: I don't know.

WOMAN: What if September is a boy?

MAN: I don't know.

WOMAN: I hate that.

MAN: Yes…Not knowing can plunge you into an abyss. The fact is we know very little about anything. Like before the big bang. What was there where the universe is now?

[Lights change.]

WOMAN 2: What did you get him for Christmas?

WOMAN: Nothing.

WOMAN 2: Don't you believe in Christmas?

WOMAN: What does that mean?

MAN: I don't know.

WOMAN 2: Did you get a Christmas tree? Did you decorate it with a dozen-for-three-ninety-nine shiny colorful balls? Did you see the Christmas display at Macy's? Did you notice the cotton ball and tinsel decoration in the drugstore window on Christopher Street? Did you send out Christmas cards with some stranger's generic greeting already written on them? Did you go to a Woolworth on Sunday and try to get to the kitchenware section against all odds?

WOMAN: Why?

WOMAN 2: Participating in Christmas makes people feel better about their lives. Can't you forgive them?

WOMAN: I saw a woman today. Old. Homeless. Cold. She was so ashamed. She had no socks.

HOMELESS WOMAN: Please spare me some change. I haven't eaten since breakfast. This morning I had...*[She looks down and thinks really hard.]* Eggs, I think. Maybe it was macaroni and cheese. Yes, that's it. Ham and cheese.

[Lights change.]

WOMAN: When I was a child, I couldn't distinguish right from left. I got them all wrong on the test in whatever grade you learn the difference between right and left. I couldn't understand why when I'm facing you, my left is your right, and the only way we can experience the same space, the same leftness and rightness, is for you to turn your back to me. So I got the questions all wrong. When I showed the test to my mother, she was standing in her apron with a bunch of very long carrots in her hand.

MOTHER: *[Angrily]* How will you ever become a doctor without being able to tell right from left?

WOMAN: She lifted the carrots and beat me on the head with them. They shattered and flew. I don't remember if we had carrots for dinner that night.

[Lights change.]

WOMAN: Sometimes I still stop and think—
In my right hand,
I hold a pen
I hold a glass of water
When I lie on top of you,
I touch your face with my right hand.
When I sleep closer to the window,
I hold you with my right arm.
[Music]
In my left hand,
I hold nothing.
When you are driving,
I reach over
and touch your face with my left hand
only when the act doesn't burn my hand.
When I sleep next to the wall,
I hold your body
with my left arm
only when my arm doesn't turn into
a hollow piece of wood.

WOMAN 2: Why is my left always your right?

WOMAN: I know my right will never be yours.

[Music. Lights change.]

MAN AT THE DELI: What can I get you, honey?

WOMAN: I'll have tuna fish with lettuce and tomato on…

MAN AT THE DELI: What is it, honey?

WOMAN: Tuna with lettuce…

MAN AT THE DELI: What? Honey, honey?

WOMAN: Tuna with…

MAN AT THE DELI: Honey, honey, honey, asoooo?

WOMAN: Tuna.

MAN AT THE DELI: What do you want? Speak up.

WOMAN: Ham and cheese!

MAN AT THE DELI: Coming right up.

[Lights change.]

WOMAN: Fire.

WOMAN 2: Where?

WOMAN: In the rainforest.

WOMAN 2: Yes.

WOMAN: How much can burn before…

WOMAN 2: Before?

WOMAN: Before there is no more Rosy Periwinkle left in the world.

WOMAN 2: But it doesn't mean anything.

WOMAN: What if September gets leukemia? How would I find the medicine woman?

WOMAN 2: I don't know.

MAN: Not knowing can help you stay sane. Not knowing when the end will come to this endless time we call history. But this may not be the last.

There may be a life after this one. Another chance to tell Paul "I love you." You don't know.

WOMAN: *[hopeful]* I don't know.

[Lights change. Music.]

WOMAN 2: So what does he do?

WOMAN: He pierces my breasts with a spear, punctures my heart, puts his hand in the wound, and turns my heart inside out. His words circulate in my blood veins.

WOMAN 2: Why are you always so fucking dramatic? I just want to know what his job is.

WOMAN: He is a carpenter.

[Lights change.]

WOMAN: Paul, I brought you some miso soup. Do you think you can eat it? Paul, I'm pregnant. It's a mistake. How would I know what's the right thing to do? How can I be sure she won't grow up to be a Republican or a born-again Christian? How do I know September won't eat my soul to survive? He says,

PAUL: Who is the father?

WOMAN: He is a carpenter. Paul is delighted to hear this.

PAUL: Jesus was a carpenter.

WOMAN: Paul, would you eat something? He looks at the soup sadly and says,

PAUL: I should get Chekhov out in the world, but some days I just can't stop throwing up.

[Lights change.]

MAN: *[sings "But Then/And Then"]*

We hug good-bye, I turn, but then
I abruptly turn around again.

And I am now a sorceress—
A blinding beam of light
Infinite in might.

I reach inside your sallow skin
And with a razor's ease
Excise the disease.

I fling it far into the air
Then summon forth the force
To reverse its course.

So you are well and strong again—
All scars and signs of waste
Instantly erased.

Victorious, I then decree
Forever you'll remain
Free from harm and pain.

We hug good-bye, I turn, and then
I go out into the rain again.

WOMAN: *[to* WOMAN 2*]* Will Paul be here to teach September all that he taught me? Will he grow old with us?

WOMAN 2: September will know him anyway. You will teach her. You'll teach her how to perform Antigone.

WOMAN: What if the audience thinks she is performing a nice Duck? How can I save her from the hurt?

WOMAN 2: You can't.

WOMAN: *[Pause]* If you think I'm a duck, that's because I am. An ugly duckling.

[Lights change.]

WOMAN: Once I saw my mother's photograph when she was in high school. She was very beautiful. Nagano, 1956. A small town surrounded by mountains they call Japanese Alps. My mother is leaning on a tree in her navy school uniform. Her hair is long and straight. Her two friends are also in uniforms. They look rural, with red cheeks and messy hair. Not at all like my mother.

Shortly after this photograph was taken, she married my father and went from a wealthy landowner's house to a poor journalist's one-room apartment. She was nineteen and he was thirty-one.

I remember when I was little, my noisy aunts would gather around a table at my house and talk about how adorable my little sister was.

Such white skin. Such big eyes. My mother would say I had been out in the sun. When I look at photographs of my childhood, I see a girl, usually in a blue dress, always clenching her fists. I also see my sister, usually in a soft pink dress.

When I became a teenager, the same noisy aunts would come over and say I looked so much like my mother.

MOTHER: Not at all. Impossible. She doesn't look anything like me.

WOMAN: I remember my beautiful mother in the photograph. And I grew up to be an ugly woman.

[Lights change. Music.]

WOMAN: Kennedy Airport. I'm back to become a citizen. Maybe September is the missing piece of my life. Maybe I can figure out the puzzle finally.

[Lights change.]

WOMAN: The Maya were the first to live peacefully in the forest. Farming. Caring.

WOMAN 2: I guess we've forgotten.

WOMAN: Chain saws to bulldozers. A revolution.

WOMAN 2: But it doesn't mean anything in Poughkeepsie or Louisville or New York City. It won't affect September. September will be safe.

WOMAN: Are you sure? According to the Mayan calendar, this world ends on December 23, 2012.

[Lights change.]

WOMAN: Keep this for me.

WOMAN 2: What is it?

WOMAN: It's a chime box. Someone threw it out on the street. I found it.

WOMAN 2: It's beautiful. Why?

WOMAN: In case something happens to me.

WOMAN 2: *[Pause.]* Over September?

WOMAN: Over September. One way or another.

[Pause.]

WOMAN 2: I don't think having one baby means destruction of the rainforest. September alone won't cause ten million species' extinction. You
think you are Medea, don't you?

WOMAN: No. But you may have a baby, too. They will grow up together and
use hairspray and eat at McDonald's.

[Lights change.]

WOMAN: Paul had a mission to get Chekhov out in the world, but some
days he just couldn't stop throwing up because of the medicine that
prevented the dreams in his eyes from fading. He got tired of dealing
with macro and micro at the same time, dealing with approaching
death and nausea at the same time. He held his hand to me, long fingers with square tips, as I sat on the edge of his hospital bed. On the
edge of the abyss.

WOMAN 2: September will know Paul anyway.

WOMAN: You know I'm an orphan.

WOMAN 2: I know.

[Lights change.]

WOMAN: I sleep alone in New York City. A Gray Line bus parks under my
window at four A.M. every morning with its engine running. I wait for
the humming of carbon monoxide to blend into the first sign of light.

September will be my shaman. She will also be my destroyer. I know
this.

[WOMAN leans on the piano. She is reading from the citizenship application.]

WOMAN: "List your addresses during the last five years. List your employers
during the last five years. If you are between the ages of fourteen and
seventy-five, you must submit your fingerprints."

I step into the N train going downtown.

[Music.]

WOMAN: The subway car is filled with a song. A young black man, slightly
disheveled, is sitting in a seat singing. Beautiful. There is a black woman
in a business suit. She wears a Walkman, with her back to the singer.
She is turning the volume up and up and up, so she doesn't have to listen to him. After the song is over, he stands up and says,

MAN: I'm a subway singer.

WOMAN: No one moves. I take out all my change—only seventy-five cents—and place it in his palm. He bows and serenades me. Two songs. On the N train going downtown. On my way to get fingerprinted. Two beautiful songs, for seventy-five cents.

MAN: *[reprises "the bridge," ending it with a new coda.]*

> In a leaden river
> I am spun away
> Whirling in its water and decay
>
> And the hanging branches
> I so vainly clutch
> Brittle, snap off at my fingers' touch
>
> Should I scream or cry out
> Not a soul would come
> So I float in silence, growing numb
>
> Closer comes the ocean
> Fierce and black as night
> As the shoreline disappears from sight
>
> I am taken under
> Lost in the debris
> Then above beyond my reach I see
> A bridge
> A bridge
>
> A bridge
> Spanning two shores
> Level with the sky
> Light bouncing off

[Lights out.]

END

I got you under my skin

V. Thandi Sule'

Seven days before I embark upon the new year, my skin starts to peel. I awaken each morning with dead skin hanging from the sides of my cheeks, my forehead and underneath my chin. But I am still perplexed, because you are still here. Despite the face lotions and oils that I've been experimenting with to rid myself of blackheads, I view my irritated skin as merely a symptom of change. I regard my shedding as an awakening. But you are still here?

As I face the mirror, surveying my skin with equal amounts of fascination and horror, I wonder if the lifeless shreds of flesh are my destiny. I wonder if I should simply rinse pieces of me down the drain or gather the withered flakes and place them in a sacred place. I wonder if they know why I am renewing myself. Yet you are still here.

I am on a precipice. The new year is on my back and the ache in my spine warns me that it is hastily inching towards my head. So, I kneel as not to lose my balance. I caress my face and thank gods, goddesses, spirits and ancestors for allowing me to regenerate. I request everything that will keep me whole during the coming year. My ramblings are very specific and empathic, yet I make no mention of you.

I become still. I listen for anything that will give me direction about what to do about you. I can feel my thoughts of you weaving through my cerebellum. These thoughts become a nuisance, diverting attention away from things that I am more confident about. But I cannot help but wonder why you were placed in my life. Is the creator trying to test my threshold of pain? Is she a jokester giving me life by bringing me closer to death?

So, I remain gasping for air, suffocating in my orgasmic juices. Shamed that I gave all of myself to you, yet overjoyed by my willingness to do so. I bathe in this quandary—this maxim of my life. My hyper-pigmented, acned, dry-yet-oily and recently scaly skin is only a symptom. My preoccupation with it is only a deterrent.

You have drained me and no amount of ointments will halt my body's natural instinct to regenerate. I am comforted by the new year, so I realize that this change is welcome. However, every so often, I feel a twitch just below my left eye or numbness just above my upper lip. And these signs serve to remind me of why my body is not turning over—replenishing—unhindered. I have taken you in subcutaneously. Your flesh is meshed with mine, making it very difficult for my body to instinctively break free. To do that would surely mean death—though momentary, death just the same.

It is the truth of my pending death that keeps my mind on anything but you. I believed that if I did not think of you, then I could remain forever in this evolutionary limbo. I could investigate skin treatments and try various holistic therapies in order not to succumb to the reality that *maybe this relationship must end.*

It is the *may be* that has got me perplexed. Because in the *may be* is my laughter, the tingle in my labia, my imaginings and wonderment, your neediness and my embrace. *May be* has brought me hope and confusion on the first day of the new year.

Yet.

It is the *maybe* that keeps life just below the surface of my skin—stirring things up.

Discussion Questions

Positive Women

1. Presented all together on a single night as one continuous theatrical experience, each of these plays is authored by a different playwright and based on the life of a different woman. Do you think that this format gives audiences a different kind of experience from that offered by single author, single subject plays? If so, what do you think the differences are?

2. The creators of this series want audiences to experience a kind of emotional arc as they watch (or read) the plays together, with *Loves That Kill* representing discovery, *Mariluz's Thanksgiving* representing anger, *Delia's Race* representing fear, *now and then* representing hope, *Ilka's Dream* representing love, and *Elba's Birthday* celebrating life. Discuss how each of the plays embodies its chosen theme.

Prologue: Loves That Kill by Sandra Rodríguez

1. What does each woman's decision about whether or not to disclose her HIV status tell us about her own attitudes toward HIV, especially as these reflect attitudes we see in the society as a whole? What other kinds of things factor into whether or not people disclose their HIV status?

2. How does the setting of the doctor's office shape the interaction of the characters?

3. How do the songs and dances at the play's opening establish a mood and a context for what follows in the doctor's office?

4. How does this play function as a prologue to the series? That is, how does it foreshadow or lay the groundwork for what follows?

Mariluz's Thanksgiving by Migdalia Cruz

1. Like *Loves That Kill*, *Mariluz's Thanksgiving* opens with visions of childhood. How do Mariluz's memories of her younger self relate to how she thinks about her current situation?

2. Are we meant to see Mariluz as angry at Felipe? If so, how does she express and not express that anger? Why?

3. How does the nature of Mariluz and Felipe's courtship and marriage play out in the way they approach dealing with their HIV?

4. Do you think it's significant that most of Mariluz's dialogue is directed

toward the Virgin Mary? Similarly, do you find it significant that Felipe is present but asleep?

5. Do you think Mariluz is a strong person?

Delia's Race by Carmen Rivera

1. Early in the play, what do we learn, both through what Delia says and what other characters say about her, about how Delia has dealt with being HIV positive up to the point of the play's beginning?

2. How does Delia react to learning that her T-cell count is zero?

3. What do you think Delia means when she says to the Doctor, "It's not like finding out you're HIV positive" and when she says to her daughter, "When I found out I was HIV positive, I thought I was going to die."

4. How does Delia's HIV status affect how she and her daughter relate to each other?

5. What is the significance of Delia finishing the race?

now and then by Michael John Garcés

1. Monica speaks both in monologue and in dialogue with others. How connected to others does she seem to you? Is she isolated or in community, or some combination of both?

2. What are the main conflicts between Monica and Eric? As his disease progresses, how do his expectations change? How does she respond to those expectations? Overall, how would you characterize their relationship?

3. What are the main conflicts between Monica and David? Does their relationship change over the course of the play? If so, what do you think causes that change?

4. Although Tanya is mostly supportive of Monica, a number of disagreements nevertheless emerge in their exchanges. How do these disagreements help us to think about the play's major themes and issues?

5. What is the relationship between "now" and "then"?

6. How might some of the stylistic choices—i.e., use of the lower case, no stage directions, first initials only for characters' names—impact an actor's interpretation of these roles? What was the impact of these stylistic choices on your reading?

Ilka: The Dream by Candido Tirado

1. Why is Ilka having trouble letting go? How do Manolito and Victor try to help her?

2. Why do you think the characters are wearing masks at the beginning and end of the play?

3. Why do you think the playwright chose to tell the story of Ilka's life from the vantage point of her death? What impact does this choice have on your reading of the play?

4. This is a play that is in some sense *about* a play, depicting as is does Victor and Manolito staging Ilka's life. What does *Ilka's Dream* seem to say about the function of drama?

5. What different perspectives on HIV/AIDS do the varioius relationships in the play reveal?

Epilogue: Elba's Birthday by Louis Delgado

1. How are the behavior and attitudes of the four main characters different from and/or similarly to their behavior and attitudes in the Prologue? Do the intervening plays help you to understand any change that might have occurred?

2. What is the significance of their ritual in celebrating each other's birthdays?

3. How does this play act as an epilogue to the series as a whole?

Love & Danger by Imani Harrington

1. What kind of world do the Players flee from, to, and why? How does this relate to society?

2. The playwright invented three specific roles for each character to play. What do you think the significance is of each character playing the roles of Player, Agent, and Social Chorus?

3. Salome is the object of Winter's and Candice's hostility. What are some of the reasons for this hostility? What role does Selena play in this conflict? How does this affect the course of dramatic action?

4. Why do you think Player E is the only character that does not get named? How do the possible reasons for this choice relate to HIV/AIDS?

5. What different forms do both love and danger take in this play?

6. In the beginning of the play, the words "positive" and "negative" simply

represent HIV status. As the play evolves what other kinds of meanings do these words take on?

7. Showing their palm markings is one of the ways the characters reveal themselves. How do the further revelations that the women make to each other change the dramatic course of the play?

8. The playwright uses a number of metaphors throughout the play. Identify some of those metaphors and discuss how they function in the play.

9. How does the play suggest new ways of thinking about living with HIV/AIDS in the future?

So... by Migdalia Cruz

1. How do various meanings of the word "so" function in this play?

2. As the play ends, each of the characters refers to kissing, and all together they ask, "So what's a kiss?" How would you answer that question based on your reading of the play?

3. In the cast of characters, the characters are identified as a "hopeless romantic" (A Woman), a "tender fatalist" (A Man), a "grounded realist" (Another Woman), and a "scared pragmatist" (Another Man). What elements of what each character says corresponds to these descriptions? Do these descriptions relate to the characters' various attitudes and beliefs about HIV/AIDS?

4. How do we see the different views of the characters about HIV/AIDS reflected in people, policies, and institutions in the larger society?

5. What role does God play? Would it make a difference, for instance, if the characters were talking to each other?

One Less Queen by Mario Golden

1. The relationship between Juan Gallo and Chuyis sets into motion the violent events that drive the narrative of this play. What are the dynamics between them (how they treat each other, see each other) that contribute to Chuyis shooting Edgar? How do the choices that Juan Gallo and Chuyis make reflect their social and cultural context, not only in terms of broad categories such as race, class, gender and sexuality, but in terms of more particular contexts as well, such as gang culture, child sexual abuse, HIV status?

2. Another important relationship in the play is that between Alfonso and Salvador. What kinds of conflicts emerge as they negotiate their relationship? Do you see any connection between what happens between Alfonso and Salvador and what happens between Juan Gallo and Chuyis?

3. Luz Paloma and Celia also face a number of conflicts. How are these conflicts, and the couple's way of dealing with them, different from and/or similar to what we see happening between Alfonso and Salvador and between Juan Gallo and Chuyis?

4. What is the function of the spirit world in this play?

5. During one of the courtroom scenes, Luz Paloma questions Juan Gallo about the significance of his nickname. How does she connect that name to his character and the nature of his relationship to Chuyis? Do any of the other characters' names provide similar insight into who they are or what they do?

6. How do the courtroom scenes help to develop some of the important themes this play is dealing with?

7. What do you think this play is saying about "family"? Can you relate its ideas about "family" to your own experience of "family"?

The Watermelon Factory by Alfonso Ramirez

1. How does the relationship between Connie and Gabriel change over the course of the play? What is revealed about these characters that would seem to draw them together? What things seem to drive them apart?

2. What is each character's relationship to religion and the Catholic Church?

3. How have gender, ethnicity, class, and generation shaped the experiences and perspectives of Connie and Gabriel?

4. What is the significance of Gabriel's HIV/AIDS status to the action of the play?

5. What does the ending suggest about the possibility of a future relationship between Connie and Gabriel?

Ashes to Ashes by Marijo

1. Why is it important for Mother Dumpler to get her son's ashes from the pipe?

2. What is the function of the ladder? Why, do you think, does the ladder get personified?

3. What are the attitudes of the church people toward people with HIV? How do we see their views reflected in what they do and say?

4. What is distinctive about the play's use of language?

5. *Ashes to Ashes* tells a serious story in a very exaggerated and humorous way. What is the effect of that choice on your response to the characters and events in the play?

6. Why is so much of the story told through the narrator rather than just acted out by the characters?

Black Power Barbie by Shay Youngblood

1. Discuss Tabitha's relationship to Black Power Barbie. What does the doll mean to her, especially in terms of her family history and her sexual and social identity? In what ways does Tabith use Black Power Barbie? Is this use or are these uses benefical or detrimental to Tabitha—or both? Does her use of the doll change over the course of the play?

2. We see a number of dreams in the play, for instance, Tabitha's dreams about Jackson and Paolo. What do you think the significance of these dreams is?

3. How do events from the past, and the characters' memories of those events, affect the present action in the play?

4. In some ways, what happens to Tabitha and Jackson may seem unique and specific to them, especially given their dramatic family history. Nevertheless, do you find it possible to relate to the issues they are dealing with or the way they deal with those issues?

5. How does Jackson having AIDS impact Tabitha?

6. What do Tabitha's fantasies tell us about her psychology?

7. How much of a part do you think gender plays in the difference between Tabitha's and Jackson's response to their experiences, both as children and as adults?

Nothing Forever by Chiori Miyagawa

1. How does the title *Nothing Forever* reflect what's going on in the play?

2. How do the playwright's stylistic choices—in terms of language, form, tempo, etc.—contribute to the play's meaning?

3. What kinds of cultural misunderstandings has the main character faced as she has moved back and forth between Japan and the United States?

4. What kinds of concerns does the main character have about bringing a child into the world?

5. Toward the end of the play we learn that Paul, a close friend of the main character, is dying of AIDS. How does this connect to the perspectives and concerns expressed throughout the play?

6. What do you make of the playwright's choice to leave all of the characters except for Paul unnamed?

7. The play begins and ends with "the bridge." How do the lyrics speak to the themes expressed in this play, such as loss, identity, and hope? How do the other songs contribute to the play's meaning?

POETRY, PERFORMANCE, AND MONOLOGUE

december song by Kehinde Apara

1. What is the emotional tone of this poem?

2. In what way does the language of this poem offer hope?

I'se Married by Sweet Potato Pie

1. What are some of the challenges of living and loving with HIV that the narrators recount?

2. What attidude do they take toward these challenges?

3. What do you think the significance is of using "I'se Married" from *The Color Purple* in this piece?

Allah appears as an eyelash in brooklyn by Dorinda Welle

1. How do you think the metaphor(s) in this poem contribute to the reader's thoughts about the poem's subject matter?

2. What is sensual about this poem? What is humourous?

Numb by Zelma Brown

1. What is the feeling and tone of this poem?

2. How does the speaker relate to her HIV consciousness?

3. What changes for the speaker?

Elegy by Joanne Bealy

1. How does the narrator express the emotion in this piece?

2. What impact does death have on love and memory?

3. What does the narrator gain by this loss?

Dolly: Old Lady, Love, and Life by Q.V. Atkins

1. What are the significant things we come to understand about the character?

2. How does the character view HIV?

Like Mama Like Daughter by Kulwa Apara

1. What do we learn about the relationships between these characters?

2. What kind of feeling do you get for the character as she speaks to her mother?

3. How does HIV infection get talked about?

I got you under my skin by V. Thandi Sule'

1. Who is the "you" in this poem?

2. In what way do the body and mortality collide in this poem?

3. What is sensual and erotic about this piece?

Theater, Acting, and Writing Exercises

INTRODUCTION

Purpose of the Exercises

These experimental exercises, based on the principles of acting, playwriting, and Augusto Boal's "Theatre of the Oppressed," are written to help readers and theater participants identify and discuss major issues, themes and sub-themes from the plays, poetry and monologues in *Positive/Negative*, as well as generate new ideas for those who are creating their own work. These exercises have been designed for individuals Boal refers to as "actors" and "non-actors." This idea of accessibility is being further extended to any and everyone, especially "writers" and "non-writers" who may be interested in creating a body of dramatic work for the stage and/or the page.

The exercises will help those writing, sculpting and creating images for scenes, monologues, and short plays, and are useful sources when creating and inventing characters. They are also intended to stimulate creative responses to various situations and ideas stemming from the works in the anthology. Through the processes of "doing" and "being" they will help users explore the aesthetic discipline of acting and express their creativity and intellectual imaginations. They are also skill-building exercises in which participants can learn to trust their impulses, take risks they might not usually take, and acquire techniques for performance. Importantly, these exercises teach participants that their thoughts matter and that they may in fact "write" text. And finally, these exercises will help to build a way of looking at the world and effecting social transformation through understanding, debating, and exploring oppression through various perspectives.

Suggestions for the Facilitator

A trained facilitator should oversee these exercises, guiding group participants in their process of discovery and intervening only to clarify physical exercises or offer suggestions to group participants. There are a number of ways to conduct these workshops (and to perform the role of facilitator) and there are many resources and locales which offer training; these exercises are designed to help the facilitator get a group started doing the basics. For additional exercises, as well as information on Theatre of the Oppressed and training resources, please see the reference list at the end of this chapter.

We suggest that before workshop participants begin exploring these exercises they generate a critical discussion on the aesthetics and standards of theater, and what purports to make theater theater. For example, there are many critics of "Aristotelian" theater who believe that "true" life experiences destroy theatrical illusion and should not be reflected on the American stage, or that new forms of theater and writing do not go well with the old forms. Do you agree? Why or why not? What aspects of the human experience have the right to be on the stage?

Group Sharing

At various points during the workshop, the facilitator should split the group into smaller units and take turns discussing their discoveries, insights, etc. After smaller group discussions have taken place, the facilitator should have participants gather again as a large group and share their observations, experiences and perceptions. Group sharing can be a very rewarding experience, especially when work has been created collectively because it can help participants recognize the value of the overall group process.

PLAYWRITING

Discuss some of the themes and sub-themes that appear in *Positive/Negative*. Stemming from your own ideas, use one of these themes (or your own, related theme) and write a 10-minute short play/one-page play/scene/2-5 minute dramatic monologue.

Note: To help beginning writers and theater participants accomplish this task, it may be helpful to start by discussing "conventional" versus "non-conventional" standards of playwriting. "Conventional" tends to refer to the standard elements used to write a play, including: conflict/crisis, action, plot, character and dialogue (presented in a linear, but sometimes non-linear way), etc. A few of the plays in this anthology are written using both standards of playwriting. Review and discuss what you think those conventions are and compare them with other plays in the anthology, or other plays. Once you have identified them, try writing a play for the stage and/or the page that uses either of these conventions, or both, as a method to tell a story. It may also blend aspects of fact and fiction. This process will help beginning writers experience what methods and approaches of writing work for them, and will help as they create, redefine, and reinvent fresh play ideas of their own.

IMPROV EXERCISES FOR WRITING DRAMATIC SCENES, MONOLOGUES, AND PLAYS

In small groups, explore creating characters by doing an improv on theme(s) from the anthology (or your own themes) using character(s) from any of the plays or your own character(s). Place your main character in a situation that oppresses her/him and then have the character break through that oppression. The situation can be one in which oppression takes the form of a moment when racism, sexism, classism, etc., is experienced or it can simply be an "oppressive" and/or "conflict" situation or circumstance—i.e., you are in a room with two other persons from your group and the room is on fire. In this case, it is the fire that acts as the oppression. What will you and the others do in order to get out of this situation? Or, the situation can be from one of the plays—for example, in *Delia's Race* there is a critical moment where Delia is feeling particularly oppressed by her circumstances pertaining to her HIV status. That moment is a great opportunity to explore various ways of "breaking through" oppression.

After doing an improv, pen a one-page or short play, scene, or a monologue that shows the progression of the "break" and which incorporates non-conventional or conventional dramatic qualities, or both.

Note: Another way to approach this writing exercise is to have one of your group members tape-record your improv. After the first try at the improv, you will have established the beginning of a body of new work with fresh ideas that will continue to develop each time you play it out. By recording the improv, you will always have a place of reference for possible alternate versions. This allows you to go back and choose a particular moment(s) that is particularly powerful.

SPECT-ACTOR: SEEING/DOING

Note: This exercise can be done in conjunction with any of the other exercises.

Choose a group of spect-actors (in Boal's terminology, "spect-actors" are active spectators who take part in the action; in this context, they are participants who are observing the exercise) to write a scene together based on what they observed in another group's creation on the stage (watching others perform an idea will spark new ideas). These scenes can either be "written" on the stage or with an actual pen. After the group has come up with their scene(s) (there might be two versions of the scene—one constructed for the stage as an improv and the other to be written language), have the group and/or individuals present a stage reading of their work. This can be done at both the group and individual level. This process illustrates another way to write, and helps participants to create fresh ideas from observation and apply their new ideas. It also allows individuals to see what the role of a spect-actor might look like when invited to participate in something someone has created. It also shows the role of an audience member who does not take part in any of the action, but rather, sits and watches the drama unfold.

CHARACTER CONSTRUCTION/DEVELOPMENT

Note: This biography exercise is a standard method for creating characters.

Participants draft a character biography which details specific character data and do an improv on the character. Then another participant interviews the character, asking questions that help to build the character's reality. The interview material should be used to inform the first participant as to what was previously not known about the character.

Next, the facilitator should plan a time to take the character outside of the workshop, allowing the character to experience being in another environment. Participants are to document what they notice about the character's development. Ideas from this research about the character and her/his relationship to society, self and others can be brought back to the lab and put towards developing the character. (These characters are not meant to be directly "provocative" to others in society, as in Invisible Theatre. Rather, this is a character development exercise to help make characters multidimensional and interesting). Finally, a group discussion should take place in which participants talk about the experience and their discoveries.

SOCIAL CHORUS

Note: This experimental exercise utilizes the concept of the Social Chorus (which appears in the play Love & Danger*) to explore moments of oppression. It is an adaptation of Augusto Boal's "Cops-in-the-Head" and David Diamond's "Corporations in Our Heads" exercises—the difference is in how it is applied and used.*

Group members brainstorm words/themes and write them down. Next, three members are selected to be the Social Chorus, and a number of others are selected to be actors. The facilitator chooses a word/theme and gives it to the Social Chorus, who create "choruses" (refrains which will be said/sung in unison) that relate to the theme. The actors will improv a scene as a response to the Social Chorus, and the Social Chorus will voice their refrain throughout the scene.

Each time this is done, the facilitator should have the group explore the exercise. What are the voices saying to these characters? How does the Social Chorus impact the person or persons to whom the voices are directed? What might a reply be to those voices? What response does the group have to the choruses established? How does the concept of the Social Chorus relate to HIV/AIDS, and other themes in daily and social life?

SUBJECT-OBJECT

Note: The "using an object" exercise is based on the work of Armand Volkas at the Drama Therapy Institute in Oakland, California.

The facilitator chooses an object (anything from a condom or dental dam to a knife) that is real (physical) or imaginary. In a circle, the participants pass the object around until the facilitator selects someone to go into the center of the circle and use the object in either a "private" moment or a "public" one. It can be verbal or non-verbal and should last no more than five minutes. After the participant is done, the facilitator should explore with the group the experience of sharing "public" and "private" moments. What makes a moment "private" or "public"? How does the use of the object relate to the moment, the epidemic, social issues and/or Theatre of the Oppressed?

POZ/NEG

Note: This exercise helps to stimulate deeper thought about circumstances and conflict, and offers new ways to build on topics for writing along with character and dramatic development.

1. In pairs, participants take turns creating two characters and placing them in a conflict. The outcome of this exercise will reflect a particular type of consciousness, created by the experiences and perceptions of each participant, showing how different people perceive and interpret conflict(s).

2. Place the pair of characters (or two pairs) together and create a five- to fifteen-minute scene. The scene should demonstrate (through their verbal and non-verbal language, actions, dialogue and goals) what the characters want, but seem not to be able to get. The next scene should show them actually getting what they want.

3. Finally, take the pair of characters and give one HIV-negative status and the other HIV-positive status. They must explore, discuss and study possible ways to get what they want from each other. If one character is HIV-positive, she or he can, for example, see if the other character will accept her or his HIV status and, if so, what happens next, and so on. You may modify HIV to be anything else for this exercise. There are many variations that this interplay of oppositional roles/positions between individuals or between an individual and society can take. In a larger group discussion, explore what these could be.

SUB-STORY EXERCISES

Note: The term "sub-story" refers to a story being told from another person's point of view.

Image Work

Note: This image work allows participants to demonstrate and rehearse their ideas. It also lays the foundation for the sub-story writing exercises. This exercise draws on Boal's Image Theatre.

Using a main or sub-theme from *Positive/Negative* (or your own, related theme) tell a sub-story. Then, build on the sub-story by selecting members of the group and "sculpting" an image that reflects the theme(s) being constructed (as in Boal, "sculpting" here refers to using the body to make a theme or moment alive—for example, in sculpting "climbing," you might position one's arms and legs in a climbing position). As a group, discuss the image created and the process of creation. What is representational about the image and how does it relate to HIV/AIDS, or the selected themes of the exercise?

Next, tell the sub-story by acting it out. Because you will be pulling from your subconscious as you improv, new thoughts will come up for the sub-story. After you have presented your story to the group, tell it again, but this time someone will join you after a few minutes and begin to improvise with you. You should stand side by side, looking not at each other, but as if you are looking at the fourth wall. After this is done, the two people will have created their own story together. Work on the sub-stories for story and character development, including dramatic effect, using elements of playwriting to achieve this goal. You may also do more image work on them. After a few times, you should have established the beginning of a very good sub-story for performance.

Group Work

In groups of five, share your scene (story) in under five minutes. Have different members of the group do both non-verbal and action-oriented scenes based on the stories. Afterwards, share your work in the larger group.

Team Work

Tell a story about any issue, metaphor, object or character from *Positive/Negative* (for example, from *Mariluz's Thanksgiving*). Create an image of your story by depicting some aspect of the work that you believe the writer intended as their vision. Act this out in teams of two or three individuals.

Scene Work

Choose a scene from any of the plays that reflects some type of conflict. Have two participants do first a non-verbal, and then a verbal, improv about the scene's conflict. Have participants take turns exploring the scene's possibilities. Later, discuss what would help further develop the scenes and what aspects of Theatre of the Oppressed, combined with other dramatic elements, could be applied to the same scene.

BREAKING THROUGH PERCEPTIONS, STIGMA, AND FEAR

The goal is for two individuals to keep each other safe, and to explore the notion of "safety" by their experience. One person is blindfolded, and their partner must keep that person from experiencing "danger." (What constitutes "danger" and "safety" should be established by the facilitator and performed by the other group participants.) The person leading should experiment with the signals that have been designated to indicate danger and safety, the different ways the person being led can experience them. This exercise helps one develop their own instincts and intuition and to define what feels "safe" or "dangerous." It can also be used in other forms of acting and trust-building exercises.

USING YOUR FIVE SENSES: TOUCH, TASTE, SMELL, SIGHT, HEARING

A participant chooses a guide from the audience (the group members who are observing). The guide leads the participant, whose eyes are closed, through a series of items on the floor. Each item should somehow incorporate all five senses, and the guide should make sure that all of the senses are utilized. Participants should discuss the experience after each round. This exercise is used in building trust. For other ways of doing this exercise, see Rénee Emunah and David Diamond.

Note: The participant should let the guide know when she or he feels "danger" or "safety." You may use the word "danger" (or something equivalent) when it feels dangerous and "safe" when it feels safe. It is important that this exercise be explored to its fullest, so that different meanings, experiences, and perceptions of "safety" and feeling "safe" can be illustrated. This is another exercise that builds trust and allows one's creative thoughts to be stimulated and acted upon.

CONCLUSION

Throughout the workshop, participants will have experienced creating, writing, and imaging, and will have shared some of their work with the entire group. Depending on the workshop, the group facilitator may then have each person choose a story that reflects some truth for them, and a story (perhaps the one that has a majority of people) will be selected to become a public "forum." Another option is to have a staged reading of the short plays for further development.

Positive/Negative: A Workbook

In order to let the reader experience the real voices of women and the actual voices of the writers, we designed a workbook separate from this anthology. A host of oral narratives, interviews and essays have been documented in order for the reader to have a more direct relationship to those whose voices we've unveiled. Our interviews provide insight into our contributors' experience as writers and spect-actors writing on the epidemic. We learn what aspects of the artists' visions were realized, and to what extent their work impacted social thought. They speak about how their work was influenced by those living with HIV and those who have died, along with details on their process and relationship to the work created. It is a celebration of voices and an attempt to unveil the perceptions and attitudes of those living with the reality of HIV and those who are actively creating change through their artistic endeavors. We invite all our readers to use the workbook along with this anthology in their study programs.

For information regarding the workbook, please call (415) 826-1300 or email (books@auntlute.com) Aunt Lute Books.

References and Further Reading

Boal, Augusto. *Games for Actors and Non-Actors*. Trans. Adrian Jackson. New York: Routledge Press, 1992.

Theatre of the Oppressed Laboratory. Brecht Forum, New York. Exercises and games created in this anthology are based on trainings received at the Brecht Forum with Augusto Boal.

Catron, Louise E. *The Elements of Playwrighting*. New York: Collier Books, 1993.

Collins, Patricia Hill. *Black Feminist Thought: Knowledge, Consciousness, and the Politics of Empowerment*. New York: Routledge, 1991.

Diamond, David. *A Joker's Guide to Theatre For Living*. Vancouver, BC: Headlines Theater, 1991, 1992, 1994, 1995, 2000. David Diamond has created a wide compendium of theater exercises and games. He also uses them in various training workshops on Theatre of the Oppressed.

Du Bois, W.E.B. *The Souls of Black Folk*. New York: The Modern Library, 1996.

Emunah, Renée. *Acting for Real: Drama Therapy Process, Technique, and Performance*. New York: Brunner/Mazel, 1994.

Goldstein, Nancy and Jennifer L. Manlowe. *The Gender Politics of HIV/AIDS in Women: Perspectives on the Pandemic in the United States*. New York: New York University Press, 1997.

Long, Lynellyn D. and E. Maxine Ankrah, eds. *Women's Experiences with HIV/AIDS: An International Perspective*. New York: Columbia University Press, 1996.

Mahone, Sydné. "Seers On The Rim," *American Theatre Magazine*. March 1994: 22-24.

Mahone, Sydné, ed. *Moon Marked and Touched by Sun: Plays by African American Women*. New York: Theatre Communications Group, 1994.

McTeague, James. *Playwrights and Acting Methodologies for Brecht, Ionesco, Pinter and Shepard*. Westport: Greenwood Press, 1994.

Roth, Nancy L. and Katie Hogan. *Gendered Epidemic: Representations of Women in the Age of AIDS*. New York: Routledge, 1998.

Squire, Corrine. "Neighbors Who Might Become Friends: Selves, Genres, and Citizenship in Narratives of HIV." *The Sociological Quarterly* (1999): 109-137. In this essay the author discusses and demonstrates, through the voices of HIV-positive women and men, the power of self in creating narratives about the self.

Schutzman, Mady and Jan Cohen-Cruz. *Playing Boal: Theatre, Therapy, Activism*. New York: Routledge, 1994.

Whitehorn, Laura. "America's Most Unwanted." *POZ Magazine* August 2000: 44-49.

The Contributors

Ernest Andrews has written and performed numerous solo and collaborative poems with Sweet Potato Pie, a performance art group dedicated to addressing AIDS from an African-American perspective. The group gained national attention when they performed at the San Francisco's AIDS Theatre Festival in 1993. Sweet Potato Pie's performances are known by many to be an emotional roller coaster ride–truthful, daring and full of honest grit.

Kulwa Apara is an accomplished young poet. A second-place winner at the Martin Luther King, Jr. Oratorical Fest 2000, Kulwa has performed her poetry in the play *Russian Roulette: Poison Places*; at M&M Special, a performing arts collective; and at various cafes in Oakland, California. She is involved with the Brazilian dance troupe Fogo Na Roupa, as well as Ballet Kiizingu, a Congolese troupe. She also enjoys painting. Kulwa says, "I am born from two magnificent beings that always made it a point to instill creativity and history. Creativity enables me to communicate with the Most High, and History allows me to continue paving the path first initiated by my ancestors. I am an illumination and reflection of the light I see in everyone and everything. My primary goal in life is to reconnect Black and brown children to the beauty from whence we came."

Kehinde Apara has been writing poetry, passionately, for six years, often creating visual art to accompany it. An avid dancer, she is involved in African, Brazilian and Polynesian dance troupes. Kehinde says, "I am the one who believes in the magic of life. I am open-minded and curious. I believe in looking past artificial barriers. I embrace unity amongst all people, and live a life full of love. And fun…lots of fun. I love the ocean and the sun; they sustain me greatly. I believe in God(dess) because I know (s)he believes in me."

Q.V. Atkins loves people and gets energized when onstage. An HIV/AIDS educator and writer, she prefers to work on projects that have a positive message, meaning and/or a mental healing effect on people. At her high school, she was a peer educator and directed student groups on issues about HIV/AIDS, STDs and other relevant teen issues. In September 2001, she traveled to Denmark to perform her written work. Q.V. says, "It is my goal to continue doing this work because it is an excellent way to openly express issues that some people think or wonder about, but feel uncomfortable talking about to others."

Joanne Bealy is from Montreal, Canada and currently lives between British Columbia, Canada, and Oakland, California. Her poetry and essays have appeared in various journals throughout the United States, and a chapbook of her poetry, *Crooked Love*, was published in 1999. Joanne says, "*Elegy* was first conceived at a time when it seemed every time I turned around, another friend was sick, dying, or dead. It was written particularly for one very good friend, but more generally as an antidote, as a means for me to try and give some meaning, if that was at all possible, and some hope." Joanne is currently working on a manuscript of poems and essays.

Zelma Brown, a native San Franciscan, is an artist and published poet. She was the mother of twin sons by age thirteen and had experienced both homelessness and foster/group homes by age sixteen. Her experiences have guided her present vocation, on the staff of the Women's Daytime Drop-in Center in Berkeley, California. She has collaborated with photographer Meredith Stout on *The Sisters Project* as well as the multi-media presentation *My Sister, My Sister*. *The Sisters Project* and *My Sister, My Sister* serve as tributes to the dignity and courage of women and children engaged in struggle within a disorderly world. Zelma and Meredith realize the projects' ability to heal, change and empower, and hope to share this work with recovery centers, shelters, churches and schools around the country. Zelma currently attends Solano Community College.

Mark Campbell has written lyrics and libretti for traditional and non-traditional musical theatre, as well as for performance art, opera and dance. His work has been performed in diverse venues—from BAM's Majestic Theatre to the Joyce Theater, to off-Broadway. Mark has been awarded the first Kleban Foundation Award for Lyricist by a panel headed by Stephen Sondheim; the American Academy of Arts and Letters' Richard Rodgers Development Award for *The Sweet Revenge of Louisa May;* a Richard Rodgers Production Award and a Drama Desk Award nomination for *Splendora;* and a Rockefeller Foundation Award for *Nothing Forever*. He also received a New York Foundation for the Arts Playwriting Fellowship for his adaptation of Emile Zola's novel, *Thérèse Raquin*. Mark is a MacDowell Fellow and a member of the Dramatists Guild.

Migdalia Cruz is a prolific writer who has authored over thirty plays, operas and musicals. Her work has been produced in numerous venues, including the Houston Grand Opera, New York's Class Stage Company, Steppenwolf Theatre, New York's INTAR, and Camposanto in California. Among her numerous awards and fellowships are a NEA fellowship in playwriting,

Sundance playwriting and screenwriting residencies, and the TCG/PEW national artist-in-residence award. Migdalia has been commissioned to pen *El Grito Del Bronx* by the Public Theater/NYSF, and the University of Connecticut at Storrs has given her the Sackler Fellowship to complete *Featherless Angels*, her play about the effect of war on children. She has been writer-in-residence at the Latino Chicago Theatre Company since 1996. Born and raised in the Bronx, Migdalia is an alumna of New Dramatists.

Louis Delgado received the 1996 Obie Award for his play, *El Cano*, as part of the Repertorio Espanol New Voice Series. In 1993, he received the Roger L. Stevens Award for Promising Playwright for his off-Broadway drama, *A Better Life*, which was published in *Ollantay Theatre Magazine*. Louis was a member of the Puerto Rican Traveling Theatre Writers Workshop, and a founding member of the Puerto Rican Intercultural Drama Ensemble (P.R.I.D.E.), which produced four one-act plays entitled *Ricanstruction Stories from El Barrio* and his one-act drama *Men Don't Cry*. He also wrote *Tony and Son*, performed at the Tribeca Performing Arts Center, and *Pitito Revolver, the Broadway II Mystery*, an interactive comedy co-written with Gloria Feliciano. At the time of his sudden death on December 1, 1998, his play *Juanita's Trip* was in the midst of a successful run at La Tea Theatre. He was also writing a collection of short stories, two of which have been published in *N.Y. Latino Magazine*, and was working on a television sitcom.

Michael John Garcés is an accomplished playwright, director and performer. He has worked at numerous theaters, including Cherry Lane, Atlantic Theater Co., Actors Theatre of Louisville/ Humana Festival of New American Plays, INTAR Hispanic American Arts Center, Repertorio Español, Coconut Grove Playhouse, O'Neill Playwrights Conference, The Directors Company, Puerto Rican Traveling Theatre and Sna Jtz'ibajom ("The House of the Writer") in Chiapas, Mexico. His one-man show, *agua ardiente*, ran off-Broadway at the American Place Theatre as part of *Dreaming in Cuban and Other Works*. He is the recipient of a TCG New Generations Grant, a Princess Grace Fellowship, and playwriting fellowships from NYFA, NYSCA and the Mark Taper Forum.

Mario Golden is a Mexican-born and raised bilingual actor, playwright, producer and director. Over the past ten years, he has performed onstage and in film both in the United States and in Mexico. Mario co-wrote, co-produced and co-starred in the Spanish-language feature film *Del Otro Lado*, and has recently completed his one-man show, *Angel's Journey*. He is the co-founder and co-director of OneHeart Productions, a San Francisco-based nonprofit theater company dedicated to exploring the truth of the human experience through theatre, film and educational programs. Mario has studied method acting at the Rob Reece Actors Workshop and is a graduate of Stanford University, where he earned a B.A. in Psychology and an M.A. in Education. He lives in New York City.

Ntombi Howell is the Program Director for the Extended Family Recovery Program for the Glide Foundation in San Francisco's Tenderloin District. She has designed and developed programs at the Program in addition to facilitating culturally-based and gender-sensitive groups. Ntombi is a member of the faculty at the New College of California. As a survivor of domestic violence and a woman in recovery from substance abuse, she is wholly dedicated to helping people empower and heal themselves, utilizing culturally-based interventions inspired by the African concept of the extended family. A writer and performance artist, Ntombi, together with the well-known AIDS activist/writer/performer, Ernest Andrews, and the late Peter Barclay, a celebrated composer/lyricist/musician, formed the performance group Sweet Potato Pie, dedicated to addressing AIDS from an African-American perspective.

V. Thandi Sule' was born in Camden, New Jersey. She holds an M.A. in Africana Studies from Cornell University, and an M.S.W. from Rutgers University, and has served as an administrator of various health and education programs. While an undergraduate at Temple University, her commitment to women's health and education issues prompted her to establish the Daughters of Kush, which published several editions of the creative arts magazine *Ululation*. In 1991, Ms. Sule' won first prize in the Herman McCalmon playwriting competition for her drama *Echoes: Love, Politics and a Sister's Womb*. A single parent, Ms. Sule' is currently co-editing an anthology on Black female sexuality.

Marijo is an actress, storyteller, writer and arts educator. She uses her work and images to educate, entertain and to reveal the common bonds between cultures. A self-described Griot/Shaman, Marijo is a truth-teller and keeper of history who has performed around the world. In 1997 she spent the summer living in a rural village in Zimbabwe with the Shona Sculptors, where she exchanged stories and learned to sculpt from world-class artists. She received her training at the American Conservatory of Theater, and has been a storyteller-in-residence in the public school system, as well as an artist-in-residence with the California Arts Council. Marijo has worked as a voiceover actor for the California Newsreel video series *In Black & White: Conversations with African-American Writers* and is penning a book of short stories addressing AIDS in the African American community.

Chiori Miyagawa is the author of numerous plays, including *Woman Killer* (HERE, published in *Plays and Playwrights 2002*), *Nothing Forever* and *Yesterday's Window* (New York Theatre Workshop), *Yesterday* (published in *TAKE TEN*), *Jamaica Avenue* (New York International Fringe Festival, published in *Tokens? The NYC Asian American Experiences on Stage*), and *FireDance* (Voice&Vision Theater). She is the Artistic Associate of the New York Theatre Workshop, Associate Professor of Theater at Bard College under JoAnne Akalaitis, and co-founder of a theater company, Crossing Jamaica Avenue. Chiori met Paul Walker, actor, director, and legendary acting teacher, when she worked with him to create a theatrical event, *A Passenger Train of Sixty-one Coaches*, for the 1991 Humana Festival of New American Plays at Actors Theatre of Louisville. Paul and Chiori collaborated on her first play, *America Dreaming*, which was produced by Music-Theatre Group in co-production with Vineyard Theatre after his death in 1995. Chiori's vision and philosophy as playwright and theater artist were greatly influenced and shaped by Paul during the last year of his struggle for life.

Alfonso Ramirez's interest in the theater began at a very young age and has continued for over thirty years. He began as an actor before moving into dance and performance, but considers himself a writer first and foremost, having decided a decade ago that there were no interesting and realistic opportunities for Latinos because there were no Latino writers creating these roles. He received a full four-year scholarship to the University of Southern California's B.G.F.A. program and moved to New York. He hit the Big Apple in 1975 to study acting at HB Studio, and has lived there ever since. He has performed, and had his work performed, at several New York City companies, including LaMaMa ETC, the Puerto Rican Traveling Theatre, the Public Theater, Circle in the Square, and at Nosotros Theatre in Los Angeles. In 1982, he and a group of friends founded the now-defunct group, the Neighborhood Group Theatre. Working as one creative force, they wrote, directed and produced original works along New York's Theatre Row. An avid traveler who has visited Brazil, Mexico, Asia, Europe, Puerto Rico and cities in the U.S., Alfonso is a proud member of the Screen Actors, Writers and Dramatists Guilds, and AFTRA.

Carmen Rivera holds an M.A. in Playwriting and Latin American Theatre from New York University. As a founding member of L.E.F.T. (Latino Experimental Fantastic Theatre) she was one of the producers of "Positive Women." Her off-Broadway productions include *La Gringa* (in repertory at Repertorio Español; OBIE Award 1996); *La Lupe: My Life, My Destiny* (Puerto Rican Traveling Theatre [PRTT]; 2002 ACE Award, Best Production), *Julia de Burgos: Child of Water* [PRTT]; *To Catch the Lightning* (PRTT; 1997 Nomination ACE Award, Best Production); The Next Stop (INTAR/ Repertorio Español); *Under the Mango Tree* (INTAR). Her other work includes *Betty's Garage; ameRICAN; Plastic Flowers; The Power of Words;* and *The Nightmare,* which have been featured at LaMaMa ETC; Women's Project; SOHO Rep; Nuyorican Poet's Café; Theatre for a New City; City Lights Youth Theatre; in theater festivals in New York, Chile, Russia, Colombia and Bolivia; as well as on National Public Radio. Carmen was a Van Lier Fellow at New Dramatists in 1995. Her publications include: *One-Acts at the Women's Project, Women Who Write Theatre* (Smith and Kraus) and *Nuestro New York* (Penguin USA).

Sandra Rodríguez is a writer, actor, singer, co-host and producer for stage, television and radio. For over fifteen years written and produced educational theatre for young audiences and she consults, conducts and organizes short storytelling and playwrighting residences for children within the New York City school system. Her plays *The Return of Margarita,* which honors Puerto Rican women, and *Tales from the Flats* (Colors and Familias) were bilingual plays commissioned by The New WORLD Theater for their Latino Theater Project sponsored by the Lila Wallace Reader's Digest Arts Partners Program. Her play *Familias* was presented on a staged reading at the renowned Repertorio Español (Spanish Repertory Theatre) and premiered in New York at the Latin American Theatre Ensemble in April 1999. She has also authored an original short piece of the life and work of Paul Robeson. Ms. Rodriguez holds a B.A. in Political Science and Sociology from the University of Puerto Rico and is pursuing a M.A. in Educational Theater at New York University.

Cándido Tirado is the author of numerous plays, including *The Barber Shop, Some People Have All the Luck, Hey There, Black Cat, Hands of Stone* (which is being made into an independent film), *The Missteps of Juan Pachanga, The Second Son, Abuelo, The Fish Market, The Missing Colors of the Rainbow* and *Momma's Boyz.* His play *When Nature Calls* was chosen by Alberto Minero of *El Diario* as the "Best Latino Play of 1993" and *King Without a Castle,* which has been produced by Castillo Theatre and the

American Ensemble Theatre, was workshopped at the Sundance Playwright's Lab. Cándido, who is a three-time recipient of the New York Foundation for the Arts Playwrighting Fellowship, co-authored the award-winning short film *Getting to Heaven*, and has been nominated for a Humanitarian Award for his writing for the television show *Ghostwriter*. He has also written plays dealing with teen pregnancy and AIDS. Cándido's work has been published in *Recent Puerto Rican Theatre: Five Plays from New York* (Penguin, Mentor Books), *Nuestro New York: An Anthology of Puerto Rican Playwrights* (Penguin USA); and *Conducting a Life: An Essay About Maria Irene Fornes* (Smith and Kraus Books).

Dorinda Welle is an anthropologist who has done HIV-related life history research for over ten years. Her current research focuses on sexual identity and adolescent development in the context of the epidemic. Her poetry has appeared in *The Lewis & Clark Review* and *A/Z: The Journal of Weird Anthropology*. She has a book forthcoming on incarcerated women in drug recovery, and is currently working on a series of wit-o-sophical Divine Lectures, weaving Buddhist, Sufi, Native American, African American and Esoteric mysticisms with Old Testament stories.

Evelyn C. White is the author of *Chain Chain Change*, editor of *The Black Women's Health Book: Speaking for Ourselves*, and was the original biographer of Alice Walker. She teaches at Mills College in the Women's Studies Department and has written extensively for numerous publications, including *Essence*, *POZ* and the *San Francisco Chronicle*.

Shay Youngblood is the author of the novels *Black Girl in Paris* and *Soul Kiss* (both published by Riverhead Books) and a collection of short fiction, *The Big Mama Stories* (Firebrand Books). Her plays *Amazing Grace, Shakin' the Mess Outta Misery* and *Talking Bones* (Dramatic Publishing Company), have been widely produced. The recipient of numerous grants and awards including a Pushcart Prize for fiction, a Lorraine Hansberry Playwriting Award, an Edward Albee Honoree award, several NAACP Theater Awards and an Astraea Writers' Award for fiction, Ms. Youngblood graduated from Clark-Atlanta University and received her M.F.A. in Creative Writing from Brown University. She has worked as a Peace Corps volunteer in the Eastern Caribbean, an au pair, artist's model, and poet's helper in Paris as well as a creative writing instructor in a Rhode Island women's prison. Ms. Youngblood was born in Georgia.

Editors

Imani Harrington's writing and ideas on HIV/AIDS have been featured in numerous magazines, newspapers and abstracts, as well as at local and international conferences. She also writes reviews and interviews on theater and psychology. In addition, Ms. Harrington leads groups and performances, acting as co-director, drama facilitator and dramaturg. As playwright-in-residence for TheatreWorks Playwrights Project, she collaborated as dramaturg along with playwright Cherylene Lee. She was also dramaturg and drama facilitator for Girls After School Academy (GASA) and for Oakland Ensemble Theatre (OET). Ms. Harrington has received numerous awards for her writing and her social and community activism, including the Bay Area Poets&Writers Award for fiction, the Giorno Poetry award and a PEN American West grant. She has a number of plays in the development pipeline, such as *In Seven Moons*, a compendium to her play *Ashes to Dust*. Her play *Master Swimmer* was first presented at the Exit Theatre and her play *Do You Have Time to Die?* was first produced for development at the Cleveland Public Theatre. Ms. Harrington studied performing arts at the Cornish Institute of the Arts, and holds a B.A. in Humanities with an emphasis in Theater and an M.A. in Clinical and Social Psychology from New College of California. She has worked in the fields of mental health and counseling for over six years.

Chyrell D. Bellamy (Bellamy-Sarr) has been an educator, advocate and activist in the AIDS field since 1987, specifically on behalf of women and people of color. She has collaborated on various projects with Imani Harrington for the past five years. Ms. Bellamy was formerly an assistant director for the New Jersey Women and AIDS Network (NJWAN). She received both a B.A. in Psychology and an M.S.W. from Rutgers University, and is currently a Ph.D. candidate in Social Work and Social Psychology at the University of Michigan. Her practical and research interests include prevention and treatment issues of women living with HIV and, more recently, understanding individual experiences of recovery from psychiatric illness. She has written and published articles and chapters in both of these areas. Ms. Bellamy grew up in Trenton, NJ.

Aunt Lute Books is a multicultural women's press that has been committed to publishing high quality, culturally diverse literature since 1982. In 1990, the Aunt Lute Foundation was formed as a non-profit corporation to publish and distribute books that reflect the complex truths of women's lives and the possibilities for personal and social change. We seek work that explores the specificities of the very different histories from which we come, and that examines the intersections between the borders we all inhabit.

Please write, phone, or e-mail (books@auntlute.com) us if you would like to receive a free catalog of our books or if you wish to be on our mailing list for news of future titles. You may buy books from our website, by phoning in a credit card order, or by mailing a check with the catalog order form.

Aunt Lute Books
P.O. Box 410687
San Francisco, CA 94141
415.826.1300
www.auntlute.com

This publication of this book would not have been possible without the kind contributions of the Aunt Lute Founding Friends:

Anonymous Donor   Diana Harris
Anonymous Donor   Phoebe Robins Hunter
Rusty Barcelo   Diane Mosbacher, M.D., Ph.D.
Marian Bremer   Sara Paretsky
Marta Drury   William Preston, Jr.
Diane Goldstein   Elise Rymer Turner